AN
ORDINARY MAN
AN
EXTRAORDINARY GOD

Dr. Ernest S. Martin

CONTENTS

But they that wait upon the Lord shall renew their strength; they shall mount up with wings as eagles; they shall run, and not be weary; and they shall walk, and not faint.

—Isaiah 40:31

PREFACE

God has always had a plan to accomplish His purposes. Moses, an Israelite, was born in Egypt. Because Pharaoh had ordered the Israelite male children to be killed, his mother placed Moses in a homemade cradle which she put in the river where Pharaoh's daughter found him.

Moses was raised in Pharaoh's palace where he was educated and lived like a king's son. At forty years of age, Moses went to see his people who were the Hebrew people, and in his own way and strength, set out to deliver his people from slavery. But because he killed an Egyptian, he fled for his life and spent the next forty years as a shepherd. Then God met Moses at the burning bush and told him that He had chosen him to deliver His people from bondage in Egypt. Moses entered the presence of God, and God spoke to Moses directly. Moses walked in the Spirit of God, proclaiming God's Word unto Pharaoh and unto the Hebrew people. He became God's man that through him, God might be magnified, and he was used to deliver the Hebrew people from bondage. Moses as an ordinary man became empowered by the Spirit of God to accomplish God's purpose through him so that God was glorified.

Jesus Christ, the Son of God, became the Son of Man, and He said that He came only to speak His Father's words and to do His Father's works. Jesus did not begin His ministry until He was baptized in the Holy Spirit. Jesus as the Son of Man became empowered by the Holy Spirit to do the works of His Father that he might glorify His Father. Jesus showed us, as men, that we might walk in the Spirit of God and accomplish God's will to glorify the heavenly Father through His Son, Jesus Christ.

When I received Jesus Christ as my Lord and Savior on August 21, 1970, I came to realize that God's Word was true. When He saved me, I realized that God's Word was His Word, and it could not fail. Then God spoke to me from His Word.

John 14:12 says:

> Verily, verily, I say unto you, He that believes on me, the works that I do shall he do also; and greater works than these shall he do; because I go unto my Father.

I said to God that I wanted to see these works that He might be glorified by using me, an ordinary man, to accomplish His work that He had set out for me to do.

Over the last few years, I have related many stories to friends, to grandchildren, and to strangers from the variety of things in my life that I have done, and they asked me if I had recorded the stories. I was amazed that anybody would be interested in my stories. Many people have begged me to record my stories and write my life story.

On June 23, 2015, I had two rods placed in my lower back from L2 to S1. I was in a back brace for six months and pretty much laid up. God spoke to me and revealed to me that many things that happened to me in my childhood and throughout my life had affected my walk with God. I believed that God wanted me to record my life story, how an ordinary farm boy from North Dakota could meet such an extraordinary God who does things beyond man's imagination that glorify His Son, Jesus Christ. I hope that as you read this book, you will come to understand that if God can use a country boy, He can use you to honor and glorify Him. My purpose in writing this book is to show how God taught me from His Word the principles, knowledge, and wisdom to walk in His Spirit to accomplish His purposes so that God might be glorified through His Son, Jesus Christ, by the anointing and power of the Holy Spirit.

CHAPTER 1

An Ordinary Man Used by an Extraordinary God

In 1971, just a few months after I had been saved and filled with the Holy Spirit, a young Baptist journeyman missionary dove off a cliff in the Union of South Africa. His spinal cord was severed at C1 and C2. He was supposed to have been flown to Houston, but Houston was fogged in, and the plane could not land in Houston. The plane was diverted to Dallas, and this young man was taken to Baylor Hospital. God told me that if I would go to the hospital and pray for this man, He would heal him.

Now you must understand that I was a nobody without any reputation. God was asking me to meet someone who did not know me, I did not know them, and there was absolutely no connection. I asked God to give me a sign, and God told me to go meet his mother at the hotel in the hospital. At first, she would be hostile. But when I would tell her that God had sent me and if she believed in miracles that God would heal her son, then she would be friendly. So I went to the hospital, found the hotel, went up to her room, and knocked on her door. She came to the door, and in a very hostile tone of voice, she asked, "What do you want and what are you here for?" She told me to sign the guestbook and be gone because she was busy.

I told her that God had sent me and if she believed in miracles, God would heal her son. She immediately became friendly, apologized for her abruptness, and asked if I would get on the elevator with her as she needed to be someplace. As we were going down the elevator, she asked if I could come back and pray for her son the next morning. I told her that I would be there. She told me that she only had five minutes with him every four hours, and I needed to be exactly on time at ten o'clock.

I went to the hospital the next morning and arrived before ten o'clock but ended up in the wrong waiting room. At 10:15, I started looking for her, and I found her in the hallway next to the correct waiting room. When I found her, she was crying so hard that I could hardly understand her. She was very upset with me because the doctors had just informed her that her son's paralysis was so severe that he would not live another hour. It would be four hours before he could be seen, and he would be dead by then.

I told her that I would go to the nurse's station and explain that I had gone to the wrong waiting room, tell them that I was Dr. Martin and had come to pray for her son, and ask if it would be possible for me to see her son. I went to the nurse's station and explained what happened. They said that I could see him.

When I went into the room, he was on the striker frame, face down. I knelt beside him, told him that I believed that God wanted to heal him, and prayed for him. Nothing appeared to happen, and yet I knew that God had moved in a mighty way. It just wasn't to be instant. I gave his mother my business card, told her that she could call me, and that if I could do anything else, I would be glad to do it.

The next morning, as I arrived at my animal hospital, the telephone was ringing off the hook. I answered the phone, and it was his mother. She was extremely excited and said, "You must come back. You must come back. You must come back."

I asked her what had happened, and she explained that during the night, he started breathing on his own. The doctors told her that it was impossible because his paralysis was so complete. I planned to meet her at the ICU at two o'clock in the afternoon. My associate, Dr. Reeves, wanted to go with me, so we went to the hospital and met his mother and his fiancé at the ICU. We asked permission to talk to the young missionary alone because we wanted to establish that he was born again. This time he was face up. Because he could breathe on his own, we were able to talk to him, and he could talk to us. We were convinced that he had a personal relationship with Jesus Christ as his Savior.

I asked him if he believed that God could heal him. He said that before I had prayed for him the day before, he could not believe that God could heal him but that something dramatic happened in his body, and he began to breathe on his own during the night. He wanted to believe that God could heal him. I told him to ask God to heal him, and just like when he invited Christ to come into his life to save him, God could also, by His Word through His Spirit, heal his body. He started to pray, hoping that God would heal him, and then the power of God through his Spirit settled upon this young man. Faith blossomed, and in a second, he cried out to God, "I thank you for healing me."

I said, "If you believe that God healed you, raise your left hand to the glory of God."

I noticed that his left hand was tied down because that was the arm where they had placed the IVs. I reached down and took hold of his hand, and he exclaimed, "I can feel you."

I said, "Your right arm is not fastened down, and if you believe God healed you, raise your right hand to the glory of God."

We watched as the muscles in his shoulders began to tighten, and he raised his right arm to the glory of God. The presence and the power of God was so strong in that sterile hospital room that this ordinary man fell to his knees, raised his hands, and praised and worshipped an extraordinary God. His mother and fiancé were watching through the window. They were jumping up and down and crying with excitement as they watched him raise his arm to the glory of God. They came in the room, celebrating the healing and glorifying God.

Three months later, this young man that was told he would not live because his spinal cord was completely severed at C1 walked out of Baylor Hospital. This man had been miraculously healed by an all-powerful extraordinary God.

As I have related this story to many people, they raised the questions as how you knew God spoke to you, how you knew God was going to heal this man, and how you could believe. Recently God began to show me that there were things in my childhood that prepared me for how God wanted me to trust in His Son, Jesus Christ. I will go back into my childhood and share some of the experiences that prepared me to meet an extraordinary God. I hope that as I share these experiences and how I came to know Jesus Christ as my personal Savior as well as how God taught me in His Word to hear His Voice in my spirit and to be able to walk with Him and trust Him that it will help you to understand that God is no respecter of persons. If He could do it for me, He can do it for you, and you can experience an extraordinary God.

CHAPTER 2

Christian to Atheist to Born-Again Believer

It was a big day for our family. My brother and I were both dressed in suits, and my sisters had on their best dresses. I was five years old, and it was the day that we were to be baptized at the First Methodist Church in Williston, North Dakota. We were presented as a family. The pastor took the lid off a large wooden container and dipped his hand into a glass container inside. He placed his wet hand on top of my head and spoke the words, "I baptize you in the name of the Father, the Son, and the Holy Ghost." He did the same for my brother and two sisters.

I spent the whole day going around, feeling the top of my head because I was sure that the water was somehow holy, and it was going to change me some way. I didn't want my hair combed that day or the next day because I was still certain that water was going to change me. It did not change me, and I was disappointed.

We were raised in a community that had a Catholic church but no Protestant church. My mother and dad started a nondenominational Sunday school for the families that were not Catholic. Every third Sunday, a Methodist minister would come to the community hall and do a service. They continued to do this until I was twelve years of age when my parents felt like we needed more. Twelve years of age was the usual time when one joined the Methodist Church. So that summer, my brother and I went to classes on Saturday morning for several weeks to learn about the Methodist Church and what it was to become a member. They talked about being baptized. I asked the question about my baptism as a five-year-old boy, told the pastor that it wasn't my choice to be baptized, and that the baptism did not mean anything to me. He said that if I wanted to be baptized again, he would be happy to do it, but that would bring embarrassment to my mother and dad, so I decided not to.

We joined the church after completing the class. Now that we were members of the church, we could take communion, and as a twelve-year-old boy, I knelt at the altar to take communion. I was taking too long, so the pastor came to me and asked what the problem was. I asked him, "How can I be forgiven?" And he said that he did not know, so I got up and went back to my seat.

At age fourteen, when I was a freshman in high school, I woke up one morning, vomiting, which was something that I just could not do in normal circumstances. I continued to vomit during the day. Around suppertime, my dad had me pull up my shirt. He looked at my right lower quadrant, and it was rigid and very tight. He said, "We need to get you to the hospital."

We arrived at the hospital around 7:00 p.m. We met the doctor at the hospital, and after he examined me, he said that I had acute appendicitis and he must operate. He was trying to assure me that everything would be okay, but I was in so much pain that all I wanted was to get out of the pain. The doctor operated on me and afterward said that they got to me just in time because when he pulled the appendix out of my abdomen, it ruptured. Little did I know at this time that this surgery was to be my first surgery of well over thirty surgeries in my lifetime.

When I was sixteen, I began to run a real high fever, and my parents took me to the doctor. They put me in the hospital and ran a bunch of tests. My fever would rise really high and go back to normal and then go back up really high. This continued for several days. During this time, they put me on aqueous penicillin. After eight days, the doctor said, "You're getting too sore from the injections every two hours, so we are going to switch you to oil-based penicillin." They gave me an injection about nine o'clock at night. My dad was sitting in the room, visiting with me. I had my hand lying on my chest, and after a short time, I noticed when I moved my hand off my chest there was a big imprint of my hand upon my chest. My entire body was swelling up like a balloon. When I told my dad about the swelling, he told me to push the nurse's button. He ran out of the room, and within minutes, there were three nurses and three doctors in the room. They were giving me all kinds of injections to counteract an anaphylactic reaction to penicillin. They did not figure out at that time what was causing the fever. Later I was diagnosed with brucellosis, and it was traced back to that time in my life.

Also, when I was sixteen, we had to pick the rocks from the fields with a rock picker in the spring before we seeded the crops. The rock picker had teeth that would go about two inches below the surface and pick up the rocks. When the teeth were full, then you would lift the teeth up and dump the rocks in a trough behind the teeth. When the trough became full, you would go from the field and dump the rocks into a rock pile.

We had a 300 Case tractor that had a front-end loader that we used to pull the rock picker. It had a scoop with two-foot teeth that we used to dig big rocks out of the ground. I had finished the first field where I was picking the rocks and had moved on to another field. I had filled the rock picker with rocks and had dug out a very, very large rock that I had on the scoop. There was a draw next to the field, and I had been taking the large rocks over to the draw, dumping them off the scoop, and watching them roll down the steep slope. It was great fun watching the rocks roll down the hill as they gained speed and crashed into the trees at the bottom of the draw. This time I had the biggest rock that I had ever dug out on the scoop of the tractor. I wanted to make a big crash at the bottom, so I raised the scoop all the way up and then tipped the rock off. I did not know that it would cause the tractor to pull over the steep hill which was about an eighty-degree slope.

Suddenly the tractor was sliding down that slope, gaining speed. I pulled the teeth up on the scoop, lowered the scoop down, and dropped the teeth on the rock picker. About halfway down the slope, when I lowered the scoop and slowly tilted the teeth into the ground, the teeth completely grabbed and stopped the tractor with the back wheels higher than the front wheels. The rock picker was hanging off the tractor at a great angle. I don't know how the tractor kept from rolling over, end over end. Now I had to figure out how to get the tractor to the bottom of the draw and then back out so I could go back to work.

I eased the teeth up slowly. I dumped the rocks out of the bucket of the rock picker, and then I continued to ease the teeth up until the tractor started to move forward very, very slowly. When it would start to move, I would put the teeth back in the ground. After several minutes, I got the tractor flat, the back wheels back on the ground, and eased the teeth up just a little bit. When the tractor would move forward, I would tip the teeth back in so that it would not gain speed. I continued this process until I reached the bottom of the draw. The only way back out was to go up the other side that had about a sixty-five-degree angle.

The tractor was not capable of pulling the rock picker up the hill, so I would stick the teeth of the scoop in the ground and pull the tractor forward. Then I would place big rocks behind the big tires and get back on the tractor. I repeated this process with the teeth and scoop until I slowly worked my way over the top of the hill. It took about one and a half hours to get the tractor out of the draw.

I seem to have a knack for keeping God's Guardian Angel busy taking care of me, but it is the only explanation that I have that I was not killed that day.

One day, when I was eighteen, my brother was running the mower to cut hay, and I was running the hay conditioner that crushed the stems of the alfalfa which should make it more palatable for the cows to eat and would also help the hay to dry quicker so it could be baled sooner. The conditioner kept plugging up, and the only way to get the alfalfa that had wrapped itself around the roller was to get underneath the steel shield, take a jackknife, and cut the alfalfa off the roller. The temperature that day was well over a hundred degrees, and the conditioner had plugged up many times. I was angry because it kept plugging up, and I had to keep getting under there and cutting it off, so the next time it plugged up, I was stabbing and cutting with a furious pace.

I stopped sweating while I was cutting the hay off the roller. When I finished, I got back on the tractor and started down the field. I was lightheaded, and as I approached the end of the field, I realized I was about to pass out. I managed to get the tractor out of gear and stop it. I don't remember anything from this point on until I woke up in the hospital, packed in ice with IVs and oxygen. I had a heat stroke, and my brother had taken me off the tractor, put me in the Jeep, and took me about three miles to my uncle's place where they called for an ambulance to meet them. I was transferred from the Jeep to the ambulance after about five miles. When the ambulance attendants took my temperature in the ambulance, it was 110. They took me the next seven miles to the hospital while they were traveling close to a hundred miles an hour.

When I arrived at the hospital, my temperature was still 110 degrees. With the temperature that high for that length of time, all my organs should have been cooked, and there was no way that I should have survived. I woke up and felt fine. The doctors and the nurses were absolutely amazed.

Jeremiah 1:5 says:

> Before I formed you in the belly I knew you; and before you came forth out of the womb I sanctified you, and I ordained you a prophet unto the nations.

Even though I did not know God personally, I had a sense that God had a calling on my life. Shortly after this, we had been out, working all day, and when we came in to eat in the evening, suddenly I passed out and fell on the floor. They told me my body was as rigid as a steel post, and the only way they could get me into a car was to pass me through the windows because they could not bend my body. They called the ambulance to meet us, and I was transferred after about seven miles into the ambulance. I woke up in the hospital again, packed in ice with IVs and oxygen. They said I had a relapse of the heatstroke.

It had been raining for several days, and the road that we took to our main fields in the hills had a lot of clay on it. Around some curves and some hills, the road was nothing but pure clay. I don't recall why it was necessary for me to go into the hills where we had been working on the tractor, but something needed to be done, and my dad sent me to do it. I was driving the big truck, and the inside duel was missing because it was flat. My dad had removed it to get it fixed.

As I came to one large curve going around this clay hill, I was going less than five miles an hour. The truck was not turning, even though I had the wheels completely turned. The truck was just sliding forward. I applied the brakes, but it was fruitless on that wet clay. The truck just kept sliding toward the cliff. I knew that sometimes on a slick surface, if you apply just a little bit of speed, a vehicle will turn. So I applied just a little bit of speed, and the truck turned, but it didn't stop turning, and it slid over the hill backward. It was somewhere between two hundred and three hundred feet down the hill. I would have been okay, but there was a big boulder at the bottom, and the truck hit the boulder with such force that it sheared the blinker lights off. The truck was twisted in a funny shape.

I didn't seem to be hurt, so I climbed up the hill, and when I got to the top of the hill, my uncle and his son were there. My uncle turned white and could not stop shaking when he saw the truck. I said that I was fine and asked to go to the top of the hill to get the tractor to pull the truck up. We got the tractor and pulled the truck off the boulder. Then I was able to drive the truck out and get it back up on the road.

I had enrolled in college at North Dakota State University which at that time was known as North Dakota Agriculture College. The freshmen had to be there a week early to get enrolled and go through orientation. My high school curriculum and my intent were to in enroll in electrical engineering. I had been raised on a farm, but now I was in a town of fifty-thousand people, and I felt claustrophobic. I said that there was no way that I could live in a big city where I would need to live to find work as an engineer. So they recommended that I enroll in pre-vet and become a veterinarian.

After enrolling, I went over to the veterinary science department to apply for a job. I was sent to the third floor where there were three veterinarians and two lab technicians, and I asked them if they had any work that I could do. I noticed a small room to the side that was full of dirty test tubes, culture dishes, flasks, and beakers that needed to be cleaned. They told me that they did not have any jobs available, so I asked them about the dirty test tubes and the rest of the dirty glassware. Their answer was, "No one wants to do that."

I said that I would be glad to do it.

Again, their answer was, "We do not need you."

So I went into the room, found soap, and a motor with a drill chuck on it. I took a test tube brush, put it in the motor, ran some water with soap, and put the test tubes in the soapy water to soak in the sink. Next to the soapy water, I ran clear water. I would reach into the sink and get a handful of test tubes and run them up and down on the test tube brush on the motor to clean the test tubes. Then I cleaned the culture dishes, the beakers, and the flasks. I rinsed them thoroughly and set them up to dry. After I finished, I went out of the room, told them that I had cleaned the test tubes and the other glassware, and didn't know if they had a place that they wanted me to put them.

One of the lab technicians went into the room, came out of the room, got one of the veterinarians, and took him into the room. They were astonished that I had cleaned up all the dirty filthy glassware that was full of bacteria and mold and had done it in such a fast time. The veterinarian came to me and asked when I could start working. He said that they had never had anyone that had taken initiative on their own to do work and to do it so well. I started working that day.

I would go by every evening after class and clean up the necropsy room. Then I would take a band saw and cut the heads of animals (wild and domestic) in half to get the brains out so they could run the rabies test on these brains.

After I started my fall quarter, I was very unsettled inside, so I went to the youth minister at the Wesley foundation on campus to get counseling because I felt like I owed God my life. He talked with me for quite some time and told me that because of my near-death experiences where God protected me, he felt that I did not have a true calling from God to be a pastor but should continue to pursue veterinary medicine.

I was raised in a family that did not drink alcohol, did not smoke, did not curse, did not use God's name in vain, and was taught to practice the golden rule. I joined Farmhouse Fraternity, which was the only fraternity on campus that did not allow alcohol at any of their social functions. However, there were several men in the fraternity that did drink alcohol. I would go with them when they were drinking, and I would be the designated driver to bring them back. At no time did they pressure me to drink.

One of my high school classmates roomed in a basement apartment with my brother and me the first year. Gary was a Catholic, and his family drank alcohol. He saw nothing wrong with going out on Friday nights and coming home totally drunk. He would go to confession on Sunday and thought everything was fine. Over the two years that I spent at North Dakota State University, I saw many people that claimed to be Christians, but their deeds did not line up with what I believed were Christian principles. In the world, I was not a bad person, but I knew that my life did not follow what I believed were Christian principles. There were people of all types of beliefs in college. I met several atheists, and their biggest reason for being an atheist was that they did not see Christians following God's teachings. When I looked at other's lives, I saw hypocrisy. But I also knew that by confessing to be a Christian and not living up to the standards of Jesus Christ that I was also being a hypocrite. I believed that as a Christian, a man's word had to be his word. My incorrect interpretation of being a Christion meant that I must live up to all the standards set by God's Word, and I decided that it was impossible to live a Christian life. So I rejected God and everything that He stood for.

I spent my first summer at North Dakota State University, taking classes so that I could meet requirements to get into one of four veterinary schools that would accept North Dakota students. That summer, I stayed in the fraternity house. I managed the house, and if I could get enough people to stay in the house, I could stay free. I also cooked for seventeen guys in the evening. Now most of these people that stayed in the house were not members of the Farmhouse Fraternity, and they did not have the same values that my brothers in the fraternity had. So as I begin to socialize with these men, I started drinking whiskey and beer, never to the point of being drunk but to be sociable with these new friends.

I was accepted at Oklahoma State University into the school of veterinary medicine, and in the fall of 1962, I started the pursuit to becoming a veterinarian. In the school of veterinary medicine, students went to class from 7:30 to 12:00 and from 1:00 to 5:30 on Monday through Friday and from 7:30 to 12:00 on Saturday. It was a tough curriculum that required a tremendous amount of studying. I developed some friends that helped me study, and when class was over and I had completed my part-time job of taking care of hemophiliac beagles, we would meet at the bar.

Before supper, five or six of us would drink one pitcher of 3.2 percent beer. Later, we would meet at someone's house to study (usually until at least midnight or sometimes one o'clock) knowing that we would have to be up for class the next day. With these long days of studying and my jobs, there wasn't much time for a social life.

During my second year in pathology class, I learned that the Egyptian cattle died of anthrax because they were in the river bottom, and the Hebrew cattle were in the desert. Anthrax goes into a spore form in desert conditions and is non-infective, but in wet conditions, it becomes a very progressive highly fatal disease that can cause death in hours. Now the week that I learned this in pathology, I decided to go to the Methodist Church on Sunday morning. The pastor was preaching on Moses delivering the Hebrew people out of the Egyptians' hands. He talked about the plague of the Egyptians' cattle and said it was an act of God.

I wanted to jump up in the church and tell him that he did not know what he was talking about because I knew that it was anthrax that killed the Egyptian cattle. At that time, I did not realize that God used natural conditions that He created to accomplish His work. But that just further confirmed my belief that there was no God, and at this point, I became a full-fledged atheist.

Between my last two years in veterinary school, I had won a scholarship to stay at the school and work on a research project in reproductive physiology. The school offered me a position to stay on after I graduated from veterinary school to get a master's degree in reproductive physiology. The project during the summer was supposed to count towards that degree. At that time, Stillwater Oklahoma was a town of about eleven to twelve thousand people. The college had over twelve thousand students of which most went home during the summer. There was nothing to do during the summer, and it was very, very boring.

I had two roommates: one was a Methodist but did not go to church, and the other one was a Jew. I was an atheist. The Baptist Student Union ran ads that they had ice-cream socials on Friday nights. The three of us decided that this would be a good place to meet girls. We went on a Friday night and enjoyed the ice cream and volleyball. I played volleyball almost all evening, and I found myself going back throughout the week to play volleyball and to socialize with the people at the Baptist Student Union.

One day, one of the members of the Baptist Student Union complained that there were people coming for the social activities, but they were not participating in the Bible studies and the services. Now I had a good thing going with free ice cream, fellowship, and volleyball. What was the big deal? I thought if it would keep him happy, I could give one hour to go to their vesper services. I went to the first vesper service where a lieutenant in the air force spoke, and all that he did was to criticize the Catholics. I didn't see much love in that.

At this time, I had five part-time jobs to try to make enough money to live during the summer and hopefully save some for the next school year. One evening, while at the Baptist Student Union, I met a beautiful young lady who was even more beautiful inside. She just had such a wonderful peace and such a sweet spirit that I was deeply drawn to her. I asked her for a date, and she accepted. On Sunday, I was going to pick her up at 1:30. We were going to go to the zoo in Oklahoma City and have dinner before returning to Stillwater. I thought that I needed to impress her by telling her I had gone to church that morning, so I got up early to take care of my hemophiliac beagles.

For the first time, I began to realize that I hated what I was doing, but there was a deeper dissatisfaction with my own life. That morning, I found myself throwing those beagles into their cages rather than treating them gently and kindly. I possibly could have killed one of them by bruising them and causing them to have bled to death. I finished caring for the beagles and then went to the dairy barn where

I was a student veterinarian. It was my responsibility to treat the sick cows and calves, and if there was something I could not handle, then I could call a veterinarian on staff that was on call.

They came to me and told me they had put a new cow in the line with the other sick cows that needed to be treated. She had mastitis, so I went to the medicine cabinet to get medications. I picked up a tube of antibiotic ointment and went back to infuse the cow's utter with the antibiotic ointment. When I began to fill out the record, it said temperature, and I thought, *I'll just leave it blank.* I could not do that because my word was still my word. So I went back and took the cow's temperature, and it was 106 degrees. She would have been dead in a few hours from septicemia caused by the mastitis. Then I had to get IV antibiotics, put a needle in her jugular vein, and slowly drip the antibiotics into her system.

All this was taking extra time and was possibly going to keep me from making church. I was ready to walk out of the barn when they caught me and said that we have twenty calves with bloody diarrhea. This didn't make me happy because this was caused by the fact that they were not keeping the calves' pens clean. The calves were transmitting coccidiosis to each other because of lack of sanitary conditions. Now this meant that I would have to give each one of these calves a bolus by mouth.

I finally finished at the dairy barn, rushed home, took a shower, and just barely made it to church. As I sat in the church, I began to take inventory of my life, and I did not like what I was finding. I hated what I was doing, I didn't like myself, and I did not feel that anyone loved me. I was completely broken and felt totally unworthy.

I picked up the young lady, and we traveled to Oklahoma City. We went to the zoo, stopped at a very nice restaurant, and had dinner. There was just something about her that was totally different from anyone I had ever met. She was at peace. She was kind, sweet, and caring. We did not talk about God, but her life and actions spoke volumes. We arrived back in Stillwater at around 9:00 p.m., and I took her to her home. I went home, changed clothes, and went to the barn to take care of my beagles.

When I walked into the barn, suddenly the presence of God filled that barn, and I recognized for the first time in my life that there was a God. I don't fully know how to describe it, but His presence just completely filled that barn, and I loved on those beagles. Normally I cleaned them at 5:30 in the evening, and for every thirty minutes I was late, they were just twice as dirty. They were not pleasant to handle nor pick up because of the dirtiness of the cages. They were filthy, but I just loved on them as I cleaned the cages.

That night, I lost a third of my vocabulary because before that, about every third word was a curse word. Meeting God changes a person. I could not wait to tell people that I had met God and that I had become one of His. People would come up to me and say, "We don't know what happened to you, but you are totally different." My answer was that I became a Christian.

When I was in high school, I did not think that I was good enough looking so that girls would want to go out with me. Also I was doing my best to study and make good grades. I had two dates when I was in high school, and these were both arranged to take two different girls to the junior senior prom. When I was a junior, there was a girl that I had known since I was in grade school, and we were good friends. She did not have a date for the junior senior prom, so I was told I would take her to the prom.

When I was a senior, my brother's girlfriend was a junior. My brother could not come back for the junior senior prom, so I was told that I would take his girlfriend to the prom. Those were my two dates in high school. In my undergraduate work at North Dakota State University, I found that schoolwork was relatively easy for me because of my high school background. My thoughts about dating girls were that they don't know me, and I don't know them, so if they turn me down, there will be another girl that won't. So I became quite good at asking girls out and getting dates.

My first year of veterinary school was extremely difficult, and my time was spent studying with very little time dating. But after the first year of veterinary school, I found that the classes that followed built up on the foundation of those first-year classes, so school became much easier for me. At Oklahoma State University, almost everyone studied in the library. After an hour or an hour and a half of study, it was time to walk over to the student union fourth floor and have a cup of coffee or Coke. I would survey the girls that were studying. When I was ready to go for a break, I would stop and ask a girl if she would like to go for a Coke, and I was rarely turned down as Oklahoma State was a very friendly outgoing campus. It was not uncommon for me to have three different dates in one night. The underclassmen had to be in at eight o'clock, the upperclassmen had to be in it at ten o'clock, and those that lived off-campus did not have a time limit. So I would take an underclassman for a Coke and then walk her back to her dorm.

I would go back to the library to study, take an upperclassman for a Coke, and walk her back to her dorm. Then I would go back to study and take a girl that lived off-campus for a Coke, and if she did not have a ride home, I would take her home. Otherwise, I would walk her to her car so that she could go home.

One year, we lived in a house that had a rosebush that produced the most beautiful roses. I had a date with three different girls, so I took three roses and put them in the car in vases to give to each girl. The first girl, the underclassman, was thrilled with her rose, and I walked her back to the dorm. The second girl, the upperclassman, was really thrilled with her rose. She wanted to go to the car to properly thank me for the rose, and I had a hard time convincing her that we did not want to go to the car. Because I had the other rose, she would have found out that there was another girl. That would have messed up things completely. She was very persistent, but I finally convinced her that my car was parked too far away, and we would not have time to make it back to the dorm. The girl that lived off-campus loved her rose, and we did go back to the car.

My last year in veterinary school, I went back to mainly studying for the national boards, and my dating life became pretty much nonexistent. The year itself was standard, but the emphasis among the veterinary students was this constant push to study for the national boards. I graduated from veterinary school, moved from the house where I was staying, and rented an apartment in Scholars Inn. I started my work that summer on my master's program. I had a government grant which paid $467 a month tax-free, which was enough to pay my tuition and books to do this research in reproductive physiology and take the class work necessary to get a master's degree.

My master's adviser changed things up on me, and he told me that the project that I had done the past summer would no longer count as my master's research. Instead, they would give me three hours credit toward my degree, and I would have to do the work that he was doing on a federal grant in reproductive physiology. His work meant leaving Stillwater at four in the morning to be at the slaughterhouse at five-thirty in Oklahoma City, collecting ovaries from pigs, flushing the ovaries with cold ACD solution, and then packing them on ice before returning them to Stillwater where they would be put on an artificial perfusion machine to revive them. We would introduce carbon-14 in the blood with different hormones to measure the effect on the ovaries. The ovaries would be on the machines for six hours.

While they were on the machines, I could not leave the area because I had to be sure that the ovaries remained alive and that everything worked the way it was supposed to. This meant that I would be there through my lunch hour. After I moved into the apartment, I started dating again. I would call one of the girls that I was dating and ask her to bring me lunch. Some of the girls would make me lunch and bring it to me. Another would stop at fast-food to pick up lunch. I would pay for it, and she would eat it with me in the lab. I had two girls that I was dating on a very regular basis; one was a blonde, and the other was a brunette.

One Saturday, I went to the pool, laid my raft on the water, and jumped on the raft because the water was still cold. I wanted to get a suntan without having to get in the cold water. Sitting along the side of the pool was a very beautiful brunette who had the most beautiful legs. She spoke, "That's a new way to do it."

I took it that she was interested, so I paddled over to where she was sitting and introduced myself. Her name was Janice Smith, but she went by Jan. I invited her to my place for a steak dinner that I would cook. She said that she did not go into a single man's apartment, and the only way that she would come was if I would leave the door open. I told her that she could have the door left open, and we would have a steak dinner. She told me that she would not do laundry for a man unless she was married to him, and that was okay because the blonde was doing my laundry. She also said that she would not cook for a man unless she was married to him, and that was okay because the other brunette was cooking for me.

After the date, I walked Jan back to her apartment, and she showed me her senior class picture from Hardin-Simmons University. When she showed it to me, I knew I was going to have that picture and that I was going to marry her. On the second date I had with Jan, I took her to a very nice restaurant, and she spent the entire evening questioning me about my salvation with God. Our relationship was going nowhere. I thought that she was a straitlaced Baptist, and how could I have any fun with her? She thought that I was a conceited doctor, which was probably true. We had a date for the Fourth of July, but she broke the date, saying that she was going home to see her parents.

I was sitting at the pool, and there was a new redhead that I was trying to get to know when Jan walked up to me. She said that she had started home, had a tire blowout, and when the man tried to fix it, he almost tipped her car over. She did not want to go home without a spare. I said, "Then does that mean our date is back on?"

Jan replied, "I guess so."

I was not very happy at the moment because I wanted to meet the redhead. I went back to my apartment. One of my part-time jobs was helping a man at a service station, so I called Jan and asked if she would like me to help her buy a new tire. She was not thrilled but said, "Okay."

I picked her up, and we went to the service station. My friend made such a good deal on four tires that her dad said to put all new tires on the car. After we got the tires on, we went out to eat. Now all the façades and trying to impress each other had broken down, and we both became just who we were. Next Sunday, I was at the pool, and Jan was talking with Donna, the blonde that I had been dating. Donna said, "I will never go back to that church again." Jan had invited her to go to church with her that Sunday morning.

I asked Donna why she would not go back to the church, and she said that the preacher had preached an hour and a half, and that was just way too long. Jan turned to me and said, "Will you go to church with me?"

I said," Yes, I will go to church with you if you also go to my church with me."

So the next Sunday, we went to the Methodist Church for the morning service, and the message was pretty dead. Sunday night, we went to Hillcrest Baptist Church. When the pastor, Brother Harry, got up to preach, there stood a man with a hook on his left arm, three fingers missing from his right hand, and a big scar on his face. As a nineteen-year-old boy, he had a baseball career where the scouts said that he was better than Mickey Mantle. He was drafted into World War II, was blown up by a bomb, lost his left hand and three fingers on his right hand, and was scarred deeply with shrapnel to the face. This man opened his Bible, started to speak about the Scriptures, and used scripture to explain scripture. He preached at least an hour and a half. He said, "All of my time is up, and I must quit."

It was all I could do not to jump up and say, "Do not stop, keep on!" I turned to Jan, and I said. "I don't know if anything will happen between us, but I know that I have found the church that I will go to from now on."

At this point, Jan and I started seeing each other every day. I was by the pool on a beautiful Sunday afternoon, and I said, "It would be a great day to go for a canoe ride." I asked if anybody wanted to go for a canoe ride.

Donna the blonde, the brunette that I was dating, and another girl that I had not dated but wanted to date me were all standing there and saying, "Yes, we want to go." I said that I would have to go call the doctor that offered me his canoe to see if he was home and I could get the canoe.

I called Dr. Pancier, who was home, and said that I could come get the canoe. I went back to the pool, walked directly to Jan, and said that the canoe was available. I asked, "Do you want to go with me?"

She did not think I was going to ask her, but she said, "Yes, that sounds great." So we left the other girls disappointed as we left and picked up the canoe. We carried the canoe to the river from Dr. Pancier's house, and we had a lovely canoe ride.

Jan had questions about my salvation, so she talked to Brother Harry. He asked her to have me come to see him. I visited with Brother Harry for about an hour and related my experience that I had in the barn. He talked with Jan afterward and said that every person's salvation experience is different. He said that I had an experience similar to Paul's on the road to Damascus, which is commonly referred to as the Pauline experience. On a Tuesday evening, five and a half weeks after we met, we had been out on a date, and I told Jan, "You're the kind of girl I want to marry." I was afraid to ask her directly to marry me because I was afraid that I would be turned down.

She told me that she needed to talk to her parents, and I needed to meet her parents before she could give me an answer. We went to church on Wednesday night, and as the service was coming to an end, she turned to me and said, "I will marry you."

We went down to the front after the service, met with Brother Harry, the pastor, asked him if he would marry us, and he replied, "Yes." Jan wanted to go home on Wednesday to tell her parents and talk to them before I came. I said that was fine because I was taking pilot training and was far enough along that I could fly solo to Spearman, Texas. I could fly out Thursday morning. However, Thursday morning, the weather conditions were such that I could not fly, so I called her and told her I could not fly. She wanted to be sure that I was still coming. I said that I would drive to Spearman to meet her parents.

I drove to Spearman, met her mother and dad, and asked them if I could marry their daughter. Her dad's response was, "If you're going to get married, why not just get married right away?"

We had planned a December wedding because we thought an earlier wedding would be too shocking to both sets of parents. We hurried around, found we could get the church in Spearman on September 2, and planned the entire wedding that weekend.

On the Wednesday night that Jan and I were engaged, we called my parents. I told my mother that I was getting married. She said, "Let me sit down while you talk to your dad." They did not know that I was dating anyone, let alone seriously dating someone and was about to get married.

I explained to my dad that I had met the girl that I believed God wanted me to marry, that we were planning a December wedding, and was wondering if they could come to a December wedding. I then talked to my mother some more, and Jan talked to both of my parents. When we came back from Jan's parents with the September date, I had to call my parents to tell them that we were getting married in September and wondered if they could come to the wedding. Since it was such a quickly planned wedding and then the date was moved up, a lot of questions were raised if this was going to be a shotgun wedding. We remained faithful to God and His values of abstinence until married. There were many disappointed people that were counting the months.

Jan's mother offered to address and send the wedding invitations we ordered if I would bring them to Spearman. So I decided to fly to Spearman and give her the wedding invitations. On the way to Spearman, I needed to stop at Gage, Oklahoma, to refuel the plane. About twenty miles east of Gage, I noticed what was appearing to be a black cloud forming. The Panhandle area was notorious for thunderstorms, so I radioed the tower at Gage to ask about the weather. They said that the weather was fine, that a pilot had just come in, the weather was clear and to come on.

I said, "It sure looks like a thunderstorm forming," but the man in the tower assured me that there was no thunderstorm, that he was looking out the window, and it was clear. I continued to fly, and in a few minutes, my Cessna 150 was being thrown around like a rubber ball. It would jump up two hundred feet, fall three hundred feet back and forth, up and down. I made it through, and I landed in Gage. I immediately went to the tower and jumped all over the man for sending me through a thunderstorm.

I took on fuel and flew on to Spearman. The aerial maps showed that there was a tower in Spearman, but when I arrived, there was no tower, no one to talk to on the radio, and the windsock was missing. The runway ran parallel to the railroad track with many tall grain elevators next to the runway. This was not conducive to landing a plane when you did not know in what direction the wind was blowing, so I tried to estimate the direction of the wind by the way the plane was handling in the air. I decided to do a full forty-degree flap landing because you can land the plane at a very slow speed with full flaps. I made my approach with power off, and about forty feet above the runway, suddenly a huge gust of wind hit my plane and lifted it beside the runway. I was not high enough to get back on the runway, so I landed on the grass. Many times during flight training, my instructor had me land the plane on the grass, so I just landed the plane on the grass, taxied up to the runway, and taxied to where the tower was supposed to be.

I called Jan's mother. She came out to the airport and picked me up with the invitations. We went to her house, visited for a while, and then she took me back to the airport as I needed to get back to Stillwater. The temperature that day was approximately 104 degrees, and Spearman was a thousand feet higher elevation than Stillwater's airport. The runway was very strange. It was extremely long, half of it was on one side of the highway, the other half was on the other side, and you had to cross the highway to use the entire runway.

I looked at the runway from the highway to the end, and it was at least three times longer than I ever needed to take off in Stillwater. I did not want to cross that highway at forty-five to fifty miles an hour, so I decided to take off at the highway. I put my plane in position, gave it full throttle, and reached fifty-five to sixty miles an hour as I was going down the runway. In Stillwater, I would have been well into the air at that speed. I was not lifting off and was running out of runway. I was going too fast to stop before the end of the runway, and there was a fence at the end of the runway. I could see that I was not going to clear the fence because I was not lifting off, so I reached up, grabbed the lever to the flaps and, with all my strength, pulled it to forty degrees. The plane lifted off, and I just cleared the fence. Once I had the plane flying and was in the air, I slowly released the flaps to normal wing position. Once again, God was watching out for me.

In July, I received notice from my draft board in Williston, North Dakota, to report to Oklahoma City with duffel bag in hand and be prepared to enter the army. I called the draft board and told them that I had gone there in February and had been classified 4F. This was during the Vietnam War. They told me, "We are redrafting you anyway" and that I was to take my physical and be prepared to go to Fort Hood.

I went to Oklahoma City, but now that I was a doctor, I did not have to go through the regular line. I was ushered through a private line for all the blood work and for the physical. I came to the doctor that had classified me 4F in February. He said, "Get on the bus. You're going to Fort Hood." I asked him why that was when I was not eligible in February, and now in July, I was suddenly eligible to go into the army. His answer to me was, "If you're seeing- eye dog is not blind, and your wheelchair doesn't have a broken wheel, and because you are now a veterinarian and can practice, you can serve in the military. Now get on the bus."

I told him that I was not getting on the bus and that I had thirty days to apply for a commission. They locked me in a room and told me I would stay in the room until I got on the bus. At five o'clock, they came, released me, and told me to go apply for my commission. I went back to Stillwater. My major adviser, along with the dean of the College of Veterinary Medicine, made some phone calls and wrote some letters. I was reclassified 2A so that I might finish my federal grant and my master's degree. Then I would have to go into the service.

Jan went to Spearman the last week of August to prepare for the wedding, and I came on August 31. Her sister and brother-in-law came that day. My parents and my two sisters arrived on September 1. Because of travel and scheduling, we had rehearsal on the morning of the wedding, and the rehearsal dinner was at lunch. On September 2, 1966, Jan and I were married in the First Baptist Church of Spearman, Texas. The wedding ceremony went well, but thirty minutes before the wedding started, it began to pour down rain. Several people didn't come because of the heavy rain. Before the wedding, my dad kept telling me to check my shoes. I told him that I already had checked my shoes and they were okay. He kept insisting that I check my shoes, so I showed him my shoes.

You must understand that there were a lot of people from North Dakota that were after me because when I was in North Dakota, I was the person that padlocked bells to the bedsprings of one couple's bed. I also jacked up one couple's car and put blocks under the back axles so that when they came out, it would appear that their car was not decorated. The husband had made all types of threats if we decorated his car. He thought he had won, and they got in the car. The rear wheels just spun, and we proceeded to decorate his car with them sitting in it.

We drove another couple up and down Main Street in a manure spreader. I painted "help" on the bottom of several men's shoes so that when they knelt to pray, the snickering and laughing went through out the audience. So my sisters were well-instructed by those friends to get even. They had painted "help" on the bottom of a new pair of dark brown shoes, but they did not go with a black tuxedo, so I had polished my old black shoes to wear in the wedding.

After the wedding, her sister, brother-in-law, and my two sisters tried to decorate my car, but it was raining so hard that the rain washed everything off before they could get it decorated. My wife had a '65 Impala Chevrolet, and we took it out to hide it before anyone arrived. She had used shoe polish on her sister's car when they were married, and it stayed on the paint, so they were also lying in wait for her.

When her sister arrived, I told her, "I guess I should wash my car, even though you guys will mess it up." No one asked about her car. We left on our honeymoon and spent the first night in Dalhart, Texas. We went merrily on our way, not knowing the chaos and confusion that was taking place in Spearman. Because of all the rain, when her dad took my best man out to get my car, he had an accident. Somehow it got back to people at the house and the church that my wife and I had been in an accident. This was before cell phones, so there was no way that anyone could check up on anybody.

We were going to the Taos Mountains in New Mexico. We had asked a friend of Jan's dad where he stayed when he was in Taos. We didn't have much money, and we needed some place economical. He suggested the Golden Indian and said that was where he stayed while he was building the Shadow Mountain Guest Ranch. We got to the Golden Indian rather late in the evening to check in. When we got into our cabin and turned on the lights, the floor was covered with cockroaches and all other kinds of bugs. We managed to stay that night, but the next day, we found the Shadow Mountain Guest Ranch. They agreed to take a check because we knew the contractor. There was an A-frame cabin that had just been completed, but it did not have any type of heat. It had a fireplace, but the only wood was scrap two-byfours, so they told us to turn on the oven and the burners of the stove to keep warm. We stayed there for three nights.

We started the fall semester at Oklahoma State University. Jan continued her graduate work in organic chemistry, and I pursued my degree that was supposed to be in reproductive physiology. When I went to enroll, my major adviser had changed my curriculum. He gave me two biochemistry courses; one needed to be taken before the other one. I was going to end up with a degree in biochemistry, and this was not my agreement with the physiology department. Also, about one and a half months into the program, I was told that my research project that I had spent all summer working on did not show any significant changes, so I would have to repeat the project with different criteria.

God continued to deal with me, and after a short period of time, I surrendered to preach. My desire was to go to Southwestern Baptist Theological Seminary in Fort Worth, Texas, and I did not want to finish the program that I had started. However, my major adviser gave me an out when he asked me to lie for him and to do things that were out and out fraud. When I refused, he told me to either do it or resign. God had made a way for me to get out of the program that was not at all what I had agreed to and signed up for. So I resigned and started looking for a job.

Finding a job was almost impossible because it was the wrong time of the year to hire veterinarians. Also because once I left school, I would immediately be drafted into the military. Dr. Edmondson in Perry, Oklahoma, wanted me to go to work for him, but he told me they couldn't pay me what I was worth. He said he was embarrassed to tell me that $400 a month was as much as he could pay. This was just a little less than what I was making, so I took the job.

In November, Jan and I went to Dallas, Texas, to look for jobs so that I could go to seminary in Fort Worth. I was offered a job by Dr. Self to run his branch clinic in Oak Lawn. Jan was offered a position to teach math in Oak Cliff. We both accepted the positions that we were offered. However, I did not have a Texas license to practice veterinary medicine in Texas and was told that I could not practice unless there was another veterinarian with me. The next exam would not be offered until February.

Dr. Self agreed to let Dr. Campbell be with me in the practice until I could take my state board exam. We located an apartment in Oak Cliff and returned to Stillwater. I gave Dr. Edmondson notice that I would be leaving toward the end of December. He had given me a $25 raise every two weeks. He told me, "I have never been as happy with a veterinarian as I am with you, and I've never done this before, but if you stay with me, I will make you a partner in my practice."

I was extremely honored, but I felt the call to go into the ministry, thus we were moving to Dallas. While I was working for Dr. Edmondson, a man brought in a cow that he had tried to help her have her calf six weeks earlier. She got away from him, and he just now found her with part of the dead calf hanging out of her uterus. It was amazing that the cow was still alive. The odor from the dead rotten calf was so bad that no one else could stay in the room with the cow without vomiting. I had the assistant get buckets of very hot water with Lysol and throw it on the floor under the cow about every five to seven minutes. I put on shoulder-length gloves and took the dead decomposed calf out of the cow's uterus bone by bone, piece by piece.

When I finished removing the calf, I flushed the uterus, put in antibiotic, and gave the cow an IV dose of antibiotic. I sent the cow home with injectable antibiotics and instructions for the owner. I told him once the cow recovered, he needed to fatten her up and sell her because she would probably never have another calf. When Dr. Edmondson came back from a farm call and found out what I had done, he said, "Why did you do that? No one should have to do that."

I told him that the cow needed to be treated and that I was hired to treat whatever came in. I did what I was hired to do. He said that he would never ask his employee to do something like that. I asked him, "Then who would do it?" and he said that he would. I said, "If you would do it, then why shouldn't I do it?"

We went to North Dakota for Christmas. It would be the only Christmas that we would spend there with my parents. I spent three days vaccinating heifers for ranchers against brucellosis while my dad showed my wife around the area where I grew up. The day that we left North Dakota, it was twenty below zero. After we arrived in Dallas, on January 1, 1967, it was seventy-two degrees. Most of the apartments at that time had heated pools as natural gas was very cheap, so we sat around the pool during the afternoon and went swimming. On January 2, I started my job as a veterinarian, working for Dr. Self. The practice was quite old, the building fairly rundown, and it was very poorly equipped to do veterinary medicine. I had no x-ray unit, no means to do blood work, a very cheap microscope that I could check dog stools for parasites, and that was about it. I had a staff that consisted of a receptionist and a kennel man. I was happy and excited to be working as a veterinarian and making a living.

Jan started teaching at T. W. Browne Junior High, and her first day was a disaster. She came home in tears and quite distraught because the discipline of the children was just nonexistent. She was teaching eighth-grade math. They had several substitutes for the entire first semester. She said they threw paper airplanes, spat wads, passed notes, and basically ignored her the first day. At the end of the day, she was feeling very badly. The janitor told her that she ought to be encouraged because things were much better than when the substitutes were teaching.

Several days later, she called me and told me that she had locked her keys in the trunk of the car. It was my afternoon off, so I told her I would bring the keys and meet her in her classroom. I walked into her classroom at the end of the day after her last class. She had a few students around her desk, wanting help. When I walked in, two boys were having a fistfight. I walked over, grabbed each boy by their shirt collars, and lifted them up off the ground. I then proceeded to set them down in a desk with a fair amount of force. I told them they would sit there until she finished with those that she was helping, and then she would deal with their discipline.

Well, the word went out that you needed to behave in her class because she was married to this humongous man that could pick you up and hold you off the ground if you didn't behave. If you don't know me, I was only five-foot- eight tall and weighed 120 pounds, but I was quite strong from growing up on a farm and throwing around hundred-pound bales of hay. It didn't solve all her discipline problems, but they did greatly improve. Today, if I did something like that, I might end up in jail, but it worked at the time.

When I graduated from veterinary school, I had all the confidence in the world that I was ready for practice until that first case came in. Suddenly I realized that I was alone and had to produce. I started out doing very well with just basic simple cases. Then I had a six-week-old Boston terrier puppy that was vomiting. It is not uncommon for Bostons to vomit when they are puppies, but there was something going on with this puppy. It had been vomiting on and off for three days before the owner brought the puppy in. I did not have an x-ray unit at my clinic, so I called a neighboring veterinarian and made arrangements to take the puppy for an x-ray.

We x-rayed the puppy at his clinic and discovered that the puppy had swallowed a dime. So I took the puppy back to my clinic, called the owner, and told him we needed to operate to remove the dime from the puppy's stomach. At this time, sodium pentobarbital was about the only anesthetic that was available. I felt that the puppy was too weak for this anesthetic, and Dr. Campbell knew how to give ether. I called her, asked her to come over, bring some ether, and give the anesthetic while I did the surgery. I had never removed a foreign object from an animal's stomach.

Dr. Campbell and I put the dog under anesthesia with the ether. I operated on the dog and removed the dime. I sewed up the stomach and the muscle wall. The puppy woke up nicely and, in a short period of time, was eating and holding the food down.

A couple weeks later, a twenty-eight-year-old married woman who had cancer and was unable to have children brought in a four-pound Yorkshire terrier that had one large puppy in the uterus. The dog was in labor and unable to deliver because the puppy was too big. I told her that we needed to do a C-section. This dog was like a child to her. Her parents raised Yorkshire terriers, and they had not had good experiences with C-sections. She did not want a C-section and asked if I would come to her home to see if we could get the mother to deliver the puppy in its more natural environment. So my wife and I went to their home, and we watched the futility of the dog in labor until midnight.

I told her that we had to go to the hospital and do a C-section. She still refused, so I told her that we were going home. She called me every hour to give me a progress report. At seven in the morning, I told her to have the dog at the hospital at eight o'clock and I would do a C-section, but because it'd been so long, she should not expect to have a live puppy. When I was in school, they did two C-sections on dogs. They got live puppies, but the mothers died. When they did the C-sections, they draped the animal and removed the entire uterus with all the puppies from the dog before they opened the uterus and started removing puppies. My thought was by doing it this way, they were taking a very full abdomen and emptying it, which was causing the mothers to go into shock.

We used a drug on the mother dog that would highly sedate the dog, but if a noise was made, the animal would jump. Everyone was instructed to be very quiet and not to drop anything. I injected local anesthetic in the abdominal wall and found an extremely large puppy in the uterus. I packed off the uterus inside the dog, opened the uterus, and slowly removed the puppy from the uterus so as not to create a large vacuum in the abdomen that would cause shock. When I removed the puppy and began to massage it, the puppy started to breathe. I handed the puppy to Dr. Campbell, and she continued to massage the puppy. It got stronger with his breathing and began to cry. To my and everyone else's surprise, we had a live puppy.

I sewed up the uterus and the abdominal wall. We let the mother wake up, and the puppy began to nurse. We called the owner and told her that she had a live puppy, a live mother, and that she could come to get them and take them home. Her mother and dad had moved to New Orleans. They were so impressed with the fact that I delivered a live puppy from the mother that when their dogs became ill, they would call me from New Orleans to tell me they were on their way to Dallas. When they were about an hour out, they would call me to meet them at the animal hospital.

I had a young man working for me that came from a large family of children, and they had a very sweet brindle boxer that was super hyper. One day, after they had gone shopping for groceries, they left a two-pound glass jar of peanut butter sitting on the counter. This was before the days of plastic jars. The boxer loved peanut butter. They had some other things to do, so they left the house with the boxer inside. When they came home, they discovered that he had knocked the jar of peanut butter onto the floor and ate it, glass and all. They brought him to the animal hospital and told me what had happened. I told them that we would need to operate to remove the glass. Recovery would be very critical. His chances were not good because of the tremendous amount of glass that he had eaten and the several hours that had elapsed.

I put the boxer under anesthetic and opened his abdomen. I could feel the glass in the stomach and the first part of the small intestine, so I decided to open the stomach. When I opened it, I found it full of glass and peanut butter. The only way that I knew to get all the glass out of the stomach was to take the stomach wall and suture it to the muscle wall of the abdomen at the side of the incision. Then I removed all the glass that I could by hand, but the stomach is made up of multiple ridges and folds, so the glass was embedded in these ridges and folds. I turned the boxer on his side with the incision over the edge of the table. I took IVs, turned them on, and let them run as I went down each fold in the stomach to flush the glass out of the folds. I did this on one side and then turned him over and did it on the other side.

I used the forceps to reach into the small intestine and grab the pieces of glass that I could get with the forceps and brought them out through the stomach. When I finished, I cut the stomach away from the muscle wall, closed the stomach, closed the muscle wall, and let the boxer wake up. He was sick for about three days. We fed him a lot of bread to try to pick up any remaining pieces of glass and move it on through the intestines. In ten days, he had made a full recovery and was his own hyperexcitable self.

One day, when we were very busy, I was working as fast as I could in the examination room, treating and vaccinating dogs and cats. I started to notice the people working for me were going back into the kennel and laughing uncontrollably. I did not know why and I did not have time to ask them. Then a twelve-year-old boy brought a dachshund in, set it on the examination table, he literally fell to the floor, grabbed his stomach, and started to laugh uncontrollably. I vaccinated the dog and handed it back to him. He left the exam room, trying to control his laughter.

The next client that came in was already a friend and one of my best clients. She said, "Dr. Martin, please do not report me to the SPCA." This lady took extremely good care of her animals, and she would be the last person that would need to be reported to the SPCA. I asked her what in the world was going on. She said, "Dr. Martin, you won't believe this." She explained that a lady came in with a Kerry Blue terrier named Mary Alice. Mary Alice went over and jumped up on one of the sofas. The owner went to the desk, asked if she could leave her purse and a sack with something in it at the desk, and asked if the receptionist would watch it for her. Then she turned, started toward Mary Alice, and suddenly said, "Mary Alice, I'm so sorry. I did not know that you were thirsty and you needed a drink. Just a minute, and I will get you a drink."

She went back to the desk, and in the sack was a thermos with a very large cap that would serve as a drinking bowl. She poured water in the cap, went over to Mary Alice, spread out the napkin on the sofa, placed the cap with water on the napkin, and Mary Alice took a drink. Then she wiped the dog's face with the napkin, took the cap, put it on the thermos, and threw the napkin in the waste basket. Now I was later to discover that Mary Alice could count, she could read, and she knew her colors. Mary Alice was going to be one of the most difficult patients I would ever encounter in my practice. Her owner was a registered nurse who also had three years of medical school. When her husband died, she met a new man who she married. He talked her into quitting medical school, and Mary Alice had become her child. Mary Alice developed chronic pancreatitis and later kidney failure. I made many emergency calls at night, Saturday afternoons, and Sundays treating Mary Alice.

One Saturday evening, around seven, I received a phone call from identical twin girls who were American Airlines stewardess. They had picked up a five to six-month-old kitten that was in the street. When they went to close the car door, the kitten jumped down, and they slammed the door on the kitten's right rear leg. I told them that I would meet them at the hospital. When they brought the kitten to the hospital, the right rear leg was completely severed except for an eighth of an inch of skin that was holding the leg on. The tibia was severed just above the metatarsal joint. They wanted me to reattach the leg.

I told them that it would not heal because there was no blood supply. All the vessels had been cut, and the nerves had been cut. If I did reattach the leg, gangrene would set in, and that would jeopardize the life of the cat. The leg needed to be amputated. They would not have any part of amputation. I stressed to them that there was no way that I could save this cat's foot. They said that I must try, so I told them that I would give my best try but not to get their hopes up.

I put the cat under anesthesia, took a stainless-steel pin, positioned the foot in a normal walking position, put the pin through the tarsus and through the joint into the tibia. I buried the pin just under the skin. Then I sewed the muscle and soft tissue back together. I sewed up the skin and gave the cat a large dose of antibiotic. Five days later, the tissue seemed to be normal in the foot. There was no sign of infection, and the cat was walking on the foot, so I sent the cat home on antibiotics. The cat made a complete recovery.

Eight weeks later, I removed the pin, and the cat could flex its foot. Now if I had recommended trying to save this cat's foot, I can assure you that gangrene would have set in, and we might have lost the cat.

It was just a few minutes before twelve when a very beautiful young lady came into the hospital with a lilac point Siamese cat that was pregnant, in labor, and having trouble delivering her kittens. I asked her where she had the cat in her home. She told me that the cat had been in a box in the living room so she could watch the cat deliver its kittens. I told her she needed to take the cat home, put the box in a clothes closet, and close the door at least three-quarters of the way. More than likely, the cat would deliver her kittens because cats like to deliver in privacy. I made quite a few house calls in the practice. I told her I would stop by at lunch because her condo was on my way home, and I would see how the cat was doing.

I finished up a few things that I was doing at the hospital and then went to her condo, which was on the second floor. There was an intercom, so I pushed the button and told her who I was. She said the door was unlocked and to come on up. I got to the top of the stairs and opened the door which opened into the living room. She was sitting on the sofa in a negligée. I was very shocked. I asked her where the cat was, and she said it was in the closet. When I opened the door to the closet, I could hear tiny squeaking sounds. I looked in the box, and the cat had two baby kittens. I knew that she had more kittens to deliver. I asked her if it would be all right for me to bring my wife by after closing and check on the cat to be sure she had delivered all her kittens.

This was not what she wanted; she was very lonely because she rarely saw her husband because of the long hours that he was working. Her husband was a new lawyer that had just completed his bar exam, and he was working for a large law firm in downtown Dallas. Young lawyers were required to do most of the research for the partners that were trying the cases. They worked anywhere from twelve to sixteen hours a day. I wanted to establish with her that I was happily married and was not interested in an affair.

She said she would appreciate it if I came back in the evening to check on the cat and the kittens and that it was okay for me to bring my wife. That evening, my wife and I stopped at her place. I checked on the mother who had delivered six kittens, and everything was okay. This lady continued as a client, and we went on as if nothing had happened. I changed my policy on house calls; I would never make a house call without someone going with me.

My wife, Jan, finished out the school year and signed a contract to teach the next year at T. W. Browne Junior High. Jan started the fall semester with much better results than the previous semester. She started with fresh classes in which she established the rules that would be followed in class. Because she was a very good math teacher who could explain things so students could understand, she had the ability to motivate students to want to do well. My wife was pregnant with our first child, and she started to spot blood.

Dr. Alexander recommended bed rest to see if she could save the baby. My wife resigned her teaching position. Two weeks later, she went into labor, and I took her to the hospital. In those days, the husband was not allowed to go into the room with his wife until they got her in a gown, put her in bed, and the doctor came in. So I was confined to what they called the dad's den which was full of cigarette smoke and lots of men waiting for their wives to deliver. When my wife removed her panties, the baby fell on the floor. Naturally, she became hysterical, and the nurses wanted to give her a sedative. They refused to come and get me.

Fortunately, Dr. Alexander came in and sent for me as he talked with her to calm her. This naturally was a very stressful time for Jan but also for me. When we married, we were told that there was probably very little chance that we would be able to have children because when I was a senior in high school, I fell off a haystack with one leg on each side of a truck box. My left testicle swelled to the size of my fist. Also, as I was doing chores the day that I was headed for college, I was riding a horse which slipped and went down on its front legs. My right testicle hit the saddle horn. Before I arrived in Fargo 450 miles away, that testicle was the size of my fist. As a result of these injuries, I kept getting infections in the epididymis. This resulted in an extremely low sperm count in which the doctors felt like there was very little chance of getting a woman pregnant.

Our joy in Jan being pregnant was suddenly dashed. Dr. Alexander was not discouraged. He said miscarriages were very common and to wait two months to try again. Jan checked back at T. W. Browne Junior High, but they had already hired a replacement, so that job was not available. She found a job at Thomas C. Marsh Junior High in North Dallas to teach math.

Changes in jobs resulted in many changes in our lives, including moving and new churches. When we first came to Dallas, we joined Grace Temple Baptist Church in Oak Cliff. When Jan started to teach in North Dallas, we moved from Oak Cliff to North Dallas, and we attended Wilshire Baptist Church. My goal was to go to Southwestern Baptist Theological Seminary in Fort Worth. So after working for Dr. Self for a year and a half, I started to look for a job in Fort Worth. I found a job working for a veterinarian in Fort Worth for two and a half days a week, which were Monday, Tuesday, and Wednesday morning. Then I worked for Dr. J. M. Farrell in Arlington on Thursday, Friday, and Saturday mornings. But Dr. Farrell and I also took every other day and every other weekend emergency duty. Dr. Farrell's wife had cancer, so the emergency duties became almost a daily and weekend deal. I enrolled in Southwestern Baptist Theological Seminary at night for the fall semester.

My wife became pregnant again, and we continued to see Dr. Alexander in Dallas. One evening in October, she started into a weak labor, but it pretty well kept both of us up most of the night. I went to work in Fort Worth on Wednesday morning. When I got home at lunch, I took her to Dr. Alexander's office. He examined her and gave us two options. One was to go home until the labor became more intense. The other was that he would give her some injections in his office to see if he could speed up the labor. We chose the injections, and at 3:30, I took her to the hospital. In October of 1968, James Martin made his entrance into the world. Three days later, I took my wife and our son home to Arlington.

Dr. Farrell's and the Fort Worth veterinarian's (referred to as Dr. G) practices were on the opposite ends of the spectrum. Dr. G was very old-school. The practice was poorly equipped, the quality of medicine was very poor, and it was very difficult for me to work in this environment. Dr. G had two syringes in his animal hospital with needles on them; one in the front of the practice where he saw the clients, and one in the back where he treated his patients. Dr. G would give an animal an injection. Then he would take the syringe, rinse it out with tap water, and give another injection without sterilizing the syringe or needle.

When Dr. G did surgery, he would take towels from the laundry and use them for drapes. If he had time, he would boil the instruments in water. If not, he would just clean them and use them to do the surgery that he did barehanded. If his glasses slipped down on his nose, he would push them back up and go back in the animal to complete the surgery. He asked me one day why I thought he kept getting abscesses in his incisions. I told him that it was probably because he did not do sterile surgery. His answer was that penicillin cost fourteen cents a cc, and that was cheaper than sterile surgery.

Dr. Farrell's practice, on the other hand, was very modern with almost all the new equipment that was available in the practice. I talked with Dr. Farrell as his practice was growing, and he was spending more time with his wife who was not doing well. I asked him if I could go full-time for him. We came to an agreement that I would go full-time, and in three months, I would receive a sizable raise. His wife continued to deteriorate, and I was taking almost all the emergency calls, both during the week and on the weekends.

One Saturday afternoon, I received an emergency call that a seven-pound poodle had been bitten by a large German shepherd. When I arrived at the hospital, I found that all four canine teeth of this German shepherd had gone through the chest of this little poodle. Both lungs were collapsed, and I did not know how the dog was still alive. Dr. Farrell's son was there, and I asked him if he could hold the dog while I sewed up the holes in the chest because it would not be possible to put the dog under anesthetic without the dog dying immediately. He said he would try to hold the dog, so I grabbed some suture material to sew up the holes that were in the chest.

I took the suture material, went around the ribs by the holes, and sewed the ribs together. Then I took a large syringe, put a needle on it, and sucked the air out of the thoracic cavity to produce a negative pressure and reinflate the lungs. I gave the dog some intravenous antibiotic. I kept the dog in the hospital for several days on antibiotics. The dog did very well, and we were able to send it home. The poodle made a full recovery.

We had a five-year-old German shepherd with severe hip dysplasia. The right hip was out of joint. We could get it back in joint, but it would not stay in joint. This German shepherd had the most difficult dysplasia to treat (grade four). The acetabulum, which is the socket that the head of the femur rotates in, was extremely shallow and arthritic, so the hip would not stay in joint. There were several surgical procedures that had been developed to keep the hip in joint, but none of them were very successful. I had spent the last year and a half studying the hip joint because hip dysplasia was so prevalent in large breed dogs. I developed a procedure that I believed would work to keep the hip in the joint.

I talked to Dr. Farrell about the procedure, and he agreed that it was worth a try if the owners were willing to let me do the surgery, knowing that it was a new procedure that had never been done before. The owners really loved their dog and said that it was worth a try. I put the dog under anesthetic, opened the hip joint, and drilled a hole through the head of the femur that came out just behind the head of the femur. Then I cut a strip of the tensor fasciae latae which is commonly used in the repair of anterior cruciate ligaments in the knees. Instead of pulling the tensor fasciae latae distally like you would for the knee, I pulled it proximally and threaded it through the hole from the neck of the femur to the opening of the round ligament. I drilled a hole in the pelvis where the round ligament would normally attach in the acetabulum. I then threaded the tensor fasciae latae through a hole in the acetabulum. I used the forceps, reached under the pelvis, grasped the tensor fasciae latae, pulled it around the pelvis and, with stainless steel wire, tied it to the pelvis. Then I closed the joint capsule, sewed up the muscles, and sewed up the skin.

The next day, the dog was walking on the leg, and the hip remained in place. We only allowed the dog to walk on a leash and never to pull or run for six weeks. The dog's hip remained in place and did not dislocate again.

When we moved to Arlington, Dr. Farrell recommended that we buy a house and thus gain some equity rather than rent an apartment. Jan and I found the last house that a builder had just finished in a development, and he was willing to make a very good deal on it so he could move on to another development. It was a three-bedroom house with a fireplace in the den and two-car garage in a very nice neighborhood. I completed my first year at Southwestern Baptist Theological Seminary. Dr. Farrell had promised me a large raise after three months. Six months had passed, and I had not received a raise. Dr. Farrell was not in the office much because his wife had become terminal, and he was spending most of his time with her at home. One day, when he came to the hospital, I asked him about the raise, and he said he would have to think about it. He was extremely happy with me as a veterinarian, and he would get back with me in the next week or two. I had a feeling that the raise was not going to be what he promised.

We were not making ends meet, so I spent some evenings and my afternoons off looking for a place to open a practice in Dallas. I located a building that had some space to lease on Sherry Lane in Preston Center. I could lease it, and the owners would pay for the remodeling.

Dr. Farrell came in the hospital about two weeks later, and I asked him about the raise. He offered me a very minimal raise that would not meet our needs. I told him that I had no choice but to give him a three months' notice that I would be leaving the practice.

He became very angry and told me I was through. I was to pack up my stuff and to get out of the hospital. He paid me up to that point. We had no savings and no means to support ourselves. I had just essentially been fired for asking for a raise that was promised. Fortunately, I had made friends with several pharmaceutical reps. I immediately got on the phone and asked them if they knew any veterinarians that were hiring.

One of them said two veterinarians were looking for a veterinarian to fill in while they were on vacation. One was going to take a two-week vacation in June, and another was going to take a one-week vacation in June. I called these two veterinarians, and they both hired me for the time they would be on vacation, but I still needed work during the other times.

Another rep told me Dr. Jerry Hosek was always in need of a veterinarian. So that day, I went to see Dr. Hosek. He hired me on the spot, and I went to work for him right then. He knew about the commitment that I had to the veterinarians for their vacation, and he said that was fine but that every day that I was free on Monday through Saturday, he could use me. The first week, I drove from Arlington to Dallas to work. This made very long days, and my wife didn't feel like I had enough time for her and our son, James. We went to Dallas and located a very inexpensive apartment that would be about one mile from my practice. This apartment was very rundown. The oven was so uneven that Jan could not bake a cake because if she put the pan in the oven, the batter in the front of the pan would be barely a quarter of an inch, and the back of the pan would almost overflow. But this apartment was what we could afford.

My practice was supposed to be ready at the end of June, but it wasn't going to make it. I took the last week off in June, went to the practice, and if the workers did not show up, I would immediately go to the contractor's office to demand that workers would be there. They finished the practice on July 3 of 1969. My wife and I and our son James opened the practice on July 4. The building was not very visible, and at that time you could not do any advertising other than put an ad in the paper announcing the opening of the practice.

I notified the forty clients that had followed me to Arlington that I had now opened my own practice in Dallas. Dr. Hopkins was the veterinarian that I took my animals to when I needed an x-ray during the time that I practiced with Dr. Self. Dr. Hopkins called me, told me that they were tired of taking their own emergency calls, and wondered if I would take their emergency calls. He would provide a form that I could fill out, noting what I found and what I did. I was to send the form with the client with instructions to see him within three days of the time that I saw them.

This was a godsend because he had a very large practice. I made my living to start with from the emergency calls that I took in the evenings and on the weekends. There was a telephone answering service that answered his calls at night and answered several other veterinarians' emergency calls. The other veterinarians had not made arrangements for me to take their calls; however, the telephone secretaries knew that I was available to take Dr. Hopkins calls, and if they could not reach the other veterinarians, they would call me and ask if I would take their calls. I had many of Dr. Hopkins clients ask if they could continue to come and see me, and I told them no. My arrangement was they had to go back to see Dr. Hopkins. I told them that they needed to go see him until the condition of the animal had been cleared up. Then, if they still wanted to make the change, they could make it, but it would have to be during the daytime hours when they chose to come see me. Many of them did.

The other veterinarians' clients asked me if I would continue to see their animals. Because I had no professional relationship with those veterinarians, and their veterinarian was not available when they needed them, I told them that I would continue to see their animals if they wanted me to. My wife and I bought an electric frying pan and a hot plate. We set up a playpen in the back corner of the surgery room. Jan worked for me during the summer, and we kept James at the hospital. Jan had not grown up around animals, and it was difficult for her at first to see how attached people were to their animals. It was good for her to spend several months with me getting to know the people, how much their animals meant to them, how to treat the animals, and to learn how to help me in surgery. She worked for me that summer and fall.

We were struggling to make ends meet, so Jan began substitute teaching in Highland Park. She found out about a math position at Highland Park Junior High and applied for the position. When she made her application, she was told that there was not a position available, but she knew that a math teacher was going to take a maternity leave at the end of the fall semester. The principal, Mr. Red, told her there would be a position. Also I knew the president of the school board, Dr. Ware, who was my urologist and a client. Jan was hired to teach math starting in January.

The first week we put James in day care, he immediately caught a virus and was very sick. Jan could not take time off to care for him as she had just started teaching and had no days to utilize. I had to take care of him while he was sick and run the practice. When Jan would finish teaching, she would come to the hospital, and then we would do the surgeries that I had scheduled. We usually ended up eating supper at the hospital. James was a very good baby, and I could leave him in the playpen or highchair, eating while I saw clients. I cooked for both of us for lunch, and it worked out quite well.

The infection in my reproductive organs continued to be a problem. Dr. Ware told me that if I was going to have more children, I had better try now because he did not know if he could keep me free of infection without surgery that could render me incapable of having more children. Jan became pregnant and took a maternity leave from teaching. We were making a living now in the practice. I did not reenroll in Southwestern Baptist Theological Seminary.

We became very active at Royal Haven Baptist Church. My wife had met a pastor of a small Baptist Church who was also a schoolteacher, and we became friends. When he was going to be gone on a Sunday, he would ask me to fill the pulpit and preach for him. One Sunday, I preached a message on how to be saved. A sixteen-year-old boy came forward during the invitation and told me that he wanted to receive Jesus Christ as his personal Savior. I told him how to ask for God's forgiveness, how to ask Jesus Christ to come into his life, and to ask

Jesus to be Lord and Savior of his life. I knelt beside this young man as he asked God to forgive him and asked Jesus to take over his life.

I watched as the peace and the joy filled this young man's life. I thought, *Boy, I wished I had what he had.* My wife and I were teaching the senior high youth group in Sunday school. She taught the senior girls, and I taught the senior boys. Dr. Colton asked me to preach a Sunday evening service, sharing my testimony how I met God in the barn and how it changed my life. My life at this time had become one of great turmoil. I was down to 112 pounds and was going through a box of Di Gel a day to keep my stomach settled so that I could eat. I was afraid to go to sleep because I was afraid that I would not wake up.

As the world describes it, I was not an evil or wicked person, but I could not get rid of the guilt that had plagued me since I was a twelve-year-old boy. I would stay up all night for two nights reading the Bible, and the third night I would fall asleep out of pure exhaustion. There were two Scriptures that I read that would send chills up and down my spine.

Matthew 7:13–14 says:

> Enter you in at the strait gate: for wide is the gate, and broad is the way, that leads to destruction, and many there be which go in there at: Because strait is the gate, and narrow is the way, which leads unto life, and few there be that find it.

As I read "Few there be that find it," it would just send chills up my back. Matthew 7:21–23 says:

> Not every one that says unto me, Lord, Lord, shall enter into the kingdom of heaven; but he that does the will of my Father which is in heaven. Many will say to me in that day, Lord, Lord, have we not prophesied in your name? and in your name have cast out devils? and in your name done many wonderful works? And then will I profess unto them, I never knew you: depart from me, you that work iniquity.

I would read this passage and be in utter fear. I finally picked up the Bible one night, held it in my hand, and said to God, "You say in your Word that you will show us what's wrong with our lives and what we need. God, I am desperate, and I need to know what's wrong with my life." After two weeks of reading the Bible, especially Matthew 7, I turned to Acts 22 where Paul gave his testimony. He stated that when the Lord spoke to him on the road to Damascus that Jesus told him to go into Damascus, and a man named Ananias would come to him to tell him all things that he must do and that he must suffer for the sake of Christ.

Acts 22:15–16 says:

> For you shall be his witness unto all men of what you have seen and heard. And now why do you tarry? Arise, and be baptized, and wash away your sins, calling on the name of the Lord.

Paul was not saved on the road to Damascus. He did not get saved until Ananias came and told him how to be saved, that he must call on the name of the Lord and be forgiven of his sins to be saved. I now realized that I was not saved in the barn. I had met God, similar to Paul's experience on the road to Damascus. I was ready to be saved, but I did not have anyone tell me that I needed to invite Jesus Christ into my heart. At this point, I realized I was lost.

Two weeks after I had shared my testimony, we were attending the evening service at Royal Haven Baptist Church. I turned to Jan, and I said, "I am lost. Will you go with me as I tell Dr. Colton that I need to be saved?"

She said, "Yes, I will go."

I went forward, told the pastor that I was lost and that I needed to be saved.

He said, "No way. I will come by on Monday, we will have lunch, and we will get this straightened out because there's no one in this church that is serving God more than you."

We went home that night and put James to bed. I told Jan that I was not going to bed until I got this straightened out, and she said that she was not either. So with the Holy Spirit as my guide, I began to search my life. Everything in my life was about me, and I realized that it needed to be about God. So on August 24, 1970, at 12:15 in the morning, I came to God and I said, "I will accept you if I do not have to go back to that church and tell them that I was lost."

God spoke to me in an audible voice and said, "Depart from me, Ernie. I never knew you."

I had been shot at; I had people that were going to initiate me; I was threatened in many ways; but never in my life did I know such fear as I knew at that moment. I threw myself onto the coffee table and cried out, "God, I'll go anywhere! I will tell anyone, I will do anything that you ask me if you will forgive me of my sins. Jesus, will you come into my heart and be my Lord and Savior?"

Jesus came into my heart, and for the first time in my life, I felt no guilt. I felt complete peace, complete joy, and I couldn't wait to go back to the church to tell them that I had accepted Jesus Christ as my Lord and Savior. I took Jan in my arms, hugged and kissed her, and she said that was even different. She was not surprised that I was lost because from the very beginning, she questioned my salvation. The pastor told her that he thought I was saved, but she never was at peace that I was saved. She said her only hope was that I was searching after God with all my heart. God said in His Word if you search for Him with all your heart, He shall be found.

The next day, Dr. Colton came to have lunch, and I told him that I would have lunch with him but that we did not need to talk about it because I had received Jesus Christ as my Savior last night. He said that he had trouble believing that I was not saved. I told him to watch me, that he was going to see a big difference in my life. I told him that I wanted to be baptized and I wanted to share with the church that I had gotten saved. He told me, "I think it will cause a lot of confusion in the church if you give a public testimony of having just gotten saved."

I told him, "Great, if it causes confusion, maybe others that are in my same condition might accept Jesus Christ as their Lord and Savior because, hopefully, it will cause people to examine their hearts to be sure that they knew him as their Savior."

We had to be out of town the next Sunday. I was having a hard time waiting to go back to the church to tell them I had received Jesus Christ as my own personal Savior. I went to work the next day, and

Sal, a technician from Morton Cancer and Wadley Institute, came to the hospital as we were doing research trying to find the LD50 for L-asparaginase in dogs. Sal asked me how I was doing, and I told him, "Great since last night."

He asked what happened last night, and I told him that I had received Jesus Christ as my Lord and Savior. Sal said to me, "I don't know him as my personal Savior." Sal and his family were Catholics. Sal told me that he would like to receive Jesus Christ as his Savior. I opened my Bible to show him the scriptures.

Romans 3:10–12 says:

> As it is written, There is none righteous, no, not one: There is none that understands, there is none that seeks after God. They are all gone out of the way, they are together become unprofitable; there is none that does good, no, not one.

I was very busy seeing patients, so I told Sal to read the Scriptures while I saw patients. When I finished seeing a patient, I went back to Sal and opened the Bible again.

John 3:16 says:

> For God so loved the world, that he gave his only begotten Son, that whosoever believes in him should not perish, but have everlasting life.

I told Sal to read this Scripture while I was seeing another patient. After I saw that patient, I went back to Sal and opened the Bible.

Romans 10:9–10, 13 says:

> That if you shall confess with your mouth the Lord Jesus, and shall believe in your heart that God has raised him from the dead, you shall be saved. For with the heart man believes unto righteousness; and with the mouth confession is made unto salvation. For whosoever shall call upon the name of the Lord shall be saved.

I told Sal to read the Scriptures, and I went to see another patient. When I came back from seeing the patient, I asked Sal if he believed that Jesus Christ was the Son of God, born of the Virgin Mary, suffered and died on the cross, and on the third day was resurrected. After he said that he believed, I asked him if he would like to receive Jesus Christ as his Savior. He replied that he would like to, so we went into the surgery room, knelt on our knees, and I told Sal to, in his own words, ask God to forgive him of his sins and to ask Jesus Christ to come into his heart and to be his Lord and Savior.

Sal asked God to forgive him and invited Jesus Christ to come into his life to be his Lord and Savior. Sal got up from his knees with great tears of joy, thanking me and thanking God for the peace that he now had. We finished our work, and Sal went back to Morton Cancer Hospital. Sal went home that night and led his wife to a saving knowledge of Jesus Christ.

Something that I never realized was that a person without Jesus could not receive love nor give love because without God who is love, a person does not believe that somebody does something purely because they love them. A person without God is looking for the strings attached when someone does something for them, and they believe that they are now indebted to that person.

John 15:13 says:

Greater love has no man than this, that a man lay down
his life for his friends.

God's love is agape love which is 100 percent giving with no expectation of return. A man is not capable of loving that way nor is he able to receive that type of love without having received Jesus Christ.

As I said earlier, I was not able to go to church the following Sunday after I had received Christ because we were going out of town. The next Sunday, Sal, his wife, and family went to church with us. When the invitation was given, I went forward and told the pastor that I had received Jesus Christ as my Savior and that I wanted to follow the Lord in water baptism. Sal and his wife came forward and made their public profession of faith in Jesus Christ. Dr. Colton announced to the congregation that the three of us had accepted Christ, and we were going to follow the Lord in water baptism the next Sunday.

Many people came by to greet us after the service. More than half of them said that they would never believe that I was not saved. I told them to watch me because now they were going to see a man walking in the Spirit, not in the flesh, and that I was a changed man.

CHAPTER 3

Cancer Research

Alady that was a client of mine came into the hospital with a cat that had leukemia. Just a few days before, there had been an article in the paper about a new drug, L-asparaginase, that had been developed by Wadley Institute in Dallas, describing a young boy with leukemia who had gone into remission after receiving the drug. I told my client that it was too bad that we couldn't get some of this L-asparaginase. She had read the article also, and she asked if I was serious about wanting to try the drug. I said, "Yes."

She said that it would not be a problem because she knew Dr. Hill who was head of Wadley Institute. Her baby was the first baby that was a blue baby that Dr. Hill gave a transfusion to replace all his blood with new blood, and her baby was the first one to live as a blue baby. She and Dr. Hill were very close friends, so she could give me a personal introduction to Dr. Hill. She set up a meeting with Dr. Hill, herself, and me. I told him that I would like to try L-asparaginase on my client's cat that had leukemia.

Dr. Hill told me about the history behind the discovery of L-asparaginase. Back before there were antibiotics, many people with cancer were in the terminal stages of cancer, and their resistance would be very low. They would contract pneumonia, and a large percentage of the people died from the pneumonia. But a few recovered from the pneumonia, and then their cancer would disappear.

After doing research, they discovered that the bacteria produced L- asparaginase, and this was the active ingredient that killed cancer cells. Dr. Hill was thrilled because they were looking for animals that had natural occurring cancers that they could test the drugs on. So Dr. Hill introduced me to Dr. Khan who oversaw the development of L-asparaginase.

Dr. Khan made arrangements for Sal to bring me the drug to give to my client's cat. Before the cat could be treated, we needed to do a bone marrow biopsy, a complete CBC, lymph node biopsies, and remove the spleen. We did all these things. Then we gave 750 units per pound of L-asparaginase to the cat every day for twenty-eight days by IV injections. The cat made a complete recovery. We continued several more cases with the same results, but we found the cat was not a good model because cats could spontaneously recover from leukemia on their own. Also, 5 mg of prednisolone given daily could put many cats into remission.

We also treated several dogs that had lymphoma with L-asparaginase. These dogs would go into remission from three months to nine months, but the lymphoma always came back. I concluded that L-asparaginase worked in the people that had cancer and developed pneumonia because the body was stressed at the same time, and thus, in some people, it stimulated the body's natural immune system to help fight the cancer. I asked Dr. Khan to give me some of the E. coli bacteria that had been killed that they were extracting the L- asparaginase from; he wanted to know what I wanted the E. coli bacteria for. I told him that I wanted to stress the animal when I gave the L-asparaginase. He said that there is no way that you can stress an animal that is in a compromised condition without killing it.

I had a cat brought to me that did not have the viral leukemia but had the bone marrow leukemia like people. This cat had 140,000 WBC, and normal WBC is ten to fourteen thousand. I asked Sal to get me some of the killed E. coli bacteria, and he said that he would do his best to get it for me. This cat at the time had no hope of survival. I talked extensively with the owners of the cat, told them that the treatment I was recommending was extremely risky, and probably would result in death of their cat. They loved this cat as they loved their children, and they asked me if there was any possibility that this could save their cat. I told them that it was slim to none, but it was the only thing that I had to offer.

They said that the cat was dying and probably would not live more than three days in the condition that it was in. If there was just the very slimmest of chances that this could work, they wanted to try it. I had the owners sign releases that totally detailed the risk, the fact that this was experimental, that it had never been tried before, and that they were fully aware that this treatment would probably kill their cat. They said, "Our cat is suffering. We do not want to watch it suffer anymore, and if this treatment puts the cat into shock, it will die suddenly." In their estimation, that would be a lot less pain than the cat was going through now.

I had talked to them about euthanasia, and they would not consider euthanasia. I really did not have any basis of knowing how much of the concentrated killed E. coli bacteria that I needed to give this cat to throw it into shock and not kill it. I arrived at an amount of the concentrated killed E. coli to give to the cat and, at the same time, gave it the first dose of L-asparaginase. The cat went into shock after the injection of the E. coli and the L-asparaginase. I treated the cat for shock with standard protocol. The cat came out of the shock, and the next day, the cat was stronger.

I continued the injections of L-asparaginase for twenty-eight days. The cat made a complete recovery, and in three months, we could not find any cancer cells in the lymph nodes or the bone marrow. The cat was three years old when we treated it, and it lived another ten years with no reoccurrence of the lymphoma.

There was a family that had a large orange and white cat named Pete who became ill. I ran tests and diagnosed Pete as having the viral leukemia. Currently, there was some controversy in both veterinary and medical fields as to whether it was safe to have a cat with leukemia around small children. The family had two children less than four years of age, and they were quite concerned about keeping Pete because a family that was very close to them had a young child that had just died from leukemia. They really loved Pete and did not want him put to sleep, but they were afraid to take him home.

I offered to keep Pete at the hospital and treat Pete for leukemia. I asked if it would it be all right if I gave him to another family if he would get well and if another family would take him. They were pleased with the offer. I also told them that I might be able to keep Pete as a hospital cat in which during the day, he would be caged, but in the evening, he would have free roam of the animal hospital. They really liked that idea because they could come and visit Pete. I treated Pete with L-asparaginase, and Pete recovered.

One night, I went out on an emergency, and a client brought in a cat that was semicomatose. I've always wondered why people wait until an animal is almost beyond saving before they bring it to the veterinarian and expect miracles. They told me that they loved the cat and wanted me to do everything possible to save the cat. I gave them very little hope as the cat's temperature was too low to register on the thermometer. The cat was cold, semicomatose, and nonresponsive. But they said to do everything I can, so I pulled some blood. On a cat in this condition, it is extremely difficult to get in a vein. I was able to use a 25-gauge needle and got in the vein. The blood looked like light pink water. A cat's normal PCV is between 40 and 45, and this cats PCV was 3. I had no idea how the cat could still be alive.

The blood smear was full of lymphoblast, so I diagnosed leukemia. I did not have any L-asparaginase at the hospital. I told the owners that I did not have the drug available, and it would not be available until Monday as this was a Friday night. Morton Cancer Hospital would not be open for me to get the drug until Monday. I told them that the only option that I had to offer was completely experimental, and that was to do a blood transfusion from Pete. I was hoping that Pete would have strong antibodies against the virus and that his blood would begin to destroy the virus so that the cat might have a slim chance of survival.

They agreed to the transfusion from Pete. I pulled 20 mL of whole blood from Pete and gave it to their cat. I had packed their cat in towels and put a heating pad under a thick layer of towels so as not to burn the cat's skin. I turned the heating pad on low to warm up the cat. I also gave the cat some sub-Q fluids to rehydrate it, some antibiotics, and hoped for the best.

The next morning, the cat was conscious and able to take a little food. I gave some more fluids, and by Monday morning, the cat was standing and was eating. The cat made a full recovery and lived for several years. Pete became my life-saving donor for cats when the owners could not afford the treatment with L-asparaginase. I also discovered that I could take Pete's blood, separate the red cells, and just give the plasma to cats with the same results. I could give Pete his red cells back, and it would not cause Pete to become anemic if I needed to use him for multiple transfusions. Pete had a great life at the hospital as my boys loved to play with him; he loved to play with them, and he had full run of the hospital when we were not seeing patients.

Dr. Spears at Morton Cancer Hospital and Wadley Institute had developed a new drug called Cis platinum. Mice and rabbit studies had been done with the drug, and now they wanted to try it in cats and dogs. They believed that this drug had a wide spectrum of types of cancer that it would cure. I had a cat that had a malignant squamous cell carcinoma that had metastasized throughout the body. There was no hope for the cat to be cured with anything else that was available. I explained to the owners that this drug had never been used in a cat and that it might kill the cat, but it was the only thing that I could offer them to treat their cat. I explained all the risks with this completely experimental drug which had only been used in mice and rabbits.

It produced a lot of vomiting in these animals when it was given, but they were seeing some good results. I stressed to the people to not get their hopes up, but they wanted to try the drug because they did not want to euthanize the cat nor watch it suffer and die. Their thoughts were if there was a slight chance that their cat could get well, they wanted to give the cat that opportunity.

After the releases were signed, I gave the cat Cis platinum. Unfortunately, in thirty minutes, the drug destroyed the cat's kidneys, and the cat died within forty-five minutes. Then we knew that this drug was not safe to use in cats. We published this so hopefully no one else would use Cis platinum in cats. Unfortunately, many people did not believe us, and they gave it to cats with the same fatal results.

Cis platinum was successful in many cancers in dogs. It would make the dogs violently sick with tremendous amounts of vomiting for several days, but the end results were that many dogs recovered from their cancers. Cis platinum is a very effective drug in many cancers in humans, but it does make people violently ill.

I had clients; the husband, who was a lawyer, and his wife were the nicest people that you would ever meet, and they had a Scottish terrier mix that they brought to me because he was having trouble eating and was drooling severely. I opened his mouth and saw a tumor the size of a lemon in the back junction of the right jaw. I told them that we needed to biopsy the tumor. So they took the dog home that evening and withheld food and water. The next day, I put the dog under anesthetic and took a biopsy. The biopsy came back a malignant melanosarcoma. At that time, there was no known chemotherapy that was effective against melanosarcoma. They loved this dog, and he was like a member of their family. They were willing to try anything that I could do for the animal, and they knew that I worked in cancer research with Morton Cancer Hospital and Wadley Institute.

I called Dr. Khan to see if they had anything that they could offer for a melanosarcoma, and he told me they had absolutely nothing. I told him that the owners were emphatic and that they would try anything if it had a chance to save their dog's life. He said he would talk to the other doctors and would call me back tomorrow.

Dr. Khan called me the next day and explained that they had a drug that was a by-product of making interferon called interleukin two. He said that this drug had not even been used in mice or rabbits, and they did not have any idea what the dose would be. He asked if I could put the dog under anesthetic daily and inject the drug directly into the tumor. I told him that it could be done. He said, "I will send the drug over tomorrow with directions. Have the people bring the dog into the hospital in the morning for the injection."

I called the family to bring the dog in the next morning, and I injected the tumor with the interleukin two. They brought the dog back the next day, and the tumor appeared to be smaller. We took photographs daily of the tumor with a ruler beside the tumor, and on the thirteenth day, we could not find any tumor to inject into. It was completely gone.

About a week later, I received a call from Bill Goddard. He and his wife were very good clients of mine, and they had three very small yorkies that were family members. Mr. Goddard said, "Dr. Martin, I know you. I'm calling about the photographs of this dog with the tumor that it had in his mouth. I want to confirm that this dog was treated by you and that the tumor had disappeared."

I confirmed that I had treated the dog and that the tumor had disappeared. He thanked me and then wrote a million-dollar check to Morton Cancer Hospital and Wadley Institute to continue work on interleukin two. Because of these results, interleukin two was approved to go directly into human trials without all the lab animal testing that was normally done before human trials.

These are just a few cases that I have shared of my work with Morton Cancer Hospital and Wadley Institute. Shortly after I started using some of the cancer drugs on dogs and cats, Dr. Hill asked if I would be their staff veterinarian which would not be a paid position. It meant that I would have to go to their lab facility unannounced four times a year to be sure that they were following USDA rules and regulations in the way that they handled and treated their animals. I would also have to be available to the USDA veterinarian of the region to give him reports and answer any questions that he had concerning their research.

I accepted the position because it gave me access to drugs that were not available to anyone else, but more importantly, it gave me an opportunity to hopefully help fight cancer in humans. I was extremely careful that in no way would I ever intentionally cause pain or suffering to an animal just for the sake of research. Some of these cases could be misinterpreted that what I did might be out of that realm; however, I can assure you that the pain and suffering that the animal was going through was far greater than anything I ever created with the drugs. I know that several animals that I treated with these experimental drugs went on to live normal happy lives. And I can only hope that this translated to some children, mothers, and fathers being alive today and living healthy happy lives because of some of the work we did in my animal hospital to help find a cure for cancer.

CHAPTER 4

The Start of My New Life in Christ

My wife was pregnant with our second child. She was running a high fever, and the doctors were very concerned, but they were afraid to give her medication because of the possibility of creating defects or problems in the unborn child. I had gone to church to teach the Sunday school class and to attend the worship service. When I came home, I asked my wife if she believed that God could heal her. She said, "Yes," but it was not a convincing yes. It was a wishful thinking type of yes that says, "I know God can do it, but I don't really believe He will."

I looked at her and said, "I believe that God's Word says He can and will and wants to heal you, and I'm going to pray for you." I laid my hand on her; I prayed for her; and I felt the fever leave her and come into me. I rebuked the fever in Jesus's name, asked God to heal her in the name of Jesus, and she was instantly well.

Early the next morning, my receptionist called to say that she had the flu with a high fever and she would not be in to work. My wife told her that she had a fever for several days, but I prayed for her, and she was healed. My receptionist asked her to get me to come to the phone to pray for her. This was all new to me. The only person I had ever prayed for to be healed was my wife, and that was in person. I didn't know about praying over the phone, but I asked the Lord to heal her in the name of Jesus. She immediately said, "The fever is gone. I feel fine. I will be at work."

She came in to work with her five-year-old son who had a runny snotty nose for weeks that he got at day care. She asked if I would pray for him, so I prayed for him, and his nose immediately dried up. She took him to day care, and they said to her, "This is the first time we've seen him in a long time when he looks healthy."

In the Baptist Church, they always ended their prayers with, "We ask it in Jesus' name." I asked why they did that, and their answer was that was how they were taught to pray, but no one knew why. I got out the dictionary and looked up *name*. "By the authority of" was one of the definitions.

John 14:13 says:

> And whatsoever you shall ask in my name, that will I do, that the Father may be glorified in the Son.

Jesus said that if we ask in His name, He has the authority to do it. Thus giving us His authority to use His name to do whatever we ask in His name.

Luke 7:2–10 says:

> And a certain centurion's servant, who was dear unto him, was sick, and ready to die. And when he heard of Jesus, he sent unto him the elders of the Jews, beseeching him that he would come and heal his servant. And when they came to Jesus, they besought him instantly, saying, That he was worthy for whom he should do this: For he loves our nation, and he has built us a synagogue. Then Jesus went with them. And when he was now not far from the house, the centurion sent friends to him, saying unto him, Lord, trouble not yourself: for I am not worthy that you should enter under my roof: Wherefore neither thought I myself worthy to come unto you: but say in a word, and my servant shall be healed. For I also am a man set under authority, having under me soldiers, and I say unto one, Go, and he goes; and to another, Come, and he comes; and to my servant, Do this, and he does *it*. When Jesus heard these things, he marveled at him, and turned him about, and said unto the people that followed

him, I say unto you, I have not found so great faith, no, not in Israel. And they that were sent, returning to the house, found the servant whole that had been sick.

The centurion said that he had authority, and he recognized Jesus had the authority to heal. What incredible simplicity to faith.

My wife and I and our son James had been living in an apartment. Since my wife was pregnant and expecting our second child, we decided that it was time to buy a house. We wanted a house with a two-car garage, a den, and a fireplace. We looked at a lot of houses, but we just didn't seem to find a house that we liked that we could afford. One night, I felt impressed to pick up the newspaper to search the real estate adds for houses that were for sale. There was an ad that just jumped out at me. It wasn't anything that fit our criteria. It had no garage and no fireplace, but for some reason, it just seemed to be the house that we needed to go see.

I called the people to make an appointment to see the house, and it turned out to be a couple that was in a Sunday school class with us previously. We made arrangements to go look at the house, and when we walked in the door, there was just a perfect peace that came on my wife and on me that this was a house that God wanted us to have. We bought the house from the couple. The room that we were going to use for the nursery was not carpeted. I measured the room and bought carpet. I called to ask the owner if I could install the carpet as they were not using the room. The owner said that it would be fine for me to come over, and he would help me install the carpet.

I went over one evening to install the carpet, and as we were working on the carpet, I shared with the man how I had recently accepted Jesus Christ as my Savior. As I shared my testimony with him, he began to weep. He said to me that there was no power in his life, that he thought he was saved, but now he realized that he had never received Jesus Christ. I told him in his own words to ask God to forgive him of his sins and invite Jesus Christ to come into his heart. He spent an hour and a half confessing his sins to God. It was really late, and I needed to get home to get some sleep. But this man's soul was more important, and finally, he called on the name of Jesus and asked Him to come into his heart to be his Lord and Savior. He got saved that night.

God moves in strange and mysterious ways. He wanted us to buy that house so the owner could come to a saving knowledge of Jesus Christ. This was not the only reason that God wanted us to buy the house, but in my mind, it was the most important reason.

In December of 1970, my wife went into labor, I took her to Baylor Hospital, and Charles Martin came into this world as our second son. After three days, I took Jan and Charlie home. The house did not have central air and heat, so we had central air and heat put in. It had a very large pecan tree in the backyard, so I put a swing for James on one of the branches. This house just seemed to be a perfect fit for us, and we were very happy in the house, even though it didn't have the things that we thought were essential. God showed us that being in His will and where He wanted us was what brought peace.

After I accepted Jesus Christ as my Savior, God gave me a scripture. John 14:12 says:

> Verily, verily, I say unto you, He that believes on me, the works that I do shall he do also; and greater works than these shall he do; because I go unto my Father.

I said to God that I wanted to see these works, knowing that Jesus healed the sick, cast out demons, raised the dead, walked on water, and taught with authority. Since God said that Jesus did these works, and you will do these works plus greater works, I was ready. When I was a small boy, about seven years of age, I went to town with my dad. My dad was well known and well respected. He needed to borrow some money, so we went to the bank, walked by the bank secretary, and opened the door to the president's office. He said, "Bill, I need to borrow some money."

Bill said, "Jimmy, how much do you need?"

My dad told him how much that he wanted to borrow, and then he asked Bill how much it would cost him. Bill told my dad what the interest rate would be. My dad said that was fine and asked when the money would be in his account.

Bill told him that it would be in his account in the morning. Bill and my dad shook hands, and my dad walked out of the bank without signing a note. My dad's word was sacred, and when he gave his word, he would keep it. There was absolutely no question about the fact that his word was his word. Now if my dad's word was that sacred and assured, how much easier was it for me to trust a holy God?

Matthew 24:35 says:

> Heaven and earth shall pass away, but my words shall not pass away.

Hebrews 13:8 says:

> Jesus Christ the same yesterday, and today, and forever.

Jesus Christ is the Logos which is the Word. With my dad's commitment to his word, it was not difficult for me to believe God's Word.

As I was standing by the waiting room when we had no patients in the animal hospital, God gave me this scripture.

Isaiah 64:6 says:

> But we are all as an unclean thing, and all our righteousnesses are as filthy rags; and we all do fade as a leaf; and our iniquities, like the wind, have taken us away.

When God spoke His Word to my heart that my righteousness that is everything I do in the flesh was as filthy rags, it broke my heart. I stood there and wept because I realized that anything I did in the flesh, including even my praise, could not please God.

Ephesians 6:18 says:

> Praying always with all prayer and supplication in the Spirit, and watching thereunto with all perseverance and supplication for all saints.

When I read that verse, I said to God that I needed to know how to pray in the Spirit. The next two nights, as I sat on my bed, reading my

Bible and praying, the desire of my heart was to be able to praise God and know how to pray in the Spirit.

John 7:38 says:

> He that believes on me, as the scripture has said, out of his belly shall flow rivers of living water.

Jesus spoke these words that out of your belly shall flow rivers of living water, and as I sat on the bed, I felt a welling up in my belly; it filled my chest and then filled my throat. As I opened my mouth to pray, I began to pray in a new language that I did not know. I felt completely engulfed in the Spirit of God, and His presence was completely overwhelming. My wife walked in the room and looked at me. She said that she did not know what had happened to me but that I was glowing and looked like I was having the best time of my life. She asked if I wanted her to stay or leave, but I did not care. I was just completely involved in the Spirit of God, not knowing what had happened but knowing that it was absolutely real.

I had never been in a Pentecostal or charismatic church where they prayed in tongues. I knew nothing about it. I did not know what had happened to me, but the one thing I knew was that I could now love people that before I could not love. Also, the Word of God became more real, more convicting, and more powerful than ever before.

The next day, Dr. Brian Reeves, who was practicing with me, had invited John Jacobs to have lunch with him. John was a Jew who had received Christ and was baptized in the Holy Spirit. They did not invite me to go with them. My wife came out to have lunch with me, and I said, "Let's go to the same restaurant and sit in the booth next to them." So we did.

John Jacobs was describing to Dr. Reeves exactly what had happened to me the night before, and it was what happened to the disciples on the day of Pentecost. Many people do not believe that the disciples had the Holy Spirit until the day of Pentecost.

John 20:19–23 says:

> Then the same day at evening, being the first day of the week, when the doors were shut where the disciples were

assembled for fear of the Jews, came Jesus and stood in the midst, and said unto them, Peace be unto you. And when he had so said, he showed unto them his hands and his side. Then were the disciples glad, when they saw the Lord. Then said Jesus to them again, Peace be unto you: as my Father has sent me, even so send I you. And when he had said this, he breathed on them, and said unto them, Receive you the Holy Ghost: Whosesoever sins you remit, they are remitted unto them; and whosesoever sins you retain, they are retained.

The disciples had received the Holy Spirit after the resurrection of Jesus and before the day of Pentecost, but He told them to tarry until they were endued with power.

Matthew 3:11–12 says:

I indeed baptize you with water unto repentance: but he that comes after me is mightier than I, whose shoes I am not worthy to bear: he shall baptize you with the Holy Ghost, and with fire: Whose fan is in his hand, and he will thoroughly purge his floor, and gather his wheat into the garner; but he will burn up the chaff with unquenchable fire.

Acts 1:4–5, 8 says:

And, being assembled together with them, commanded them that they should not depart from Jerusalem, but wait for the promise of the Father, which, said he, you have heard of me. For John truly baptized with water; but you shall be baptized with the Holy Ghost not many days hence. But you shall receive power, after that the Holy Ghost is come upon you: and you shall be witnesses unto me both in Jerusalem, and in all Judaea, and in Samaria, and unto the uttermost part of the earth.

Now I knew what had happened to me that God had baptized me in the Holy Spirit. As I said earlier, my wife and I were teaching the senior high Sunday school classes at Royal Haven Baptist Church. I shared my testimony in the class the first week after my salvation.

Three eighteen-year-old boys realized they were not saved and accepted Christ that first Sunday. A couple girls also received Christ. Now this created quite a stir in the church because these children had supposedly been saved at an early age. Instead of their parents being excited that their children had now truly received Christ and were on their way to heaven, they were upset with me. These teenagers really got turned on to God, and they asked if we would have a Bible study, so we started a Bible study on Tuesday nights in our home.

Within a few weeks, another boy received Christ, and all these four boys who were new converts felt the call to go into full-time ministry. They asked if I would have a Friday night Bible study just for them so that they could really get deep into the Word. So we met for about three weeks on Friday nights and studied the Word. Then they said almost in unison, "This is great that we are studying the Word, but we want to put it to use."

Open mouth, insert foot, and swallow all the way to the knee is what I did at this moment when I asked them where the greatest need in Dallas was. They said that it was Fed Mart parking lot, which was on Forest Lane between Marsh and Midway, so I told them that we would go out there next Friday night around 9:30 in the evening after we had finished the Bible study.

I told one young man who played the trombone to bring his trombone, another young man who played his guitar to bring his guitar and to bring their Bibles. We would go out on the parking lot to witness. I had read *The Cross and the Switchblade* written by David Wilkerson. He had a person play a trumpet on the corner of the street in New York City, and after a crowd gathered, he preached to them about the saving knowledge of Jesus Christ. I knew God was no respecter of persons. If he could do it for David Wilkerson in New York City, he could do the same thing for us in Dallas, Texas.

The next Friday, the boys came to Bible study, we studied the Word, and then we drove to the parking lot. I had no idea what went on in that parking lot, but my eyes were quickly opened to the ways of the world. There were kids out on the parking lot, some as young as twelve years of age, with a fifth of whiskey. They ranged up to the early twenties and were openly passing and using drugs of all types. People were having sex in the backs of the pickups parked on the lot. I could not believe my eyes. We got out of the car and leaned up against the fenders of the cars, hoping that people would come by and ask why we were there, but they just looked at us like we were complete weirdos.

Finally, I said to the young men that the people were not going to come to us, so we needed to go to them. I turned to the young man that played the trombone and asked him if he could play "When the Saints Come Marching In." He was so scared that he couldn't even make a noise on the trombone. I then turned to the young man with the guitar and asked if he could play something on the guitar; and he likewise was so nervous and scared that he couldn't play his guitar.

We decided to just walk the length of the parking lot, hoping that maybe we could get some people that would listen to us. As we were walking, people were looking at us like we were weird and strange. We walked almost the full length of the parking lot, but no one had shown an interest in us. Then a young man came up to us and said, "What are you guys doing out here?"

I told him to follow us, and I would tell him.

He said, "No way. You guys are strange, and I don't want anything to do with you."

We walked on to the end of the parking lot, turned around, and started back. The young man came up to us again and he said, "Seriously, what are you doing here?"

The Holy Spirit anointed the young man that had the guitar. He had written his testimony to music, so he played his guitar and sang his testimony. Then one of the other young men who had been involved in drugs before he got saved shared how drugs almost destroyed his life and how Jesus had restored his life. Then I opened my Bible and preached a short message on how to receive Jesus Christ. When I finished preaching, I bowed my head and prayed that God would touch their hearts that they might receive the freedom of Jesus Christ.

When I finished praying, the young man who had asked us what we were doing there had his face right in my face where our noses couldn't have been more than two inches apart. He asked me if I meant that this Jesus that I have talked about could forgive him of all the things he had done wrong. I told him that Jesus could forgive him. He said, "You don't understand. Can he forgive me for all the girls I have slept with? Can he forgive me for all the booze I drank? Can he forgive me for all the drugs that I have taken?"

I replied, "Yes" as he asked each question. He continued, "The psychiatrist told me that my brain is fried. I no longer can think or reason, but I sure would like this Jesus."

I really didn't have the experience to know what I was doing, but I told him I was going to pray for him. I laid my hand on his head, and I asked Jesus to clear up his mind that he might have an understanding and an ability to receive Jesus Christ as his Lord and Savior. This young man started jumping up and down, yelling and screaming. I was embarrassed. He said, "I can think. I can think. I can think. God has healed my mind. I want this Jesus."

He received Jesus Christ as his Savior. While I was talking to him, the young men led two young girls to Jesus Christ as their Savior. On Sunday morning, this young man and the two girls were in our Sunday school class and then went to church. Now this caused not just a small stir amongst the deacons but a complete outburst. Dr. Colton called me into his office, told me that we are not Pentecostal, and that I could not take those boys out to the parking lot again. I replied that there were three new converts that were now attending this church because they accepted Christ on the parking lot. He repeated that we were not Pentecostal and we did not do things that way.

Now the first week we were out on the parking lot, the four young men did not have the baptism of the Holy Spirit. The next week, all four received the baptism of the Holy Spirit, and I told them that the pastor told me I could not take them out to the parking lot again. They were emphatic that they wanted to go. I felt that it was the will and the call of God to go back to the parking lot, so I decided to obey God rather than man.

We went back out to the parking lot that Friday night. These four young men each gathered their own crowds, sharing Christ multiple times to small groups, and several more people received Christ. We didn't hear anything from the church, so we went out the next Friday night. On Sunday, Dr. Colton called me into his office, and he told me, "Ernie, I warned you not to go back out to the parking lot. You're no longer welcome in this church. You and your wife must leave the church."

One of the young girls that had received Christ the first time we went to the parking lot started attending the Bible study that we had for the young people. One night, she told me that she had a nephew that was about six months of age. Her nephew was having uncontrollable seizures, and the doctors were unable to stop them with medication. The Lord spoke to me and said that the child had a demon that was causing the seizures and needed to be delivered. Now you tell me, how do you go to a young teenage girl and tell her that her nephew has a demon that is causing the seizures? So I asked God how I could tell her that her nephew had a demon and that he needed to be delivered. Then the Lord spoke to me a scripture.

Matthew 17:15–18 says:

> Lord, have mercy on my son: for he is lunatic, and sore vexed: for often times he falls into the fire, and oft into the water. And I brought him to your disciples, and they could not cure him. Then Jesus answered and said, O faithless and perverse generation, how long shall I be with you? How long shall I suffer you? Bring him here to me. And Jesus rebuked the devil; and he departed out of him: and the child was cured from that very hour.

So I took the young lady aside, read her these verses in Matthew, explained to her that God had spoken to me, and that her nephew had a demon that was causing the seizures. I asked her if she could bring her nephew to me so that I could pray for him to be delivered and healed.

The next day, she and her best friend brought her nephew to me. When I approached the young boy, he began to cry and shake. I laid my hand upon him and commanded the demon to leave in the name of Jesus. The young boy stopped shaking and crying. She took her nephew home to his mother and father, and he did not have another seizure from that day forward. Even though this young boy had multiple seizures before God delivered him and healed him, the doctors' answer was, "We must have missed our diagnosis."

The next Sunday, my wife and I went to Walnut Hill Assembly of God Church. I shared with them that we had been out on Fed Mart parking lot on Friday nights, sharing Christ. The youth pastor said they had gone out to the parking lot but without any success. They were thrilled to know that we had success and wanted to take the youth choir and a PA system on Friday nights. They would have the youth choir sing songs before I preached, and then everyone would witness to the people on the lot.

My reaction was that we needed to have permission from the manager of Fed Mart, so I planned to see him on Thursday, which was my day off. Then I would let the youth pastor know if it was okay to go and minister on the parking lot.

On Thursday, I went to see the manager. He was happy to have us come on Friday nights because they were having a lot of trouble with vandalism and littering of all types of trash so that it was a real mess to clean up Saturday mornings to be ready for business. So, on Friday, we went to the church about eight o'clock, loaded a piano and a PA system in the back of a pickup, and went to the parking lot. We were setting up the PA system and unloading the piano when a police officer drove up and asked me what we were doing. I told him that we were going to preach the gospel to the people on the parking lot. His response was, "You are going to get yourselves killed because this parking lot is so dangerous and out of control that the police officers do not come on the parking lot after nine o'clock. They stay on the perimeter and control what they can from there."

I told him that we were going to set up and preach. He reemphasized that we were going to get killed and that they would not do anything to help us. He said, "You're on your own because we've had our heads rubbed in the asphalt by this mob."

We finished setting up, and at 9:30, the youth choir began to sing old-time hymns. There were several people that gathered around to listen. When the youth choir finished, I took the mic and preached a short message on how to be saved. While I was preaching, there was a young man standing with a beer can in one hand, a cigarette dangling out of his mouth, shaking his fist and cursing me. I finished preaching and gave an invitation to receive Christ, but no one came forward.

Then the youth and the adults that had come to support the youth split up around the parking lot with Bibles in their hands, hoping that maybe a few people would come up and ask for more information. I finished the night, feeling like a failure because I did not see the results than I had expected.

This feeling carried into Sunday morning when we went to church. I felt so bad and so low that I just hung my head. I didn't look up at anybody or anything. We went to the worship service, and as they sang, I was still looking down. When the pastor got up to preach, he said, "Before I start to preach, there is someone that would like to share something with you." I still was not looking up as I heard a young man start to speak, and he said that he was out at Fed Mart parking lot on Friday night. I recognized the voice as the young man that was cursing me. He told everyone that there was a man preaching. "I was shaking my fist in his face and cursing him and God. After he finished preaching, Leonard Brandon came up to me and started to talk to me about Jesus Christ. On Friday night, I gave my life to God and accepted Jesus Christ as my Lord and Savior."

After we had been out on the parking lot for three weeks, I received a call from the captain of the regional police office. The captain said to me, "I don't know what you're doing on Friday nights at the Fed Mart parking lot, but we have never seen anything like it. Our crime rate has gone from astronomical to almost nil. Whatever you're doing is really working, and we would like for you to start what you are doing all over the city of Dallas."

I told him that we were proclaiming Jesus Christ and that this was the answer to what these people were searching for so that they could be set free from drugs and alcohol. Jesus could set them free and start them with a new life in Christ. I told him that we only had enough people to work the Fed Mart parking lot and that I was sorry that we could not help him by starting other ministries.

We continued to go out to the parking lot on Friday nights for seventeen weeks. The choir would sing, and I would preach. Then we would stand up against a fender or trunk of a car with our Bibles, and within minutes, we would have a group of people around us, asking questions about God and how to receive Jesus.

One night after I had finished speaking, a young man came up to my wife, and he began to talk to us. He said that he had given his life to Satan because Satan gave him power to heal and to destroy. Then he proceeded to tell us about a time when he and his best friend had gone to California. He became very upset with his friend, and he prayed to Satan that Satan would harm his friend but not take his life. Just after he had prayed, his friend went surfing and had a serious accident on the surfboard that broke his neck. They were able to get him to shore before he drowned. He ended up paralyzed from the chest down.

I asked this young man if he had peace. He said that he did not have peace and that he was tormented day and night. I told him that if he would turn from Satan, turn to God, and ask Jesus Christ to forgive him of his sins and to become the Lord and Savior of his life, then God would give him peace. He replied that he would not give up the power that Satan had given to him for peace.

A few minutes later, a car drove up; the man in the passenger seat put down the window and yelled at me, "I need to talk to you." This young man was paralyzed from the chest down, and as it turned out, he had been the best friend of the man we had just talked to. I then shared with him how he could receive Jesus Christ as his Lord and Savior. He said that he would think about what I said, and he asked for my phone number. I gave him my phone number, and I prayed for the Lord to not let that man sleep tonight until he realized that he was dealing with God.

At 3:30 in the morning, I received a call from this man. He wanted me to meet him the next day at his sister's place. He gave me the address and asked if I could meet with his brother-in-law and with him. I did not realize that this young man was a member of a very wealthy family when I agreed to meet him the next day. I met with him and his brother-in-law, Roger, and after we had visited for several hours, Roger asked if I would lead a Bible study on Monday nights that had been going on for a period of time, but they needed a new teacher. This study rotated to different homes every week.

I started teaching the adult Bible study to a group of very wealthy people in North Dallas the next Monday night. I was completely overwhelmed and felt like a fish out of water because of my financial status and social status. But never underestimate God's ability to take an ordinary man who looks to an extraordinary God to meet the needs of everyone, regardless of social and/or economic status. For God is no respecter of persons, and in God's eyes, we are all equal at the foot of the cross. I was well received by this group of men and women.

One night, as we had arrived at the home for the Bible study, a man who was very angry and upset was leaving. The homeowner walked out of the door with the man who was his brother-in-law and whose sister was still in the house. The man whose home we were having the Bible study in that evening told me that the angry man was one of the wickedest men that he had ever met and that there was no way that God could save him. At that moment, God spoke to me and said that he was going to save him.

This man had been in his own home in the guest bedroom with his mistress while in the master bedroom, his wife had taken enough medicine to kill herself. He waited until he was sure that his wife was dead before he called her parents to tell them that maybe they should come and check on their daughter. They were forty-five minutes away but came right over and immediately called 911. Miraculously, she survived.

A short time later, she accepted Jesus Christ as her personal Savior. She told her husband to move out, and she had filed for divorce. I went into the house with the brother-in-law and met the people before we started the Bible study. This man came back into the house and sat through the Bible study. The next morning, he called Roger, the man that asked me to lead the Bible study. He went to Roger's office, and Roger led him to Christ. He started coming to the Bible study on a regular basis.

After several weeks of attending the Bible studies, he went to his wife and told her that he did not see any way that she could ever forgive him and that he did not deserve forgiveness. But the Bible said that we are to seek forgiveness from those that we have deeply hurt, and he asked her to forgive him, but if she could not, he would not hold her to it. God gave his wife the grace to forgive her husband, and their marriage was reunited. Even to this day, they have one of the strongest godly marriages that I know.

Several weeks after my wife and I had been teaching the adult Bible study, I received a call from one of the ladies in the Bible study. She said her nephew would wake up almost every night at midnight and just go through the house, destroying things. His dad was a former tight end for the University of Arkansas, and he could not hold his son down because the son seemed to have supernatural powers and strength. He could pick up a three-cushioned couch and throw it. I told her that the young man was demon-possessed and needed to be delivered. She said that she would have his mother call me and asked me to tell her that her son was demon-possessed and needed to be delivered.

Now this is not the way that one would like to inform a family that their son was demon-possessed. Especially in the day and time that we lived in, if you mention demons or the devil, people will think you were crazy. The concept today of the devil is a little guy in a red suit with horns, a tail, and a pitchfork in his hands.

Within thirty minutes, the mother of the child called me and said that she understood that I believed that her son was demon-possessed. I told her that I was not sure whether he was or wasn't, but with what was happening and the way he was behaving with the supernatural powers, I believed that it was very possible that her son was demon-possessed. She asked if my wife and I could come to their house that evening at 10:30 to be there when he started his rampage so we could see it in person. She gave me her address.

I called my wife and told her that we needed to meet this family at 10:30 in the evening at their home because it appeared that their son was demon- possessed. When we walked in the house at 10:30, the first thing that I noticed was an extremely expensive piece of artwork, a tapestry of a Buddhist temple hanging on the wall. Also, the walls were filled with paintings that were very valuable, but most of them were demonic. I told them that in the book of Acts that the Ephesians, after they had come to Christ, realized that the things that they had used in the worship of demons needed to be destroyed.

Acts 19:18–20 says:

> And many that believed came, and confessed, and
> showed their deeds. Many of them also which used curious

arts brought their books together, and burned them before all men: and they counted the price of them, and found it fifty thousand pieces of silver. So mightily grew the word of God and prevailed.

I had them open their Bibles to this passage as I read it to them. They were both new converts that had accepted Christ recently. I asked them to look around their house to see if they could spot anything that would be related to Satan and possibly demonic worship. The husband lit a fire in the fireplace. They started taking these valuable paintings that were demonic off the walls and threw them in the fireplace and burned them. They also took tarot cards and a Ouija board and burned them.

I ask them about the tapestry of the Buddhist temple, and they said it was not theirs but they had borrowed it. They rolled up the tapestry and said that they would return it to the owners the next day. They asked me and my wife if there was anything else that needed to go. I told them that I was asking God to lead them to the things that were not pleasing to Him. They said that if there was any question about anything, they wanted to get rid of it. They may have thrown some things in the fire that didn't need to be destroyed, but they felt good about their choices. However, there was one thing that they missed; it was a ceramic Siamese cat with emerald eyes.

I asked them about the cat, and they both immediately said that everything started when that cat was given to their son by his grandfather. The grandfather had bought this Siamese cat that came from one of the pyramids in Egypt. In Egypt, they worship the Siamese cat as one of their gods. The husband said he knew that this cat was a big problem, so he took the Siamese cat out on the driveway, used a sledgehammer, and pulverized it.

At twelve o'clock, the boy did not get up. We waited until 12:15, and their son still had not gotten up. We went into the bedroom where he was churning and restless but was not getting out of bed, so I asked the parents to lay hands on the boy with me. Then I bound Satan, commanded that the demon leave the boy, and reminded Satan that the children are sanctified by the parents that know Jesus Christ as their Lord and Savior. This young boy had no more episodes, and in a short period of time, he accepted Jesus Christ as his own personal Savior and is serving God today.

When we were out on the Fed Mart parking lot, we discovered that there were several children from wealthy families that their parents showed very little attention or love to these children. It wasn't uncommon to meet a twelve-year- old child with a fifth of whiskey. When he was asked what he was doing with the whiskey, he would reply that his parents were having a party, they gave him

$20, told him to get lost, and not to come home before one o'clock when the party was over. These children did not want to be out there in this environment. They wanted parents that loved them enough to tell them that alcohol and drugs were wrong and they should not be doing it, but instead their parents were encouraging this type of behavior. The people attending the adult Bible study were aware of these children from twelve to eighteen years of age that were staying with friends or living on the street because their parents had either kicked them out of the house or didn't care enough to care for them properly.

So after much prayer and seeking God, it was decided to form a nonprofit corporation, buy a large house on Walnut Hill Lane, and establish a ministry not to the down-and-outers but to the up-and-outers. So a nonprofit corporation was formed, and a director was hired to run the ministry. The ministry started out with Bible studies for these young people, and if they did not have a place to stay, room and board was provided.

The ministry got off to a good start and then began to have financial problems. People that were giving to the ministry were having trouble figuring out why it was having financial problems because they knew how much they were giving. After an audit and some research into the finances, it was discovered that the director of the ministry had embezzled $175,000. The director was called in to a meeting and confronted with the facts. He denied that he had embezzled the money, and we had no choice but to fire him. We hired another man and his wife to direct the ministry, and again it was moving forward with really good results. Then the couple got involved with some false doctrine, and when they were confronted about the false doctrine, they were not willing to turn from the false doctrine. So we had to let them go.

Several men on the board had contact with Youth with a Mission and Loren Cunningham, the director and founder. After much prayer and meeting with Loren Cunningham, it was decided to give the ministry and the building to Youth with a Mission. They brought in a very young couple that was not seasoned or experienced to run the ministry. After a short period of time, the ministry lost its purpose and direction. Youth with a Mission decided to sell the building and buy property in Lyndale, Texas.

Loren Cunningham came to our home, had lunch with us, and spent several hours visiting. He had just returned from Russia with Brother Andrew where they had smuggled Bibles. This was still during the Communist regime, and if anyone was caught with Bibles in Russia, they would be imprisoned. I was ready to leave the next day to smuggle Bibles into Russia, but my wife had other ideas. She said that I was not leaving her alone with two small children and no income so that I could smuggle Bibles into Russia. It turned out that my wife was my best check and balance in my walk with God.

CHAPTER 5

A New Walk with God

I was teaching a Bible study to the people from North Dallas, teaching the youth Bible study, and we were going to the parking lot on Friday nights to minister. God spoke to me and told me to give up all my ministries or he would take them away from me. I was not obedient to God and had not canceled my ministries. I went to the church on Friday night to prepare to take the youth to the Fed Mart parking lot.

The youth pastor told me that the youth were not going out that night, so I asked him why. He said God told him that that ministry was over. I asked him how he could make such a decision when the ministry was reaching so many people, people were being saved, and it had been written up in road magazines that you could find Jesus on Friday nights at the Fed Mart parking lot in Dallas, Texas. There were people coming from Waco and Houston on Friday nights to find Jesus as their Savior. He told me that God said it was over and that was final. So I went home very upset and angry.

God reminded me that He told me to give up the ministries or He would take them away. I got on the phone, canceled the Bible studies, and then sat down on the couch, very angry at God. I asked God why He stopped these ministries that were reaching people who were being saved. He told me it was time for me to grow up in the full stature of Jesus Christ, and that would not happen if I was spending all my time ministering to other people. Instead, I needed to spend the time with

God so that He could teach me how to walk in the power of His Word and Spirit. Then God told me that He wanted me to spend as much time studying and praying as I had been ministering to other people.

I told God that I had been ministering for two to five hours a day, and He replied that He wanted that time spent with Him. I got a notebook and my Bible. I started that night spending several hours studying the Word of God, praying, and taking notes on the things that God was teaching me. God told me that for me to grow up into the full stature of Jesus Christ and to understand His Word that there were certain ground rules that needed to be laid. The first thing was that He was not the God that I wanted Him to be because that would be filled with human characteristics, thoughts, and understanding. I was not to bring God down to my level, but instead, I was to let God raise me up to His level.

Isaiah 55:8–9 says:

> For my thoughts are not your thoughts, neither are your ways my ways, says the Lord. For as the heavens are higher than the earth, so are my ways higher than your ways, and my thoughts than your thoughts.

God wanted me to come to understand that He was so much more than I could ever imagine Him to be, and I was to enter the journey as an ordinary man to find an extraordinary God that would be beyond my wildest imagination.

The second thing that God wanted me to understand was if I read His Word with a preconceived idea of what His Word said or what I wanted it to say, I would not be open to the truth. Instead I would be trying to make the Word fit what I wanted it to say. He told me that I needed to forget every doctrine that I had been taught and let Him teach me His doctrine.

John 16:13 says:

> Howbeit when he, the Spirit of truth, is come, he will guide you into all truth: for he shall not speak of himself; but whatsoever he shall hear, that shall he speak: and he will show you things to come.

God made it clear to me that the Holy Spirit would teach me the truth. The third thing that God wanted me to understand was that I needed to forget all traditions that I had learned concerning God, religion, and church. The Pharisees who were blinded by their tradition could not see truth when it stood in their face in the form of Jesus Christ because they believed that tradition was established by truth.

Second Peter 1:20–21 says:

> Knowing this first, that no prophecy of the scripture is of any private interpretation. For the prophecy came not in old time by the will of man: but holy men of God spoke as they were moved by the Holy Ghost.

Many people believe and teach that without tradition and doctrine, one will fall into false doctrine and thus be led astray because it is necessary to be surrounded with established teaching. One reason that we have so many denominations is because people have latched on to what they believed to be the truth. They refused to search any further and thus established a denomination based on their understanding of the Bible.

Ephesians 4:12–16 says:

> For the perfecting of the saints, for the work of the ministry, for the edifying of the body of Christ: Till we all come in the unity of the faith, and of the knowledge of the Son of God, unto a perfect man, unto the measure of the stature of the fullness of Christ: That we henceforth be no more children, tossed to and fro, and carried about with every wind of doctrine, by the sleight of men, and cunning craftiness, whereby they lie in wait to deceive; But speaking the truth in love, may grow up into him in all things, which is the head, even Christ: From whom the whole body fitly joined together and compacted by that which every joint supplies, according to the effectual working in the measure of every part, makes increase of the body unto the edifying of itself in love.

God told me that for me to come to the truth, I had to be willing to admit that I could be wrong; because if a person cannot admit that they could be wrong, they are unteachable. He told me that if I would be amenable clay, He could mold me into the image of Jesus Christ and lead me into the truth. Unity can only be achieved when we become unified in the truth of God's Word, but until we grow into that truth, we must be loving and patient with each other as brothers and sisters in Christ.

The fourth thing that God dealt with me on was fasting and praying. I cannot tell you the number of times that one of my Christian friends would tell me that when they needed an answer from God, they were going to fast and pray until God answered their prayer and gave them direction. Another way of putting this was they were going to starve themselves until God found grace and mercy to answer their prayers. God made it clear that one does not have to fast for him to hear their prayers.

Isaiah 58:4 says:

> Behold, you fast for strife and debate, and to smite with the fist of wickedness: you shall not fast as you do this day, to make your voice to be heard on high.

Matthew 7:7–11 says:

> Ask, and it shall be given you; seek, and you shall find; knock, and it shall be opened unto you: For every one that asks receives; and he that seeks finds; and to him that knocks it shall be opened. Or what man is there of you, whom if his son ask bread, will he give him a stone? Or if he ask a fish, will he give him a serpent? If you then, being evil, know how to give good gifts unto your children, how much more shall your Father which is in heaven give good things to them that ask him?

I knew that if I asked my dad for something, he would give me an answer. The answer that my dad would give me was not always a yes or a no, and sometimes it would be later before my dad would answer my question. If my earthly dad heard me and was responsive to me, how much greater would my heavenly Father be responsive to me?

Isaiah 58:6–14 says:

> Is not this the fast that I have chosen? to loose the bands of wickedness, to undo the heavy burdens, and to let the oppressed go free, and that you break every yoke? Is it not to deal your bread to the hungry, and that you bring the poor that are cast out to your house? when you see the naked, that you cover him; and that you hide not yourself from your own flesh? Then shall your light break forth as the morning, and your health shall spring forth speedily: and your righteousness shall go before you; the glory of the Lord shall be your reward. Then shall you call, and the Lord shall answer; you shall cry, and he shall say, Here I am. If you take away from the midst of you the yoke, the putting forth of the finger, and speaking vanity; And if you draw out your soul to the hungry, and satisfy the afflicted soul; then shall your light rise in obscurity, and your darkness be as the noonday: And the Lord shall guide you continually, and satisfy your soul in drought, and make fat your bones: and you shall be like a watered garden, and like a spring of water, whose waters fail not. And they that shall be of you shall build the old waste places: you shall raise up the foundations of many generations; and you shall be called, The repairer of the breach, The restorer of paths to dwell in. If you turn away your foot from the sabbath, from doing your pleasure on my holy day; and call the sabbath a delight, the holy of the Lord, honorable; and shall honor him, not doing your own ways, nor finding your own pleasure, nor speaking your own words: Then shall you delight yourself in the Lord; and I will cause you to ride upon the high places of the earth, and feed you with the heritage of Jacob your father: for the mouth of the Lord hath spoken it.

God told me to fast and pray that I might enter into His presence, and He would reveal His nature, personality, and character. Knowing the nature, personality, and character of God is essential to understand God's Word.

Deuteronomy 8:3 says:

> And he humbled you, and suffered you to hunger, and fed you with manna, which you knew not, neither did your fathers know; that he might make you know that man does not live by bread only, but by every word that proceeds out of the mouth of the Lord does man live.

I felt God leading me to fast and pray during my lunch hour two to three times a week. I would lie down on the floor of my converted van during this time. My feelings were that God's Word was more important to me than the food to satisfy my flesh. I found this to be an incredible time that I spent in the presence of God. Some days I would just lie and soak up his presence without saying a word. Other days I would read the Word of God as I asked God to reveal Himself to me through His Word. There were days when God would reveal to me who He was and His imminences (secrets of His heart). These were some of the richest times in my life.

Psalm 25:14 says:

> The secret of the Lord is with them that fear him; and he will show them his covenant.

Deuteronomy 29:29 says:

> The secret things belong unto the Lord our God: but those things which are revealed belong unto us and to our children forever, that we may do all the words of this law.

When I got saved, I told God that I did not want to be a hypocrite, that I wanted to be honest, and that I did not want to praise Him unless I really felt like it. At that moment, I loved Him for saving me and setting me free from my guilt and the power of sin. But I told God that I wanted to love Him because He was worthy of my love and because of who He was, the Almighty God. We do not fall in love with someone unless we spend time with them. We may be infatuated with someone, but true love can only come about when we spend time together. God, in His infinite wisdom, was starting the process of my falling in love with Him. I did not know at that time that there was a time and a place for sacrificial praise.

Hebrews 13:15 says:

> By him therefore let us offer the sacrifice of praise to God continually, that is, the fruit of our lips giving thanks to his name.

There is a time in our walk with God when we will not feel like praising Him, but we need to give the sacrifices of praise unto our God. Our God inhabits the praises of His people, and when we praise Him, we are showing unto God that we trust Him and that He is sovereign. We are to walk with God by faith until that time comes when He lays the groundwork for us to fall in love with Him.

John 1:1–5 says:

> In the beginning was the Word, and the Word was with God, and the Word was God. The same was in the beginning with God. All things were made by him; and without him was not any thing made that was made. In him was life; and the life was the light of men. And the light shines in darkness; and the darkness comprehended it not.

John 1:11–14 says:

> He came unto his own, and his own received him not. But as many as received him, to them gave he power to become the sons of God, even to them that believe on his name: Which were born, not of blood, nor of the will of the flesh, nor of the will of man, but of God. And the Word was made flesh, and dwelt among us (and we beheld his glory, the glory as of the only begotten of the Father) full of grace and truth.

The Greek word for Word is *Logos*. The Greek term means (1) a thought or concept; (2) the expression or utterance of that thought. As a designation of Christ, therefore, Logos is peculiarly felicitous because

(1) in Him are embodied all the treasures of the divine wisdom, the collective thought of God; and (2) He is from eternity but, especially in his incarnation, the utterance or expression of the person and thought of deity. In other words, Jesus Christ who is the Logos is the expression and utterance of God, and to see Jesus is to see God, for they are One; and to know Jesus is to know God.

This concept completely revolutionized my walk with God. Jesus, the Word, became flesh and dwelt among men. Jesus the Son of God was born of the Virgin Mary, took on the flesh of man, and thus became the Son of Man and the Son of God. He came to show us how to live that we might know how to please God the Father.

John 6:26–69 says:

> Jesus answered them and said, Verily, verily, I say unto you. You seek me, not because you saw the miracles, but because you did eat of the loaves and were filled. Labor not for the meat which perishes but for that meat which endures unto everlasting life, which the son of man shall give unto you: for him has God the Father sealed. Then said they unto him, What shall we do, that we might work the works of God? Jesus answered and said unto them. This is the work of God, that you believe on him whom he has sent. They said therefore unto him. What sign show you then, that we may see, and believe you? What do you work? Our fathers did eat manna in the desert: as it is written. He gave them bread from heaven to eat. Then Jesus said unto them. Verily, verily I say unto you. Moses gave you not that bread from heaven: but my Father gives you the true bread from heaven. For the bread of God is he which comes down from heaven, and gives life unto the world. Then said they unto him, Lord evermore give us this bread. And Jesus said unto them. I am the bread of life: he that comes to me shall never hunger: and he that believes on me shall never thirst. But I said unto you. That you also have seen me, and believe not. All that the Father gives me shall come to me: and him that comes to me I will in no wise cast out. For I came down from heaven, not to do

my own will, but the will of him that sent me. And this is the Father's will which has sent me, that of all which he has given me I should lose nothing but should raise it up again at the last day. And this is the will of him that sent me, that everyone which sees the Son, and believes on him, may have everlasting life and I will raise him up at the last day. The Jews then murmured at him, because he said, I am the bread which came down from heaven. And they said, Is not this Jesus, the son of Joseph, whose father and mother we know? how is it then that he says, I came down from heaven? Jesus therefore answered and said unto them, Murmur not among yourselves. No man can come to me, except the Father which hath sent me draw him: and I will raise him up at the last day. It is written in the prophets, And they shall be all taught of God. Every man therefore that has heard and has learned of the Father, comes unto me. Not that any man who has seen the father, save he which is of God, he has seen the Father. Verily, verily, I say unto you, He that believes on me has everlasting life. I am the bread of life. Your fathers did eat manna in the wilderness, and are dead. This is the bread which comes down from heaven, that a man may eat thereof, and not die. I am the living bread which came down from heaven: if any man eat of this bread, he shall live forever: and the bread that I will give is my flesh, which I will give for the life of the world. The Jews therefore strove among themselves, saying. How can this man give us his flesh to eat? Then Jesus said unto them, Verily, verily, I say unto you, Except you eat the flesh of the Son of man, and drink his blood, you have no life in you. Whoso eats my flesh, and drinks my blood, has eternal life: and I will raise him up at the last day. For my flesh is meat indeed, and my blood is drink indeed. He that eats my flesh, and drinks my blood, dwells in me, and I in him. As the living Father has sent me, and I live by the Father: so he that eats me, even he shall live by me. This is that bread which came down from heaven: not as your fathers did eat manna, and are dead: he that eats of this bread shall live forever. These sayings said he in the synagogue as he taught in Capernaum. Many therefore of his disciples, when they heard this said. This is a hard saying: who can hear it? When Jesus knew in himself that his disciples murmured at it. He said unto them. Does this offend you? What and if you shall see the Son of Man ascend up where he was before? It is the spirit that quickens: the flesh profits nothing: the words that I speak unto you, they are spirit, and they are life. But there are some of you that believe not. For Jesus knew from the beginning who they were that believed not, and who should betray him. And he said, therefore said I unto you, that no man can come unto me, except it were given unto him of my Father. From that time many of his disciples went back, and walked no more with him. Then said Jesus unto the twelve, Will you also go away? then Simon Peter answered him, Lord, to whom shall we go? you have the words of eternal life. And we believe and are sure that you are that Christ, the Son of the living God.

When the disciples asked Jesus to teach them how to pray, He had already told them that if they would seek first the kingdom of God and His righteousness, then all of their needs for food, shelter, and the things that they needed for daily living would be given to them. And in what is known as the Lord's Prayer, He said, "Give unto us this day our daily bread."

During the three years that Jesus spent with his disciples, He struggled trying to get them to stop walking in the flesh and after the flesh but to start walking in the Spirit. What I came to realize was that the Word had become flesh. When Jesus said that we needed to eat His flesh to have eternal life, the Word of God was truly His flesh, and if I would feed my spirit the Word daily, I could grow up into the full stature of Jesus Christ. After Jesus had been baptized with the Holy Spirit and baptized with water by John the Baptist, He was defending himself against Satan when Satan had taken Him into the desert. He told Satan that man did not live by bread alone but by every word that proceeded out of His Father's mouth.

Romans 10:17 says:

So then faith comes by hearing, and hearing by the Word of God.

I came to realize that to read the Word of God without the Holy Spirit was nothing but reading words on a page and had very little effect upon my life. But when I went to God and asked Him to feed me with the bread of life, His Word became alive and living in my spirit. I now knew that I needed the living bread that came from heaven. I liked food and enjoyed a great meal, but I began to realize that the greatest meal is to feed on the bread of life.

Isaiah 55:1–2 says:

Ho, every one that thirsts, come you to the waters, and he that has no money; come you, buy, and eat; yea, come, buy wine and milk without money and without price. Wherefore do you spend money for that which is not bread? and your labor for that which satisfies not? hearken diligently unto me, and eat you that which is good, and let your soul delight itself in fatness.

God was saying that it was time to make my soul fat with His Word. I started to fast and pray two to three days a week during my lunch hour and lay before the Lord with His Word, asking Him to feed my soul the true bread of life. I was also spending two to five hours a day reading His Word and praying.

During this time, I would get up in the morning having spent hours the previous evening studying the Word and praying, and I could sense and feel the presence of the Holy Spirit. I was on the top of a mountain. Then as I would leave home, something seemed to always happen that would upset me or not go the way I thought it should, and it felt like the presence of the Lord just vanished. This went on for several months. Then, one night, as I was seeking the Lord, reading His Word and praying, I asked why He kept leaving me. My spiritual life was like a roller coaster, spiritually high for a moment, and then a nosedive to a low. It was just up and down, up and down. As I sat in the presence of the Lord, He spoke to my heart and to my spirit the scripture, "I will never you leave you nor forsake you."

Suddenly I heard the Word with faith, and I realized that it was not dependent upon my feeling God for God to be with me. The Word says that God will never leave me nor forsake me. It did not matter what my flesh felt or thought; I did not have to feel God to know that God was walking with me every moment of my life. This was the first time in my life that I truly began to understand what it was to eat the flesh of Jesus which truly brought life. His Word had just come alive to my soul and spirit and truly had become living faith in me. I was now coming to understand what it was and is to walk in the Spirit of God.

Our second son Charlie was born with both feet turned the same direction. One foot was turned out like it was supposed to be, and the other foot was turned in at the same angle as the first foot. The doctors were going to send us to a specialist to do surgery to turn the foot back. The night before we were to have the appointment with the surgeon, God gave me the following:

John 9:1–3 says:

> And as Jesus passed by, he saw a man which was blind from his birth. And his disciples asked him, saying, Master, who did sin, this man, or his parents, that he was born blind? Jesus answered, Neither has this man sinned, nor his parents: but that the works of God should be made manifest in him.

God said that Charlie was born with the foot turned in that He might be glorified when He healed him. The next morning, when we got up and went into Charlie's room to take him out of the crib, his foot was turned out in a normal position. Once again, God had glorified His name. We canceled the appointment with the surgeon. At his next visit with Dr. Baskin, the doctor was amazed that Charlie's foot was now normal without surgery.

My wife and I felt that it was time to change churches, and we went to Lakewood Assembly of God. In a very short period, the pastor asked me to teach senior high school boys. The first Sunday that I taught, they sat there with total disrespect for me while taking turns in unison, popping Styrofoam cups. After God had told me to give up all my ministries, I told him that I would not take on another ministry unless he brought it about. Because the pastor had asked me to teach the class, I felt that God was in it.

I went to the Lord Sunday evening after the class and asked the Lord how I could carry this burden to teach these young men when they showed no respect. God spoke to me and told me that He would carry the burden and that He did not ask me to carry the burden. He wanted me just to teach what He laid on my heart, and He wanted me to pray for each of these young men by name every day.

In just a few short weeks, God turned these young men's hearts toward God. They became hungry for the Word of God and began to seek God to change their hearts and lives.

God spoke to us when my wife became pregnant again and told us that He wanted to bless us with a new house. We were completely happy with our house but also wanted the blessing He had for us. Houses had appreciated in value very rapidly in the area where we lived, and they were selling very fast. I asked God to lead us to the house that He wanted us to have.

One night, as we were driving to Lakewood to go to church, we saw a new housing development south of Lovers Lane between Abrams and Skillman, and we drove into the development. There were two houses left for sale. We took down the name of the developer, and I called him the next day. We met him in the smaller of the two houses. When we told him that we had a house and its location, he told us that as a real estate agent, he took houses in on trade. After some negotiations, the builder agreed to take our house as a down payment on the new house. This house seemed to me to be above our price range, so I asked God for a sign.

This was on Monday, and I told God that the next time I drove by that house, I wanted there to be plants in the planters in front of the house because the developer told us at the price he was selling the house to us, there was no way that he could put plants in the planters. On Wednesday, when we went to church at Lakewood, we drove by the house, and there were plants in the planters. We traded our old house and bought the new house. In six months, the market completely dropped out of the area where our old house was located, and you could hardly give the house away. God knew this, and we did not. The new house was in a much better school district, was closer to my animal hospital, and closer to the church. Later I was going to have to move my animal hospital, and this house was even going to be closer to that hospital.

I received a phone call around 11:30 one evening from a young lady who was a Braniff Airline hostess. She had a very sick black cat named Lucifer. She asked me if I could meet her at the animal hospital. After examining the cat, I determine that the cat had feline leukemia. I told her that I had a drug, L- asparaginase, that had a good success rate in curing leukemia, but it would require an IV injection every day for twenty-eight days. While I was examining the cat and treating the cat, I shared with her how I had come to know Jesus Christ as my Savior. She wept profusely throughout the time that I was sharing with her.

I asked her if she would like to receive Jesus Christ as her own personal Savior. She said that she had tried many times, but it did not work. I then asked her if she would go to church with us on Sunday morning, and she agreed to meet us at church. She came to church on Sunday morning and continued to attend Sunday morning, Sunday evening, and Wednesday evening for about three weeks. She brought her cat to the hospital every day for treatment, and each time, we discussed the Scriptures.

On the third Sunday night, when the altar call was given, she went forward; my wife and the pastor's wife were trying to minister to her at the altar. My wife came to get me to minister to her because they were not getting any place with her. As I was going to minister to her, God spoke to me and said that she was demon-possessed and needed to be delivered. God told me to invite her to my house on Monday night, and He would deliver her.

I invited her to come to our home on Monday night, and she said that she would be there. I had not been taught about demon deliverance or seen God use anyone else to deliver someone. The only thing I knew was what I read in the Bible when Jesus cast out demons.

When she came on Monday night, we invited her in. She sat down on the couch, and God told me to open the Bible to Genesis chapter 1. I asked God if He knew what He was doing as I could not imagine that someone could be led to Christ, let alone delivered from demon-possession by reading the first chapter of Genesis. One thing that I had learned in my short time as a Christian was that God knew what he was doing, so I started reading in Genesis.

Genesis 1:2 says:

> And the earth was without form, and void; and darkness was upon the face of the deep. And the Spirit of God moved upon the face of the waters.

And when I read that verse, I realized how it described a person's life without Christ there was no form or direction and a person's life that does not know Jesus and that life is empty of purpose and it is full of darkness. There is no light or hope. But then God's Spirit begins to move upon that life and shows the person that there is hope in Jesus Christ.

Genesis 1:3–5 says:

> And God said, Let there be light: and there was light. And God saw the light, that it was good: and God divided the light from the darkness. And God called the light Day, and the darkness he called Night. And the evening and the morning were the first day.

Genesis 1:14–19 says:

> And God said, Let there be lights in the firmament of the heaven to divide the day from the night; and let them be for signs, and for seasons, and for days, and years: And let them be for lights in the firmament of the heaven to give light upon the earth: and it was so. And God made two great lights; the greater light to rule the day, and the lesser light to rule the night: he made the stars also. And God set them in the firmament of the heaven to give light upon the earth, And to rule over the day and over the night, and to divide the light from the darkness: and God saw that it was good. And the evening and the morning were the fourth day.

Something that I had never noticed in reading Genesis was that the first day was made for the fourth day. The first day, God created the light, and He divided the light from the darkness. On the fourth day, He put the sun for the light of the day and the moon and the stars in the darkness. He called the light day and the darkness night.

Genesis 1:6–8 says:

> And God said, Let there be a firmament in the midst of the waters, and let it divide the waters from the waters. And God made the firmament, and divided the waters which were under the firmament from the waters which were above the firmament: and it was so. And God called the firmament Heaven. And the evening and the morning were the second day.

Genesis 1:20–23 says:

> And God said, Let the waters bring forth abundantly the moving creature that have life, and fowl that may fly above the earth in the open firmament of heaven. And God created great whales, and every living creature that moves, which the waters brought forth abundantly, after their kind, and every winged fowl after his kind: and God saw that it was good. And God blessed them, saying, Be fruitful, and multiply, and fill the waters in the seas, and let fowl multiply in the earth. And the evening and the morning were the fifth day.

Now I saw that God had made the second day for the fifth day. On the second day, God divided the firmament above for the sky and the firmament below for the waters. On the fifth day, God put the birds in the sky, and he put the fish in the waters.

Genesis 1:9–13 says:

> And God said, Let the waters under the heaven be gathered together unto one place, and let the dry land appear: and it was so. And God called the dry land Earth; and the gathering together of the waters called he Seas: and God saw that it was good. And God said, Let the earth bring forth

grass, the herb yielding seed, and the fruit tree yielding fruit after his kind, whose seed is in itself, upon the earth: and it was so. And the earth brought forth grass, and herb yielding seed after his kind, and the tree yielding fruit, whose seed was in itself, after his kind: and God saw that it was good.

Genesis 1:24–31 says:

And God said, Let the earth bring forth the living creature after his kind, cattle, and creeping thing, and beast of the earth after his kind: and it was so. And God made the beast of the earth after his kind, and cattle after their kind, and every thing that creeps upon the earth after his kind: and God saw that it was good. And God said, Let us make man in our image, after our likeness: and let them have dominion over the fish of the sea, and over the fowl of the air, and over the cattle, and over all the earth, and over every creeping thing that creeps upon the earth. So God created man in his own image, in the image of God created he him; male and female created he them. And God blessed them, and God said unto them, Be fruitful, and multiply, and replenish the earth, and subdue it: and have dominion over the fish of the sea, and over the fowl of the air, and over every living thing that moves upon the earth. And God said, Behold, I have given you every herb bearing seed, which is upon the face of all the earth, and every tree, in the which is the fruit of a tree yielding seed; to you it shall be for meat. And to every beast of the earth, and to every fowl of the air, and to every thing that creeps upon the earth, wherein there is life, I have given every green herb for meat: and it was so. And God saw every thing that he had made, and, behold, it was very good. And the evening and the morning were the sixth day.

I realized that God made the third day for the sixth day. On the third day, God created the earth, and on the earth, he created vegetation to support life. On the sixth day, God created all the creatures that were upon the earth. I turned to her and said, "You see, God is a God of order, and everything that God does is good."

She jumped up off the couch and said, "There is nothing good in my life. There is absolutely no order in my life. I have been worshipping Satan, and I did not know it. I no longer want him to rule my life. I want Jesus."

What had just happened was that God, through His Word, brought revelation for deliverance to this young lady. The Logos, the Word, must bring deliverance to a person that is demon-possessed. Based on the Word, they must come to realize that they are demon-possessed and that Jesus, who is the Logos, will deliver them. I told her to tell Satan that she no longer wanted to serve him and that he could no longer control her life. Then she was to ask Jesus to forgive her of her sins and to come into her life to be her Lord and Savior.

She told Satan that she no longer wanted to follow him and that he must leave her life because she was going to turn it over to Jesus Christ. She then asked Jesus to forgive her of her sins and to come into her heart to be her Lord and Savior. At that moment, I laid my hands on her and told Satan he must leave in Jesus's name. She stated that she knew Jesus had come into her heart, forgiven her, and that she was saved.

I asked her if she wanted all that God had for her, and she said that she did. I explained the baptism of the Holy Spirit and told her to ask God to baptize her with the Holy Spirit. I laid hands on her, prayed, and God baptized her with the Holy Spirit. This is another example of an ordinary man who yielded to an extraordinary God and was led by the Spirit so that God, through His Word, could set a young lady bound by the powers of Satan free from his hold into the marvelous grace of God and the salvation of His Son, Jesus Christ. I continue to be amazed at how God can use a man to accomplish His marvelous works through His Spirit by His Word.

A short time after the ministry on Fed Mart parking lot had stopped, I was on my way to work when Satan spoke to me and told me that he was going to take everything that I had, including my family, my practice, my home, and last of all, my life. I was immediately paralyzed with fear. I was afraid to go off and leave my family, but I knew I had to go to work or I would lose my practice just from lack of being there. I struggled with this for three days.

First John 4:4 says:

> You are of God, little children, and have overcome them: because greater is he that is in you, than he that is in the world.

As I turned to God and to His Word, I began to find answers that would set me free from the fear that Satan had brought upon me. God's Word states very clearly that Jesus Christ dwells in me, and the Spirit is greater than Satan.

Revelation 12:11 says:

> And they overcame him by the blood of the Lamb, and by the word of their testimony; and they loved not their lives unto the death.

First Corinthians 15:55 says:

> O death, where is your sting? O grave, where is your victory?

God began to speak to me with this word that the hold that Satan had upon this world was the fear of death. But when Jesus Christ was crucified on the cross for the sins of the world, and on the third day was resurrected, He conquered death, and death no longer had a sting upon the child of God that had received Jesus Christ as Lord and Savior. God's Word says that perfect love casts out fear.

Second Corinthians 10:5 says:

> Casting down imaginations, and every high thing that exalts itself against the knowledge of God, and bringing into captivity every thought to the obedience of Christ.

As I began to analyze the situation, I realized that if my children should die, they would go into the presence of God in heaven where there would be no more suffering or pain but the joy of being in God's presence. If my wife died, she would also graduate from this world of suffering and pain into His glorious presence. My practice and my home were just things which could be replaced. To deal with Satan and demon-possessed people, a person needs to overcome the fear of death and the clutches of material things that have a way of strangling our spirits.

I turned to Satan and told him that he could have no hold upon me unless God allowed it, that he might be able to take my life and the life of the ones I loved as well as all my material things, but he could not have my soul because that was secure in Jesus Christ. When I made this declaration to Satan and put my trust in God's Word, a total peace settled upon me, and all fear was gone. When I put my trust in the Word, God's Spirit truly gave me the peace that surpassed all understanding.

The next night, as I sat down to pray and read God's Word, I saw a vision of thousands of demons coming at me with ferocity and anger. The demons seemed to hit a glass shield in front of my face and then bounce off. After several minutes of watching the demons trying to attack me when they were unable to penetrate the shield of God, I told God that I knew He was protecting me, and I had seen enough. God spoke to me and told me that I needed to take the authority that He had given me over these evil spirits and command that they go away. I rebuked Satan in the name of Jesus and told him to be gone. The demons turned and fled like angry dogs that had been scolded with their tails between their legs, turning back with gnarly teeth as they fled.

Ephesians 6:12 says:

> For we wrestle not against flesh and blood, but against principalities, against powers, against the rulers of the darkness of this world, against spiritual wickedness in high places.

God commands us to put on the full armor of God, and after we have put on the armor to stand against the powers of darkness in His power and strength. We must come to realize that if we are going to serve God and walk with God, we are not going to wrestle only against flesh and blood but against evil spiritual powers that come from Satan. I was talking to a pastor who was also a professor at Dallas Theological Seminary. He told me that he wanted no part of Satan or of delivering demon-possessed people: if that was my thing, he was glad that I was doing it, but he wanted no part of it. I do not understand how one can minister in this world, where Satan is the prince of this world, by sticking their head in the sand and refusing to deal with Satan because they don't know how to. People do not want to get involved and are afraid to stir up Satan.

We are fighting a spiritual battle. If we try to fight it in our own strength and in the flesh, we will walk in fear and probably be defeated. But God has given us authority over Satan and his demons so that we can walk in victory. Satan is very subtle; he has convinced the world that he is this little guy in a red suit with horns, a tail, and a pitchfork. Many people laugh and make fun of the idea that Satan is real, but he is very real, and we need to wake up to the facts.

When I went to sleep that night after studying God's Word and praying, I had a dream. Satan came to me and told me that he was going to kill me. In the dream, I was walking down the street, and a man with a knife who was possessed of Satan tried to kill me. I rebuked him in Jesus's name, and he fled. Then I went to get a haircut, and as I was sitting in the barber's chair, I realized that the barber was Satan. He was ready to cut my throat with a straight-edge razor. I rebuked him in Jesus's name. Then I went into a large room with huge sacks that were stuffed full. I did not know what Satan looked like or where he was, so I began to run to escape him.

This went on for a long period of time. Then God reminded me that they overcame Satan by the blood of the Lamb, the word of their testimony, and feared not their life unto death. I stopped running and said to Satan, "You can kill me, and I will go to be with Jesus. You cannot harm me unless God allows it. Now in Jesus' name, be gone. When I woke up, I was lying in a pool of sweat.

That is how hard and fast I had been running. When I looked up, Satan was standing in a clothes closet, ready to pounce upon me and kill me. I just spoke the words, "In Jesus' name be gone."

God had shown me through His Word, in visions and in dreams, that he had conquered Satan and that I did not have to fear him. When God asked Satan if he had considered his servant, Job, Satan said to God that he could not do anything to Job because God had put a hedge around him. God is all sovereign, and nothing can happen to you unless God allows it. I still marvel at how God can take a country boy and teach him how to be led by His Spirit. To deal with demonic spirits, one must come to a place in life that there is no fear of death, because if one fears death, Satan still has a hold.

The airline hostess that had been delivered and saved asked me to start a Bible study where she could bring her friends that they might find this same Jesus because they said they had seen such a marvelous change in her life. God told me to start a Bible study on Monday nights. Monday night arrived, the doorbell rang, I answered the door, and the man at the door was a full-blown hippie. He said to me, "Is this where the happening is?"

I told him that this was where the Bible study was. I invited him in, and he came in and sat on the floor. The doorbell rang six more times, and six more hippies came in and sat on the floor. Finally, the airline hostess came, and she sat on the floor with her friends. You must understand that the hippies hated anyone that was over thirty. They were against any type of materialism. Most of them did not work, and most of them were involved with drugs and alcohol. Everything that I stood for, they were against. I was raised with strong work ethics: you worked to make a living and cared for yourself. You could have cut the atmosphere with a knife.

They glared at me, and I tried not to glare back. I lifted a silent prayer unto God, "What do I do?"

God said to share my testimony, so I shared with them what my life was like before I came to Christ, how Jesus saved me, and how it changed my life. When I finished, one of the men said, "Like, man, you just told the story of my life."

My thoughts were, *No way!* God spoke to me and said that you just told the story of this man's life because there is a void in every man's life that can only be filled by Jesus Christ. We continued the Bible study on Monday nights where sometimes there might be one person and other nights a large crowd.

If she was not flying, the airline hostess continued to come to church on Sunday mornings, Sunday nights, Wednesday nights, and the Bible study on Monday nights. She would come to the services very down and depressed, but after the service was over, she would be very uplifted. This went on for several weeks. God told me that I needed to go to her home because there were things in her home that were causing the problem. So Dr. Reeves and I made an appointment to meet her at her home.

When we walked in, the first thing that we saw was a picture of a Spanish princess who had been involved in the occult. This picture was hanging above the mantel on the fireplace, and immediately, the eyes of the picture fastened down upon us. I looked at Dr. Reeves, he looked at me, and I nodded for him to go to the left while I watched. I stood there and watched the eyes follow him to the far-left side of the room. When he got to the far side of the room, he nodded, and I went to the right side. Immediately, the eyes fastened on me, and I watched as the eyes followed me to the right side of the room. Dr. Reeves watched as the eyes left him and followed me. Then I nodded to Dr. Reeves, and when he started to come to my side of the room, the eyes immediately went to him. I watched as the eyes followed him toward me on the right side of the room. Then I walked to the left side of the room, and he watched as the eyes followed me to the left side of the room.

Now most of us grew up watching the television program *Bewitched*. We all laughed about it, thought it was funny and totally make-believe when the eyes in the grandfather's picture followed people around the room. This was not make- believe. We changed positions in the room several times and watched the eyes jump from one of us to the other one as one of us would start moving. I opened the Bible and showed the young lady that the Ephesians brought their occult books and paraphernalia and burned them. In the house were tarot cards, many other occult things, and a Ouija board that was used in séances.

The young lady had been deeply involved in the occult when she was demon- possessed before she got saved. She had held séances and all types of occult practices in her home. She had a fireplace, so we burned everything that was involved in satanic worship, except the picture. I said we needed to burn it also, but Dr. Reeves insisted that he wanted to take the picture to show our pastor. So, we took the picture out of the frame and rolled it up. We anointed the young lady's house with oil, prayed, informed Satan that she was now a child of God, and that he had no more place in her home because she had given it to Jesus, and the Holy Spirit had sanctified the home. She was set free and no longer had oppression when she went to her home.

Dr. Reeves and I started back toward my home where we had met. Suddenly he could not breathe. He was holding the picture. I stopped the vehicle, got out, went to his side, took the picture out of his hand, shredded it into small pieces, and threw it down a rain gutter where it would be washed away and destroyed. I prayed for him, and he was able to breathe freely. We both learned a valuable lesson that you do not mess with Satan. We are not here to let Satan be glorified with his powers, but we are here to manifest the powers of God and glorify Jesus Christ.

Many of the hippies that were coming to my Monday night Bible study had started coming to Lakewood Assembly of God church. The pastor asked me to quit teaching the high school boys and start a class for the hippies. We named the class Regeneration. Then the pastor asked me to preach a Friday and Saturday night revival keyed to the hippies which would be held in the chapel of the church, so we scheduled the revival.

The first night, there were from seventy-five to one hundred people that came. Several got saved and baptized in the Holy Spirit. On Saturday night, we had a little larger crowd. Between the two nights, there were fifteen that received Jesus Christ. The fifteen that got saved were all friends, and they spent Sunday afternoon and all-day Monday reading their Bibles. When they came to the Bible study on Monday night, a young man asked me what I thought about men having long hair. These men all had very long hair, some even to their waist. I asked them why they were asking me that question. I knew why they were asking, but I wanted them to tell me.

At first, they would not tell me why they were asking the question, but they kept asking it throughout the first part of the Bible study. I usually taught from one and a half to two hours, and then we would take a break where my wife would have some Kool-Aid and cookies, and we would visit. I would minister to some of them during the break, teach another hour, and then minister to those that wanted to receive Christ or had other needs.

During the break, the man came to me again and wanted to know what I thought about men having long hair. I told him that it didn't make any difference what I thought about long hair. Then they said that they read in the Bible where it said men should not have long hair, but they wanted to know what I thought about it. I told them that it made no difference what I thought about the length of hair. If they were going to follow God, they must learn that man's opinion does not change God's Word, and the final answer will always be God's Word because God said His Word does not change. And Jesus said that He was the same yesterday, today, and forever. Jesus is the Logos.

Men and women will try to trap you into getting you to give them an opinion that will justify their sin. Moses, when leading the children of Israel out of Egypt, often stood alone with God's Word, and almost all the people were against him. But Moses never backed down from God's Word because God is the final judge.

On Wednesday night at church, I did not recognize most of these young men because many of them previously had full beards and hair so long that it covered parts of their faces. They all had real short haircuts, had shaved their beards, and did not look like the same men that had been saved the weekend before. It is not our duty or responsibility to change men and women. It is our duty to proclaim God's Word unadulterated and in its pure form. The Holy Spirit changed the lives of men and women with His Word.

After the revival, the Bible study on Monday nights jumped in numbers as those that had gotten saved invited their friends. Many in the church wanted to come because they saw the power of God changing lives, and they wanted to be part of that. One night, after I had finished teaching, we broke up into several small groups to start ministering to those that had needs. Many were praying in the Spirit out loud, and as each group was praying, they had trouble hearing their own group because the others in each group got louder until it was utter chaos.

I had two young sisters that I was trying to talk to about Jesus. They said they were going to leave because there was no order and it was total chaos. I shouted, "Shut up!" As everyone stopped praying and it became quiet, I asked them to stop praying out loud in tongues and to quietly minister to the needs of each group. The sisters then decided to stay, and they both received Jesus Christ as their Savior. I knew what had happened that night could not be of the Lord because God is not the author of confusion. I asked the Lord to teach me the proper way to minister in the Spirit. The people that joined me to help minister had come from the Assemblies of God and the charismatic movement where it was traditional for everyone to pray out loud in the Spirit all at once when they were ministering to someone with a need. In 1 Corinthians 14:1–40, God gives us directions of how we are to speak in tongues and to prophesy.

First Corinthians 14:40 says:

> Let all things be done decently and in order.

First Corinthians 14:23 says:

> If therefore the whole church be come together into one place, and all speak with tongues, and there come in those that are unlearned, or unbelievers, will they not say that you are mad?

In this chapter, God tells us that if we speak in tongues, the message in tongues needs to be interpreted. If there is no one to interpret, God says for the one praying in tongues to pray silently. He also tells us that the Spirit is subject to the bearer; in other words, the person can begin to pray in tongues or cease praying in tongues at his will. At no time will the Spirit take over so that a person will lose control and the Spirit will do whatever He pleases. God is not the author of confusion. When we are ministering, it needs to be in order and under control. With fear and trembling in my spirit, I spent time teaching what God's Word said the next week. I did not want to quench the Spirit so that God would not have the freedom that he needed.

This was a faulty assumption and fear because when we follow God's Word and obey it, God has greater freedom to accomplish what He wants to accomplish. Sure enough, after teaching what God's Word had to say about the Spirit, there was a greater move of God in the Bible study. However, many were deeply ingrained with tradition, would not accept what God's Word had to say, and were not willing to submit to the Word. They no longer came to the Bible study.

Tradition can be good, but the Pharisees were so blinded by tradition that when Jesus stood in their face, they could not see the truth and see the light. Because of their tradition, they rejected the Messiah that God had sent to save them. I was beginning to understand why God told me to forget all traditions and doctrines that I had ever been taught so that He might teach me the truth. The Word of God says that you shall know the truth and the truth shall set you free. When we follow the Word of God, God has complete freedom to accomplish the works that are His perfect will.

In February of 1972, my wife went into labor, and Mark Martin came into the world at Baylor Hospital. Everything seemed to be fine, and after visiting hours, I went home to care for the rest of the family. I received a phone call from Jan that they had placed Mark in ICU and that it did not look good. They were not sure what was wrong, but they were running some tests to confirm that he was born with kidneys that were unable to filter; there was not much hope. I went to the Lord in prayer, and God spoke to me that whatever you ask in Jesus' name, you shall have.

Romans 10:17 says:

> So then faith comes by hearing, and hearing by the word of God.

I had heard the faith, and I knew that God had healed our son. I went to the hospital and told the doctors that they could take our son out of ICU. Their answer was that they were glad that I had that faith because that was his only hope, but they could not remove him from ICU until the tests were normal. That Monday night, as I was teaching the Bible study, there were some people that needed prayer for their physical needs. Satan was sitting on my shoulder, asking me how I could pray for these people when my son was in ICU, and I could not even get him well. I reminded Satan that I could not heal anyone; it was God who did the healing.

At the Bible study, there was a young man with both of his arms completely paralyzed and hanging at his side because of an injury several years before. God spoke to me and said, "You shall lay hands on the sick and they shall recover." I asked the young man to come to me, I laid my hands upon him, and I asked Jesus to heal him in His name. The man was immediately healed and began to raise his arms high above his head. He was jumping up and down praising God, and everyone in the study was praising God for this miracle.

In those days, you could buy Cokes in a wooden case that held twenty-four glass bottles. He grabbed one of those cases full of Cokes and started carrying it around the room while praising God. The next day, he went to work at a factory, building doors. There were others that were healed of other conditions that night. My wife came home from the hospital after three days, but they would not release our son until he started to gain weight. I asked the Lord to manifest his healing and that Mark would begin to gain weight.

First he stopped losing weight, then he gained a little, and after seven days, they released him from ICU. We were told that we would have to give him a special formula. We took him home, put him on regular formula, and he did fine. When we took him back to the doctor for his two-week checkup, he was gaining weight and doing well. The doctor looked at me and said, "You didn't use the special formula, did you?" I told him that I did not use the special formula because God told me that He had healed our son, and I believed and followed God. He showed me my son's chart and written across the chart was "Miracle of God." Because of this miracle, Dr. Baskin, who was Mark's doctor, received Jesus Christ as his Lord and Savior.

After my message on the Holy Spirit and speaking in tongues based on the Scriptures, the people that had been helping me minister to the hippies quit attending, and I was left alone to minister to the needs of the people after the Word was preached. Many nights, it would be 3:30 or 4:00 in the morning before I would finish ministering to the needs. People who needed to be ministered to have a way of talking around the fringes and not telling me the real problem. Sometimes it would take forty-five minutes to an hour to get to the problem. When Jesus was upon the earth and someone came to Him, He immediately perceived the problem and spoke directly to the problem. I went to the Lord and told Him that I needed to be able to minister like Jesus.

John 16:12–15 says:

> I have yet many things to say unto you, but you cannot bear them now. Howbeit when he, the Spirit of truth, is come, he will guide you into all truth: for he shall not speak of himself; but whatsoever he shall hear, that shall he speak: and he will show you things to come. He shall glorify me: for he shall receive of mine, and shall show it unto you. All things that the Father hath are mine: therefore said I, that he shall take of mine, and shall show it unto you.

Jesus spoke and said that He was still in the world today, perceiving the needs of people. He would perceive the needs and tell the Holy Spirit who in turn would show it to me that I might be able to minister in His Spirit and in His power.

The next Monday night, after I had finish teaching, a young lady who was inappropriately dressed walked up next to me with tears in her eyes. As I looked at her, the Spirit spoke to me and said, "Jesus said to the woman caught in adultery, neither do I condemn you, go and sin no more." I had never met or seen this woman before. It was her first time at the Bible study, so I wondered, how in the world would I turn to a young lady and make that statement?

John 10:27 says:

> My sheep hear my voice, and I know them, and they follow me.

I knew that I had just heard the voice of Jesus and that He had perceived this young lady's needs. I turned to her and told her that Jesus had said to the woman caught in adultery, "Neither do I condemn you. Go and sin no more."

She fell to her knees, wrapped her arms around my legs, and began to weep profusely. I reached down, took her by the arm, and lifted her up. She told me that she was a prostitute and she did not think that God could forgive her. She wanted to give her life to Jesus Christ. We sat down at the table, and I opened the Bible to show her how to be saved. Suddenly she became deaf and dumb. She could not hear me nor could she speak. I realized that she was demon- possessed, and the controlling spirit was the spirit of deaf and dumbness.

Second Corinthians 4:3–6 says:

> But if our gospel be hid, it is hid to them that are lost: In whom the god of this world has blinded the minds of them which believe not, lest the light of the glorious gospel of Christ, who is the image of God, should shine unto them. For we preach not ourselves, but Christ Jesus the Lord; and ourselves your servants for Jesus' sake. For God, who commanded the light to shine out of darkness, has shined in our hearts, to give the light of the knowledge of the glory of God in the face of Jesus Christ.

Satan had blinded this young lady's mind that she might not receive the gospel of Jesus Christ. I laid my hands on her and bound Satan that he could no longer blind her mind so she might see and hear the gospel of Jesus Christ. After I bound Satan, she was able to see and understand the Word of God. Notice that I did not cast out any demons, but I bound them, and she came to realize that she was demon-possessed. She wanted to be delivered and she wanted to receive Jesus Christ. I told her to, in her own words, tell Satan that he could have no more place in her life and that she was giving her heart and her life to Jesus Christ. At that point, I commanded that Satan leave her in Jesus' name, and she prayed, asking Jesus to come into her heart, to forgive her sins, and to be her Lord and Savior. She said that she wanted all that Jesus had for her, and she asked Jesus to baptize her in the Holy Spirit.

At that moment, she could not hear or speak. I laid my hand on her, and I told Satan that this was a child of God; greater was He that was in her than Satan who was trying to deceive her and steal her salvation. Now she was a child of God, and he could have no more power or control of her because she belonged to Jesus. Immediately, she began to pray in tongues, worship, and praise God.

Because Satan is a liar and the father of lies, I did not cast him out again. It would have been unbelief to cast him out again because God's Word says that when Satan is bound or cast out in the name of Jesus, he must be gone. I have seen people in these circumstances try to cast them out again, and because of unbelief, Satan gets a hold. As it says in Mark, the fourth chapter, if the seed is sown by the wayside, Satan will steal it and take it out of the heart so that they do not believe the Word of God.

About seven in the evening when the doorbell rang, I went to the door, and there was a young lady with her three-year-old daughter. The lady had accepted Christ in our Monday night Bible study. She stood at the door, crying and shaking. Her face was all black and blue, and her arm was broken. I looked at her, told her to come in, and said, "Your husband did this to you, didn't he?" I told her to stay with my wife, instructed them not to open the door, and they were to call the police if someone came to the door.

I called her husband's best friend, told him what had happened, and said that I would like for him to go with me to their house that we might confront her husband. I knew that he would know that she came to our house, and he was probably on his way to our house. His friend was quite reluctant because he knew this man's temper and anger, but he agreed to go. I picked him up, and we drove to the house.

Just as we arrived at the house, her husband came barreling down the driveway in his car and exited the driveway. My first thought was that he was going to my house. But he pulled into the 7-Eleven, so we waited at the driveway. In a few minutes, he came back to the house. I drove into the driveway and blocked it. He went in the back door, and we went to the front door.

When I knocked on the door, he came to the door, and he had his pistol tucked in the front of his waistband. He said, "My wife is at your house, and I'm going over there to kill her."

I said that I was coming in, walked into his house, went to the sofa, and sat down. He went behind the sofa that was facing the one I was sitting on. I said to him, "You are the biggest gutless wonder that I have ever met. A real man does not beat up on a weaker helpless woman. You think you are a real he-man, but you are a gutless wonder and a sorry excuse for a man." I told him that he had a beautiful, sweet wife and a lovely three-year-old daughter and asked him if this was the way that he wanted his daughter to remember him.

He came around the sofa and sat down. His friend and I told him that there was help for his anger and his temper and that help was in a man named Jesus Christ; it took a real man to admit that he was a wretched sinner out of control. We shared with him how he could receive Jesus Christ. He began to weep, fell on his knees, and asked God for forgiveness. He asked God to come into his life, take it over, and make him a real man. After he got up off his knees, he sat down on the couch. He pulled out the gun, laid it on the table, and said that his intention was to go to my house to kill his wife, his daughter, and my entire family for helping them. He expressed that he did not know how he could ever thank the two of us enough for coming to his house and preventing this tragedy. After we went back to my house, we went with them to the hospital to get his wife taken care of. Once again, we had experienced the power of the loving merciful God. By his supernatural power and the shield of Jesus Christ, he gave us the courage and strength to confront this man. The Bible study to the hippies continued to grow, and lives were changed.

There was a young man who had received Jesus Christ at the revival. He was divorced from his wife. She had received Christ earlier and was one who had invited him to the revival. They had two children. She had no desire to have a relationship with him, but because he was the father of their children, she wanted him to have the peace and joy in Jesus Christ that she had found. They would both come to the Bible study, and they were pleasant to each other. Otherwise, they sat on opposite sides of the room and had no relationship.

God really had his hand on this young man. His hunger for the Word of God and his desire to obey God were extremely strong. After he had been saved for a few months, he came to me and said that based on God's Word, he believed that God wanted him to be reunited in marriage with his former wife. We invited them to come to our home one evening. My wife was raised in a good home with a very sheltered environment. As we sat with this couple, she was not prepared for the venom, animosity, and anger that would come forth from the wife toward her husband. He was a very talented musician and singer and had been in a rock band for several years. They had both been involved in drugs and alcohol, and both had extramarital affairs. We sat there for an hour and a half and watched as this venom and anger came out of each one toward the other. Then, suddenly, it just stopped. They looked at each other, basically unable to speak anymore.

Isaiah 61:1–3 says:

> The Spirit of the Lord God is upon me; because the Lord has anointed me to preach good tidings unto the meek; he has sent me to bind up the brokenhearted, to proclaim liberty to the captives, and the opening of the prison to them that are bound; To proclaim the acceptable year of the Lord, and the day of vengeance of our God; to comfort all that mourn; To appoint unto them that mourn in Zion, to give unto them beauty for ashes, the oil of joy for mourning, the garment of praise for the spirit of heaviness; that they might be called trees of righteousness, the planting of the Lord, that he might be glorified.

I stood in front of the couple, put one hand on her and one hand on him. I prayed that God would bind up the broken hearts, that he would restore unto them joy, and that the relationship might be healed in the name of Jesus Christ. As they looked at each other, all of that hate and anger just melted away. They took each other in their arms, kissed, and hugged with tears of joy running down their cheeks. In a very short time, they were remarried, and their family was reunited. After a period of time, God called the man into the ministry, and he became a pastor of a church.

As I was praying one night, God gave me a vision of an Austin stone church building, told me to buy it, and to start an outreach ministry in that building. The hippies were coming out of Lee Park on Turtle Creek in the Oak Lawn area of Dallas. I drove to that area and saw the building that I had seen in the vision. Roger, a commercial real estate agent and developer, and Bill, an attorney, were in the North Dallas Bible study. I talked with them about this building and the vision God had given me, and I talked to the pastor of Lakewood Assembly of God Church.

After everyone prayed about it, we felt that this was the building that God wanted us to buy. Roger contacted the people that were selling the building and found out how much they wanted for it. As we prayed about it, God gave me an amount that we should pay for the building, and he gave Roger the exact same amount which was quite a bit less than they wanted for it. However, they liked the idea that the building would be used in God's service.

Roger agreed to be on the board of our new ministry. Bill asked that he might be on the board in the formative stages as he was an attorney. Bill was going to incorporate the ministry as a church and a nonprofit corporation. As a founding board member, he was going to take care of all the legal requirements at no charge, and then he would not continue to be on the board. An associate pastor at Lakewood Assembly of God church named Paul agreed to be the other board member when Bill resigned. The pastor told me that we needed to ask God to provide the funds to pay cash for the building and to pray the prayer of faith that God would do this.

As Lakewood Assembly of God was growing rapidly and needed to expand, God had led the pastor to pray that God would raise up the funds that they could pay cash for new properties and buildings. With his advice along with the board's advice, we prayed that God would provide the cash to pay for the building. On the day of closing, we had $500 in the bank. I had to call the owners of the building to tell them that we could not close because I did not have any money and asked them for an extension. I was extremely embarrassed and questioned whether I had heard God or knew anything that God was speaking to me. I questioned everything about my walk with God.

When I talked to Roger, he said that he knew God was leading and that we were to buy the building. The mistake was that we did not ask God how he wanted to finance it. Roger called me back in about an hour and told me that a man who I led to Christ in our Bible study owned an insurance company, and he just called, saying that he would like to finance the building. So Roger and Bill got together, worked out the legal requirements, and the insurance company financed the building. We purchased the building at 2814 Oak Lawn Avenue, Dallas, Texas.

At one time, this building had been Oak Lawn Baptist Church, but it had been converted to an office building. The corporation was named Mount Zion Evangelistic Association. One of the great lessons that I learned out of this was that you must seek God to find out what his plan is for you, not what his plans are for another ministry because each ministry is unique. God told me that people do not appreciate a ministry that costs them nothing. This was to be an outreach ministry to reach the hippies.

In this area of Dallas, there were adult theaters, organized crime, and prostitutes congregated on the streets. Most of the churches had moved out of the area because it was no longer a safe or desirable area to live. The building inside was in bad shape. It was filthy and dirty and was divided into small office spaces so that there was no longer a large room to meet in. So the people that were involved in the Monday night Bible study took out some petitions, made a large room that we could meet in, painted the walls white, and cleaned up the building for an outreach ministry. We had Bible studies on Monday and Friday nights.

It was during this time that many Christians were picketing the 7-Eleven stores because they were selling *Playboy* and *Penthouse* magazines. Across the street from our church building was a Stop and Go market which had shelves of pornography that were far worse than *Playboy* or *Penthouse*. After seeking God and praying, God gave the direction that we were to pray for the owner of the Stop and Go markets for thirty days, and then we were to go see him and to share Christ with him. There would be no picketing. So the body of believers and the advisory council to the ministry prayed for the CEO of Stop and Go markets for thirty days.

I went across the street and asked the manager where the CEO's office was located and was told that it was in Houston, Texas. One of the men on the advisory council said that he had to go to Houston on Wednesday and that he would be leaving a car in Houston that needed to be driven back to Dallas. While he was there, he would find the headquarters of Stop and Go markets and would leave a map in the car. He would meet us Wednesday night to give us the keys to the car and directions for the location of the car in the airport parking lot. We would have transportation in Houston, and we could drive his car back.

The plan was that I would take one other person with me, and we would go to Houston to witness to the CEO. One of the young men and I took the Southwest Airlines flight out of Love Field. We needed to be in Houston by three o'clock, but our flight was delayed, and we did not leave Dallas until three o'clock. Needless to say, I was quite upset. God spoke to me and said that Satan could keep me here, but He could keep the CEO in his office; just relax and trust Him.

We arrived in Houston, found the car, and drove to the headquarters of Stop and Go. I went to the receptionist and told her that I wanted to meet with the CEO. She immediately wanted to know what it was about. I told her that it was personal and that I needed to tell him in person why we came. His secretary came out to meet with us and said that if we would not tell her what this was about, he would not see us and he would fire her. I told her, "Tell him that you did everything you could to find out what it was about but that I would not tell you."

About five o'clock, he came to the waiting room and asked us to come with him into the hallway. He asked us why we were there and said that he was a very busy man. I asked him if there was an office where we could talk. As we went down the hall, he saw an empty office and told us go in there. I told him that I would not take more than two minutes of his time, and if after two minutes he did not want to talk to us, we would leave.

As we sat down, he was quite agitated. I looked at him and I said, "Sir, in this room there are many pictures and voices, but we cannot see nor hear them unless we bring in a TV set that has a receptor that can give us those voices and pictures, just like Jesus Christ is standing at the door of your heart, knocking and wanting to give you eternal life, but if you do not turn on the receptor, you cannot receive him."

He looked like we had hit him between the eyes with a two-by-four. His response to us was if there was ever a man that needed to be saved, it was him. He told us that he was very wicked and was not sure that God could save him and not to tell him that God woke us up in the middle of the night and told us to come and witness to him. He said that he did not have time to talk to us and that he had a lot of living to do before he thought about God. I told him that as I had told him earlier. If he did not want to talk to us, we would leave; but before we left, I wanted to read him a scripture.

Hebrews 9:27 says:

> And as it is appointed unto men once to die, but after this the judgment.

For the next twenty minutes, this man would not let us go as he continued to ask questions about God and salvation. Then I sensed that we had talked to him as much as God wanted us to. I told him that I wanted him to do something for himself which was to search the Bible to see if what I told him was true. He said that he did not have a Bible, so I told him that he would have one before we left today because I was going to buy him a Bible and leave it with his secretary.

Across the street from his office was a Woolworth store. When we walked in the door, there was a display of Bibles on special. I bought him a Bible and in the front leaf wrote a plan of salvation as well as how to pray to receive Jesus Christ. I took it back for him and left it with his secretary.

The next business that God laid on our hearts was an adult theater. We prayed for the owner of the theater for thirty days. Then another church member and I went to the adult theater, asked to speak to the owner, and were told that he was not there but that he would be back in an hour. We waited an hour and went back, but he was still not there. I asked if there was any way that they could contact the owner, and they replied that they could page him, so I asked them to page him. When he called them back in a few minutes, they told him that I was there and would like to speak to him. When they gave me the phone, he asked who I represented and said, "You know the type of business that I am in. I must know who I am coming to see."

At that moment, God told me to tell him that I represented the Master of Creation. He told me to wait at the theater and that he would be right over. He arrived in about thirty minutes with two men that were his bodyguards. All three of them had pistols that were very visible stuffed in their waistbands. I asked him if he had an office or a place we could go to talk. He did not have an office, but there was a twenty-four-hour cafe across the street, and we went over there. We all either ordered a Coke or coffee. I was trying to find a way to talk to him about Jesus that would be a smooth transition. I felt like I had on boxing gloves and was trying to thread a needle. Finally, I looked him in the eyes and said, "I came to talk to you about Jesus Christ."

He looked at me and said, "My grandmother's prayers are being answered. You are here because of her prayers." He told me that a long time ago, he knew Jesus as his Savior, but he had gone a totally different direction which he knew was the road to hell. He knew that he needed to repent and come back to Jesus, but he was just not ready. As we talked about the Lord, one of his bodyguards wept profusely as he heard the words to eternal life. After about an hour and a half of conversation, I gave him my name and phone number and told them that if I could ever help them to feel free to call me. Sometime later, he was arrested and found guilty of putting a hit out for a DPS trooper. He was sent to Huntsville prison to serve his sentence. I heard through the grapevine that while he was imprisoned, he had recommitted his life to Christ.

While we were carrying on the outreach ministry on Oak Lawn, we continued to attend Lakewood Assembly of God Church, and the pastor asked me to help him minister at the altars during the altar call. I also continued to teach Sunday school class to the hippies, so on Sundays and Wednesday nights, they continued to go to Lakewood. One night, a young man came to the altar and asked if he could help minister. He told me that he was a minister traveling around the country, sharing Christ. God spoke to me and told me that he was a minister of righteousness, so I asked him to tell me how he had gotten saved. He said that he overdosed on heroin, and in the process of dying, Jesus told him if he would serve Him that He would save him from death. He told Jesus that he would serve Him, and he had been preaching His Word everywhere he went.

Second Corinthians 11:13–15 says:

> For such are false apostles, deceitful workers, transforming themselves into the apostles of Christ. And no marvel; for Satan himself is transformed into an angel of light. Therefore it is no great thing if his ministers also be transformed as the

ministers of righteousness; whose end shall be according to their works.

I asked him if he had peace, and he told me that he was tormented day and night. I opened the Scriptures and showed him that Jesus Christ came to give peace. Then he repented of his sins and received Jesus as Lord and Savior. He told me that when he overdosed on heroin, that the Jesus that spoke to him did not say anything about repentance. When Satan transforms himself into the angel of light, he represents himself as Jesus.

When I showed this man 2 Corinthians 11:13–15, he realized that he was demon-possessed and had become one of Satan's ministers of righteousness. Everything in his ministry was based on works, not the free gift by grace that comes from Jesus Christ. He said that for the first time in his life, he had found peace and rest. Over the next several months, while ministering either at Lakewood or on Oak Lawn, I met five more men that had the same experience as this man. Everyone had overdosed, and the angel of light had come to them with the promise that if they would work for him, he would save their life. They thought they were serving Jesus but were serving the angel of light as a minister of righteousness.

CHAPTER 6

Legalism to Grace

We Christians have a habit of wanting people to get saved and then putting a burden upon them of having to act in a certain way to be a Christian. Once saved, one must read the Bible, pray, go to church every time the church doors are open, go to Sunday school, and witness to their friends. Some proclaim one must not curse, drink, smoke, or even dance.

These are some of the things that are heavy burdens that are laid upon Christians. When I accepted Christ, I had determined that in seven years, I was going to be as near perfect as a man could be and almost as holy as Jesus. I did not realize at the time that I had set goals that were doomed for failure and impossible to achieve. God began to teach me step-by-step that I was walking in the flesh and not in the spirit. Somehow, I did not understand His grace and His love. I told Him I wanted to love Him, not because of what He had done for me but because He was worthy of my love.

I went to my animal hospital on a Sunday afternoon to take care of the animals and found that the drain was plugged again with pet hair. I had called the plumber more than once to clean out the drain, and the last time he came, I talked him into selling me a box of his plumber grade drain cleaner. There were four bottles which cost $25 each, and that was a lot of money in those days. I poured one bottle in the drain, waited thirty minutes according to the instructions, and then I stuffed a hose down the drain. I turned on the hot water to flush the drain, but the drain did not open. So I used a plunger to plunge the drain, but that still did not open it. I ended up pouring all four bottles of drain cleaner in the drain, and then ran water through the hose into the drain. I had several inches of water over the floor, and the drain was not open.

I used the plunger until I had worn huge blisters on the palms of both of my hands. The blisters had broken, and I had worn all the skin off down to the muscle in my hands. I was exasperated, angry, and was not thinking very nice things. I cried out to God and asked Him why He did not open these drains, and He said that I had not asked Him to. I asked God in Jesus's name to open the drains. He told me to go get a screwdriver, go in the other room, and take the brass plate off the floor. I had wondered what that brass plate was for but had no idea, so I got a screwdriver, and I took the brass plate off. God told me to stick the hose down that pipe and turn on the hot water.

Suddenly, all this black stuff began to boil up out of the pipe, and I said, "Oh my God, what a mess." Then I realized what I had said, and I began to thank God in the name of Jesus that this drain was being opened. As I began to thank God, I heard a swooshing sound, and the water immediately began to flow down the drains. As I cleaned up the mess, both of my hands were hurting severely. God spoke to me and said that He could heal my hands. I told God that I knew that I did not deserve to have my hands healed because of my anger and my thoughts toward Him. God spoke to me again and said, "Neither did you deserve my salvation, but while you were a sinner, my Son, Jesus Christ, died for you that you might be saved. He paid for your sin and has forgiven it. Because I love you, I will heal your hands."

I looked up with tears in my eyes and asked God to forgive me for the way I acted and for not asking Him in the first place to open the drains. Immediately the pain was gone in my hands, and they were healed as if nothing had ever happened to them.

I continued to teach the hippies in Sunday school at Lakewood Assembly of God Church and continued the Monday night Bible study at the church on Oak Lawn. God was saving people and delivering them from demon-possession, drugs, and alcohol. He was also performing miracles of healing. Even though God was using me, and I was trying to serve Him, I found in my own life that I was slipping away from His holiness; I couldn't live that holy life that I had promised him.

Romans 8:3 says:

> For what the law could not do, in that it was weak through the flesh, God sending his own Son in the likeness of sinful flesh, and for sin, condemned sin in the flesh.

God saved me, and then I was trying to serve God in the flesh. One night, as I laid on the bathroom floor with my face buried in the carpet because I was ashamed to look up, I told God, "With my mouth I say that I am a Christian, but my very actions deny it. How could I possibly be saved?"

God let me lie there for about forty-five minutes, weeping and broken. Then He spoke to me and asked, "How were you saved?"

And I replied, "By grace." I lay there for another fifteen minutes before He asked how my salvation was maintained. Then He spoke to me that my salvation was maintained by grace in the same way that I was saved. I laid there for another ten or fifteen minutes before He spoke the words that broke my heart and caused me to fall in love with Him. Those words were, "Now do you know how much you need me?"

I continued to struggle with sin, and I asked God why He kept using me when I kept sinning. Why did He not chastise me because I needed a good spanking at that time? God spoke to me and said, "I would rather love you into the kingdom than to chastise you."

I asked God why I kept sinning, and He said that it was because I loved my sin and that if I hated my sin, I would not do it. What a revelation because I had to realize that I loved my sin. Proverbs states that the fear of the Lord is the hatred of evil or sin. Or turning the phrase around, if you do not hate sin, then you do not fear God. And that happens to be us because we sin. When God doesn't judge our sin or chastise us for our sin, we begin to think it is all right. Nothing could be farther from the truth. I finally realized that in my flesh, I could not stop sinning.

Psalm 37:23 says:

The steps of a good man are ordered by the Lord: and he delights in his way.

I realized that God was ordering my steps and that when I got up in the morning, I needed to say to the Lord, "I give you my life anew and a fresh. Use it for your glory and order my steps today." There was one major problem in my life, and it was called sin. When the disciples asked Jesus to teach them how to pray, He said, "Lead me not into temptation but deliver me from evil."

I asked the Lord to order my steps each day to lead me not in the way of temptation and if evil crossed my path to deliver me from that evil because I was too weak and would succumb to it. I would not be able to resist or overcome, except by the power of His spirit. Knowing that He had taken my sin problem, I was able to serve the Lord.

Jude 1:24–25 says:

Now unto him that is able to keep you from falling, and to present you faultless before the presence of his glory with exceeding joy, To the only wise God our Savior, be glory and majesty, dominion and power, both now and ever. Amen.

God is able to keep us from falling into sin and to present us to Himself faultless. He is the author and the finisher of our faith.

Romans 8:1 says:

There is therefore now no condemnation to them which are in Christ Jesus, who walk not after the flesh, but after the Spirit.

Romans 12:1–2 says:

I beseech you therefore, brethren, by the mercies of God, that ye present your bodies a living sacrifice, holy, acceptable unto God, which is your reasonable service. And be not conformed to this world: but be you transformed by the renewing of your mind, that you may prove what is that good, and acceptable, and perfect, will of God.

If we renew our minds with God's Word, hide the Word of God in our hearts, yield ourselves to walk in the Spirit and not in the flesh, we will find that the Word is a light unto our footsteps that we might not sin against God.

CHAPTER 7

God's Call

I continued to minister at the outreach ministry on Oak Lawn and attend Lakewood Assembly of God Church for a period of time, but I felt God was calling me to be a pastor. I went to my pastor and told him that God was calling me as a pastor.

He said, "Ernie, I don't think so. I think you need to keep working as a veterinarian and doing the outreach ministry."

I submitted to his authority and advice as my pastor, but there was no peace. I had many friends that had been saved within weeks of the time that I had been saved, and we developed strong bonds with each other. Several of these people were called into mission fields and had gone into training to become missionaries. As I said earlier, I wanted to go with Loren Cunningham and Brother Andrew to smuggle Bibles into Russia, but my wife would have no part of it.

First Peter 3:7 says:

> Likewise, you husbands, dwell with them according to knowledge, giving honor unto the wife, as unto the weaker vessel, and as being heirs together of the grace of life; that your prayers be not hindered.

My wife was my best check and balance in my walk with God. I almost drove her crazy with all the things that I kept telling her that God wanted me to do. She maintained a steady hand and common sense that kept me grounded and prevented me from running off doing something stupid that was not of God.

One day, as I walked into the darkroom to develop an X-ray, God spoke to me and told me that all my friends were going into missions overseas, but who would stay here to be His minister? I said, "God, I will." You must understand there is nothing about my personality that would fit the pattern of a pastor. I was not a people person. I was not outgoing. I was not loving and kind. I was blunt and to the point. I was not compassionate and understanding, and I was not politically correct. But I knew without a doubt that God had called me to pastor, and I told God that He had His work cut out for Him to mold me into a pastor.

I went back to the pastor of Lakewood Assembly of God, and I told him, "Pastor, I don't care what you say. I know without a doubt that God has called me to pastor."

He put his arm around me and said, "Ernie, God's called you into the ministry. This very week, the Assemblies of God are meeting to ordain pastors. Let me go talk to the sectional board and get you an interview. You will need to take a test on the Bible and on Assembly of God doctrine."

He made the arrangements, I took the tests, was interviewed, and started the process of becoming an ordained Assembly of God minister. For two years, I would carry the title of an interim pastor, and if I successfully completed that time, I would be interviewed by the district council for approval to be ordained. I was ordained as an Assembly of God pastor.

After I received my credentials as an interim pastor, God spoke to me and told me that it was time to change the outreach ministry into a church. I sought counsel with the advisory board of the Assemblies of God and my pastor at Lakewood Assembly of God. They all agreed that this was God's leading, so we changed the outreach ministry at Oak Lawn to Mount Zion Assembly of God Church. We started Sunday services, Wednesday night services, and stopped the Monday and Friday night outreach ministries. All the messages that were preached were recorded on cassette tapes, and eventually we got an inexpensive video camera and videoed the services. I also continued my practice of veterinary medicine and did counseling at my animal hospital.

I had a ten-year lease for my first animal hospital which was on Sherry Lane in Preston Center in Dallas. As the lease came near time to renew, I went to the real-estate agent, and we came to an agreement for another five years. He told me that he would get the paperwork, then we would sign the lease. When the ten years were up, I called him and asked where the paperwork was. He said that he had just been busy, but he would get it to me. He told me to start paying the rent that we agreed upon.

Six months later, I got a letter saying that Preston State Bank had bought the building and that I had thirty days to vacate the premises. I went to the real- estate agent and asked what the problem was and why he had not brought me the papers for the new lease. He made all kinds of excuses without being honest and telling me that he knew there was a contract being worked out on the building when we agreed to the new lease. He said that he was sorry and that was it.

I went to Preston State Bank and told them that there was no way that I could move a practice in thirty days, so they agreed to give me more time to find a new location and to move my practice. I had been preaching on Isaiah chapters 41, 42, and 43. God spoke to me and said that He was going to use me as an example of His Word in these chapters. I had no money saved up, so it was going to be very difficult to get a lease on another property and be able to afford to remodel another building.

My dad said that he would loan me the money at the same interest rate that he was being paid. My wife's dad was a master carpenter with incredible skills who had built homes, and he agreed to help me remodel the practice if we could find a location.

After several days of searching, I located an empty building in a shopping center across from the old Dr. Pepper plant on Mockingbird. I contacted the owner of the property, Joe Chaffin, and set up a meeting with him. My father- in-law went with me to talk with Joe Chaffin. I told him that I believed that God had led me to this property and how God was providing for me. We agreed on a ten-year lease. The building had a roof, the floor, and four outside walls with a few interior petitions. My father-in-law would go down in the mornings, take the petitions down, and take out the nails to save the wood so we didn't have to buy as much wood. I would go to my practice on Sherry Lane from 7:30 until noon. Then I would meet my father-in-law, W. W. Smith, an expert interior carpenter as well as a perfectionist at the new location on Mockingbird.

There was a Burger King near the location, so we would eat a hamburger, and then we would work on the building. On the farm, I had to learn to do lots of things, and one of the things that I learned to do was plumbing. I rented a jackhammer and cut out the floor where I needed to put in the plumbing. I laid the PVC pipe for the drains and put half-inch copper pipe in for the water system. My father-in-law taught me how to frame the building and to frame doors; and with him, everything had to be perfect. He used a four-foot level to be sure that all the walls were perpendicular and all the corners were square. When it came time to hang the sheet rock, we were able to put the sheet rock up with no gaps between sheets. This made taping and bedding much easier. I had never done taping and bedding, so since my father-in-law knew the principles, he showed me, but he said that he was not good at it.

I was able to develop the technique to tape and bed to make the walls smooth so you could not find the joints. I hired the electrical and heating and air- conditioning done. My father-in-law and I put in a drop ceiling with ceiling tile. After forty-five days, we needed the cabinets and the counters out of my old practice, so I made the decision that on the weekend, we would take out the cabinets and countertops that we needed to install in the new exam rooms and make the move from the old practice to the new practice. In this way, I could be building when I had free time during the day and seeing patients at the same time. We had made a portable table for the treatment room, so I could use the treatment room and the portable table to examine patients and to treat them. I built thirty-six runs out of concrete blocks to board animals in. We finished the hospital in ninety-two working days. God was true to His Word.

Isaiah 43:19 says:

Behold, I will do a new thing; now it shall spring forth;
shall you not know it? I will even make a way in the wilderness,
and rivers in the desert.

God had truly made a way in the wilderness and a river in the desert. With my father-in-law's help and my dad's help, I was able to maintain my practice. I had a new location that was more visible, so the practice grew, and that helped to provide for my family's needs. The practice was now located much closer to where I lived, and it was easier for my wife to bring the boys to the hospital after school to help.

Joe Chaffin, the man from whom I leased the building for the animal hospital told me of his backslidden condition in his Christian walk. Joe told me that he normally did not go to a property after he had leased it, but he would like to come see my animal hospital once the remodeling was finished and it was open. I called him when we finished the animal hospital, he came out, and we went to lunch. He told me after he met me and my father-in-law that he realized that he needed to get right with God. He wanted to come and thank us for sharing with him when I leased the property and to let us know that he had recommitted his life to Christ.

A short time later, Joe was diagnosed with lung cancer, which was a result of his smoking when he fell away from the Lord. I sought the Lord to receive the mind of Christ in the situation to know how to pray for Joe. God spoke to me and said this was an illness caused by the abuse of one's body. Joe's salvation was secure, and He would take him home to be with Him. A short time later, Joe went home to be with the Lord.

There was a young man that I met at Lakewood Assembly of God Church who was a taxi driver and would witness to his passengers. He started to come to the outreach ministry on Oak Lawn and continued to come when we converted it to a church. This man had been a drug addict, an alcoholic, and had become a minister of righteousness, so I asked God if I should confront him. God told me to leave him alone and that in His time, He would bring the man to the realization that he was demon-possessed, had become a minister of righteousness, and needed salvation. The taxi driver would bring people to the church who would get saved, and he would bring people to my animal hospital for me to witness to them.

One day, he brought a man in his mid-thirties to my animal hospital. This man who was demon-possessed had attended another church, and during the service, he disrupted the pastor and the service. He took a two-inch leather- bound Bible and tore it in two as you and I would tear a sheet of paper in two. The pastor called him forward, and the man began to yell and scream and slither on the floor like a snake. The pastor took a hold of him and cast Satan out in the name of Jesus. He did not lead the man to Christ or use the Word to show the man that he was demon-possessed; he just cast out the demons and stopped the disruption of the service.

Matthew 12:43–45 says:

> When the unclean spirit is gone out of a man, he walks through dry places, seeking rest, and finding none. Then he says, I will return into my house from whence I came out; and when he is come, he finds it empty, swept, and garnished. Then goes he, and takes with himself seven other spirits more wicked than himself, and they enter in and dwell there: and the last state of that man is worse than the first. Even so shall it be also unto this wicked generation.

This man had been in the army and, after several years of service, was declared mentally insane. He was put in the army's psychiatric hospital where they treated him for five years but were not able to help him. So the army gave him a medical discharge and sent him home. The man was not mentally ill, but he was demon-possessed. As I tried to talk to him, I realized in about two minutes that he was not the least bit interested in what I had to say. I told him that he could not care less what I had to say, and he told me that I was very perceptive because he could not care less. I told him that I was not going to waste my or his time trying to witness to him about Jesus Christ, but I would like to pray for him before he left. He said that he must ask the spirits if that was okay. I immediately bound Satan in Jesus' name so Satan, and his spirits could not hinder me from praying for him.

Second Corinthians 4:4–6 says:

In whom the god of this world has blinded the minds of them which believe not, lest the light of the glorious gospel of Christ, who is the image of God, should shine unto them. For we preach not ourselves, but Christ Jesus the Lord; and ourselves your servants for Jesus' sake. For God, who commanded the light to shine out of darkness, has shined in our hearts, to give the light of the knowledge of the glory of God in the face of Jesus Christ.

He sat there, and I could tell he was stunned and bewildered because the spirits were not speaking to him. Finally, he said, "I guess it would be all right if you prayed for me." So I laid my hand upon his head, and I bound Satan in the name of Jesus Christ that he could no longer blind this man's mind and eyes that he might see the glorious gospel of Jesus Christ. Then I gave him my card, and I told him when he was ready to talk to come to the church, Mount Zion Fellowship on Oak Lawn, and that I also wanted him to read his Bible. He walked out of my hospital in a very stunned state.

Six months later, he came to the church, and when I gave the invitation to receive Christ as your personal Savior, he came forward. I talked with him a minute, asked him to have a seat on the front row. I told him that as soon as I finished ministering to the other people, we would go to the office where we could sit down and talk. He had a seat and waited for me. Now there were several people in our church that had been in the church where the pastor had prayed for his deliverance. I took him to the office and opened the Scriptures that talked about the peace and the love of God. He told me that he knew that he was demon-possessed, and Satan had been in control of his life for years. He said that he could not stand the torment. He wanted to turn his back on Satan. He wanted the forgiveness of God for his sins and he wanted Jesus Christ to take over his life and be his Lord and Savior.

I told him to, in his own words, tell Satan that he would no longer have any place in his life because he was turning his life over to Jesus Christ. He told Satan that he had no more place in his life. I laid my hand upon him, bound Satan, and commanded that he leave in the name of Jesus Christ.

The man immediately prayed, asked God for forgiveness, and asked Jesus Christ to come into his life to be his Lord and Savior. Then he prayed and received the baptism of the Holy Spirit. I ask him what happened when the other pastor had prayed for him to be delivered at the church service. He said that for a few moments, Satan left him, but before he left the church doors, Satan came back with a lot more demons than he had before. He thought his life was a living hell before that pastor prayed for him, but it was nothing compared to what happened after he prayed for him. After he received Christ, we went back into the sanctuary, and everyone asked me if I saw Satan manifest himself.

I replied that I saw Jesus Christ deliver this man from demon possession and set him free. He did not get saved to give Satan a showplace that he could manifest himself but rather a place where God might be glorified through His Son, Jesus Christ. Before this man accepted Jesus Christ, he had not been able to hold a job and was on disability. He went out the next day and got a job driving an eighteen-wheeler. He was stationed in Dallas for six months, and he was regular in his church attendance. It was an amazing transformation that had taken place in this man's life.

To watch the joy, the peace, and the commitment that this man had for the Lord would put most of us to shame. After six months, he was transferred to Houston, Texas. His mother lived in Houston and was a committed Christian that had been praying for him. He lived with her for a period of time. She wrote me a letter, telling me of the tremendous change in this man's life. Every Christmas, I received a Christmas card from him, thanking me first for not wasting time with him the first time he met me but praying the prayer that I prayed, and then being there when he was ready to receive Christ. He has had a very successful career and life and has continued to serve the Lord.

There are many people, including pastors, that do not understand demon powers, how to deal with them, and how to use the Word to bring the deliverance so that a man does not have to go through what this man went through. In my years of ministering, I have met several other people that had been delivered without knowing they were demon-possessed. The Word had not discerned to them that they were possessed, and the Word had not brought them deliverance. A man who had Jesus in his life and was Spirit-filled, using the name of Jesus Christ, had prayed for their deliverance, and the demons must obey him. But we need to use the wisdom of God before praying for people's deliverance lest we do more harm than good.

We have in veterinary medicine an edict to do no harm. How much greater do I think that this should apply to those of us who are ministering in the name of Jesus Christ, whether we be a layperson or a pastor? Because Jesus said that if we would harm a child, it would be better for us that a millstone was hung upon our neck and we were cast into the sea.

The taxi driver continued to come to church on an off and continued to bring people to the church and to my office. These people would get saved, and I kept praying for the taxi driver that he would get saved also. One Sunday morning, when the altar call was given, he came to me and told me that he was lost and needed to be saved. I asked him how he knew that he was lost, and he replied that he had been reading in 1 John where it says if you hate your brother, you are a murderer and not a child of God. He said that he hated his brother and was convicted that there was no love in him and that he did not know the true Christ that came down from heaven to save the lost. He said that he had been serving Satan and wanted to give his life to Jesus.

He prayed, received Jesus Christ, and was delivered from the demon powers. His life took on a whole new dimension because now as he shared Christ to his customers, it came from a heart and life that was walking with Jesus Christ.

One Wednesday evening, as I was walking into the church, God spoke to me and said that one of the nursery workers had cancer of the uterus; and after the service, I needed to send someone to the nursery to get her so we could pray for her. So after the service was over and the invitation was given, I sent someone to get the nursery worker. When she came, I asked her if she had cancer of the uterus. She said, "Yes, and tomorrow they are going to remove my uterus. The prognosis is not good."

I prayed for her, and she went to the hospital the next morning. She told the doctors that God had healed her and that she did not need her uterus removed. The doctor became very highly irate with her, told her that they had done a biopsy, and that she had a very highly malignant cancer of the uterus, and it needed to come out sooner rather than later. She told the doctor she would not sign a consent to remove the uterus unless he did a D and C first. If he found cancer after looking inside of her uterus, then she would consent to having the uterus removed.

The doctor finally agreed to her request, and they did a D and C. When they looked in the uterus, there was no sign of cancer. They took some biopsies, and they came back negative. They could not believe that the cancer was gone. Once again, God had glorified himself.

One Sunday after the service was over, I noticed an eighteen-month-old boy trying to run down the hall, and he kept falling on his face. When I looked further, I noticed that both of his feet were turned in severely. His dad came out of the sanctuary, picked up his son, and told me that the next week, they were taking him to the surgeons who were going to operate to turn his feet out. God spoke to me and said, "You shall lay hands on the sick, and they shall recover." I turned to the dad, and I said that surgery would not be necessary. I asked him to bring his son to me because God had just told me that he was going to heal him. I took the boys feet in my hands, and I asked Jesus in His name to heal the boy. We watched the feet immediately turn out in a normal position. Then his father put him back down on the floor. The boy ran down the hallway as fast as he could with no more falling on his face. God had manifested himself again in His Son's name, and in the name of Jesus Christ, this boy was made well.

One of my clients came with her animal into the animal hospital, and when she walked into the exam room, I could tell that she was extremely upset. Before I could ask her what the problem was, through tears, frustration, and anger, she told me how angry she was at God and said that she would never pray again. I asked her why she was so angry with God and why she would no longer pray. She told me that her best friend, who had five children, had just died of cancer, leaving the children without a mother. She said that her friend had been prayed for at the church, and there had been words of knowledge and prophecies that she would be healed, but she died. She wondered what kind of

God would take a mother of five young children when there were over one million people praying for this woman.

I asked her when she would visit with the woman, what were the woman's feelings toward God and her cancer? She said the woman wanted to talk about heaven, and she told her to stop that foolishness because God was going to heal her that she might raise her children. I told her that there were seven types of illnesses described in the Scriptures, and one of the illnesses was an illness unto death. And that if you had an illness unto death, it did not make a difference how many people prophesied or how many people prayed. It was not going to change God's mind because it was an illness unto death. She said, "Oh my gosh. I was not a good friend to her because I kept trying to convince her that God was going to heal her when he was not going to. When she wanted to talk about heaven and how wonderful heaven was, I would shut her off instead of listening to her as God was calling her home and preparing her for her homecoming."

James 4:1 says:

> From whence come wars and fightings among you? come they not hence, even of your lusts that war in your members? You lust, and have not: you kill, and desire to have, and cannot obtain: you fight and war, yet you have not, because you ask not. You ask, and receive not, because you ask amiss, that you may consume it upon your lusts.

The Scripture tells us we do not receive the answers to our prayers because we ask after our lust. We do not want someone to die because we will miss them, and it will be very painful for us to live without them. However, for that person, when they go to heaven, there will be no more suffering and pain. They will receive their reward, enter into the joy of heaven, and see the end of their salvation which is to be with God.

CHAPTER 8

Marriage

In 1973, a book titled *The Total Woman* came out. It was a book written by a Christian woman that talked about sexual pleasure for women and especially for Christian women. Basically, the book was how she seduced her husband and thus spiced up her sexual life. There was a lot of good in the book because many Christian husbands and wives were hung up that sex was somehow sinful and dirty. God created sex in a marriage to be fulfilling and pleasurable.

It was suggested that a wife meet her husband at the door dressed seductively to arouse him and have sex. Shortly after the book came out, my wife read the book, and she tried some of the things written in the book. At first it seemed like maybe this was a good thing. But we both figured out in a short period of time that this technique created lust and an unnatural sex life. One would say this was a five or a ten, and it seemed to create an atmosphere of reaching for that ten.

My wife and I attended a pastor's meeting with the pastors from North and South Dallas sections. When I walked in the door, there was a group of pastor's wives who came up to me and said, "Dr. Martin, we want you to tell us how God wants Christian husbands and wives to have sexual relationships, and it's sure not *The Total Woman*."

Now I was totally puzzled by these women because I was probably the youngest pastor at the meeting, and it was hard for me to believe that they had not gone to the more mature and seasoned pastors for their answer. I knew from experience that God had an answer and that there had to be a better way. So, I spent several weeks praying and seeking God for an answer. As you've probably seen by now, I use the King James Version of the Bible; however, the Good News version gives a very clear translation of what God has in mind.

First Thessalonians 4:1–4 says:

> Finally, brothers, you learn from us how you should live in order to please God. This is, of course, the way you have been living. And now we beg and urge you, in the name of the Lord Jesus, to do even more. For you know the instructions we gave you, by the authority of the Lord Jesus. This is God's will for you: He wants you to be holy and completely free from immorality. Each of you men should know how to take a wife in a holy and honorable way, not with a lustful desire, like the heathen who do not know God.

This scripture proclaims very clearly that God does not want us to lust after our wives. I will go through the evidence that God gave me from the Scriptures, and it goes back to how God brings a man and woman together in holy matrimony. I promise you that if you know God's plan for a husband and wife based on His Word, and if you are obedient to His Word, you will have the best sex of your life.

God says, "Be you holy because I am holy." In counseling young couples when they would come to me to tell me that they were in love and wanted to get married, I would ask them how they knew they were in love. They might tell me something like this: "Well, we both like mustard on our hamburgers."

I found that most young couples do not understand what love really is. They were infatuated with each other. God says that a husband is to agape his wife. Agape is God's love, and it is 100 percent giving with no expectation of return. I also found that most people would spend more time and scrutiny picking out a car than they spent picking out a mate. So I asked the Lord to show me his plan for how a man and woman would be brought together by God. The Scripture says what God has joined together let not man put asunder.

Adam said that Eve was bone of his bone and flesh of his flesh. God told me that the first thing that needed to happen was that a couple could come together in the spirit. They both needed to be born again, and when they are born again, they become brother and sister in Christ. A brother and sister should never lust after each other. Many people say, "I want to get married so that either my husband or my wife will make me complete." No man or woman is able to complete the other one. Only Jesus Christ can make you complete in Him.

When you are complete in Jesus Christ, have found the joy of living for Jesus, and have found that Jesus Christ is sufficient, then you have a life that you want to share with someone else. Once the couple become one in the spirit and find fulfillment when they serve God together, the next step is to become like- minded. If a man is called to be a pastor and the woman has no calling in that direction and cannot see herself as a pastor's wife, they are not like-minded. The couple needs to spend time together to get to know each other and find out if they are truly like-minded with the same call on their lives.

I believe that God has a perfect mate for each man and woman. If a man or woman seeks God's will for their marriage, God will direct them to the person he has prepared to be their mate. When Abraham told his servant to go back to where Abraham came from and get a wife for Isaac, he told his servant, "God has a wife for my son Isaac."

When the servant arrived at Abraham's old home, he asked God to lead him to the right woman for Isaac. And God led him to Rebecca who gave him a drink of water and watered his camels as described in Genesis. The last thing that God does is make a man and woman one in the flesh.

God lays out in Ephesians the fifth chapter the relationship between a husband and wife and how they are to treat each other.

Ephesians 5:21 says:

Submitting yourselves one to another in the fear of God.

Many husbands want to jump on the next verse where it says that wives are to submit themselves unto their husbands, but verse 21 says that we are to submit ourselves one to another. Most of us have been taught that God is first, the husband is second under God, the wife is third under God, then the children, then work, and whatever else takes place in life follows this. Try as hard as you can, this does not work out in a practical way because of many ups and downs in our lives.

God gave me what I believe is a better pattern, and that is the wheel with the hub that is on the axle and the spokes going out to the rim. If the wheel remains in balance, it will continue to turn, but if it gets too far out of balance with too much weight on one side, the wheel will bog down and not turn. God is the hub of the wheel, and the spokes represent the husband, the wife, the children, work, and the other things that are in our lives, such as vacations and schools. There are times when a husband may need more of the time; his work to support the family may require more time. There are times when the wife may require more time, especially when she is pregnant and is caring for two people; she needs more help and rest. There are times when a child will be struggling in school or with an illness, and more time is needed to care for the child.

I think we get the idea that life is not perfectly balanced, and there are times when we must shift our priorities. However, if God is the center of that priority in our lives and our lives revolve around God, we can keep the wheel balanced and keep it turning, even during the shifts in priorities. During trials and tribulations, we need to look to God for direction, wisdom, and strength to keep our lives moving in love and harmony.

Ephesians 5:22 says:

> Wives, submit yourselves unto your own husbands, as unto the Lord.

Husbands, this does not make your wife a doormat. Wives, you must come to realize that there must be one head for a body to function properly. My wife and I will have been married fifty years on September 2, 2016. When we got married, I fully realized that I had married way above myself. I loved Jan, my wife, very much, and I did not want to hurt her. We discussed before we married that we never wanted to speak words that hurt the other one. I don't care how many apologies are issued. Once words are spoken, they can never really be taken back.

We decided that if we had a disagreement and it was headed toward a full- fledged argument and fight that one or both of us would raise a hand, which meant stop. We would each go into a separate room, get on our knees, and ask God to let us understand the other one's point of view. God's Word says to be angry and sin not. Anger is a natural emotion and is not in itself a sin. It becomes a sin when you let it control you.

God's Word also says to not let the sun go down on your anger. In the fifty years that we have been married, we have not had a fight. We have had many disagreements, but because we chose to follow God's plan, they did not escalate into a fight. In 1 Peter 3, it says to give honor unto the weaker vessel. Husbands, even if you are the stronger person, this is to recognize that your wife is an intelligent person, and I have found my wife is my best check and balance with God. Most of the times that we had disagreements, when we came back together, we were able to resolve them. But when there were times that we could not resolve them, my wife told me that she would turn to God and ask Him to direct me as the head of the household, and thus she could submit unto me because she was submitting unto God.

Ephesians 5:23 says:

> For the husband is the head of the wife, even as Christ is the head of the church: and he is the savior of the body.

Husbands, as the head of the body, you have an enormous responsibility to be the savior of that body. I don't know about you, but I realized very quickly that I was not capable in my own strength and wisdom to carry out this responsibility. It drove me to my knees and to the Word that I might find God's wisdom and strength to be the head of the body.

Ephesians 5:24 says:

> Therefore as the church is subject unto Christ, so let the wives be to their own husbands in every thing.

Wives, for the body to run smoothly, you will need to learn to pray for your husband that God may direct him to lead the body as you submit unto him as unto the Lord.

Ephesians 5:25–27 says:

> Husbands, love your wives, even as Christ also loved the church, and gave himself for it; That he might sanctify and cleanse it with the washing of water by the word, That he might present it to himself a glorious church, not having spot, or wrinkle, or any such thing; but that it should be holy and without blemish.

God tells us husbands that we are to love our wives as Christ loved the church. The word for love is *agape*. I had to come to God and confess to Him that in my flesh, I was not capable of loving my wife with that kind of love. God told me that if I would seek Him with all of my heart with the desire to agape my wife that He would agape her through me. It was also my responsibility to cleanse and wash the body with His Word.

Colossians 3:5–6 says:

> Mortify therefore your members which are upon the earth; fornication, uncleanness, inordinate affection, evil concupiscence, and covetousness, which is idolatry: For which things' sake the wrath of God comes on the children of disobedience.

It is my responsibility to cleanse the body of its fleshly lusts. Marriage is a foretaste of heaven, and our marriages should glorify and honor God as we live our lives as husbands and wives. As Jesus is going to present a church without spot or wrinkle that is holy and without blemish, we as husbands must walk in God's holiness and in His Word that we may present our body to Christ without blemish.

Husbands, God has given us an incredible responsibility that in our own strength and in our own flesh is impossible. I find this awesome responsibility to be extremely humbling because without Christ in me by His Spirit, there is no way that I can even remotely do what He asked. But thank God the Word of God says that we can do all things through Christ who strengthens us. So once again, we must submit unto an extraordinary God that can take an ordinary man and create a marriage that glorifies our heavenly Father.

Ephesians 5:28–30 says:

So ought men to love their wives as their own bodies. He that loves his wife loves himself. For no man ever yet hated his own flesh; but nourishes and cherishes it, even as the Lord the church: For we are members of his body, of his flesh, and of his bones.

Husbands, if you do not like or love yourself, you will never be able to love another person or your wife. I don't think that God made any of us in the image that we envisioned for ourselves, the image that we really wanted to be. One of the first things that we have to come to grips with is that God made us in the image that He had in mind for us, and if we yield to Him, He will mold us into the image of His Son, Jesus Christ, which is far better than any image that we would have desired to be. Once we accept that God did not make a mistake and created us exactly as He desired, then we can love ourselves and love our wives.

Ephesians 5:31–33 says:

For this cause shall a man leave his father and mother, and shall be joined unto his wife, and they two shall be one flesh. This is a great mystery: but I speak concerning Christ and the church. Nevertheless let every one of you in particular so love his wife even as himself; and the wife see that she reverence her husband.

The last thing that God does when he brings a man and woman together to be married is they become one flesh in a sexual relationship as they are joined together. As we see from the Scriptures, the sexual relationship should be holy and pure that glorifies God.

The world has deceived us in that we associate love with having sex. Even in Proverbs, the prostitute says to the man, "Let us take our fill of love." We know that there are three Greek words for love in the Scriptures. *Eros*, which is erotic love, which is strictly for fleshly pleasure. Philo is brotherly love; that's the type of love that families have for each other and that we have for friends. Agape is God's love, and it is 100 percent giving without any expectation of return.

I'm going to go through a scenario that is typical of most marriages. Most marriages do not start out this way, but it doesn't take long for most to fall into this scenario, especially after there are children in the family. The husband gets up in the morning, shaves, and brushes his teeth. When he picks up the toothpaste, it has been squeezed in the middle, and this irritates him because he always squeezes the toothpaste from the end. He cannot figure out why his wife insists on squeezing it in the middle. He dresses, gets ready for work, and goes into the kitchen to eat breakfast. He's running a little late, and the eggs that he likes over easy are over hard, and the toast is burnt. He wonders why his wife can't make a decent breakfast. He grabs his briefcase and heads out the door. She wants a hug and a kiss, but he just goes out the door.

After a hard day at work, he comes home, grabs a beer, sits down, and watches television. When dinner is ready, he eats and goes back to watch television. Then he wants sex, but she says that she's too tired. If they have sex, it is quick (slam, bam, thank you, ma'am), and he rolls over and goes to sleep.

The wife gets up early in the morning. She must get the kids ready for school, pack their lunches, get breakfast, and get herself ready to go to work. She walks into the bathroom, and his dirty underwear is lying on the floor. She can't figure out why he can't put it in the clothes hamper. She goes into the kitchen and starts making the children's lunches. She goes to their rooms to be sure they have the clothes they need to put on and tells them to brush their teeth and get ready for school. She goes back into the kitchen, finishes packing their lunches, and begins making breakfast for the family. Then one of the children can't find his or her shoes. As she goes to help find them, the toast burns, and the eggs get too done. She gets the children ready and off to school, and she must finish getting ready to go to work.

When she comes home from work, she must help the children with their homework and try to get dinner on the table. After dinner is done, she must do the dishes, the laundry, and get things ready for the next day. It seems all he does is watch television. She is exhausted, and he wants sex. Frankly, she's too tired, not in the mood, and would just like to go to sleep.

Many marriages are legal prostitution and gigolos. She says that she will give him sex if he does these things for her. He says he will do these things for her if she gives him sex. He buys her a sexy teddy and wants her to put it on to arouse him. He doesn't buy it for her, but he buys it for himself because it turns him on. This type of marriage is not based on God's love but on lust and personal needs. Foreplay starts in the morning, not with the sexy lingerie. When the husband gets up in the morning, he needs to have bought two tubes of toothpaste, one for her and one for him; he has eliminated an irritant. When he went to bed the night before, he should have put his dirty underwear in the laundry. He should go to the kitchen and cook breakfast for the family so that his wife can get the children ready for school. And then as she is packing the lunches, they have time together in the kitchen.

When the children are ready for school and they are ready to go to work, a good hug and a kiss will go a long way in starting the day off better. When he comes home from work, he can ask his wife if she would rather that he helped the children with their homework or if she would like for him to grill dinner. Hey, all guys are king of the grill. If he will clear the table and put the dishes in the dishwasher after dinner, she will have time to start the laundry and get the children ready for bed.

Husbands, this kindness and helpfulness does not go unnoticed. Plus, your wife isn't going to be so tired. The thing that turns a woman on more than anything else is when she knows she's appreciated and you have helped her lessen her load. Women respond to kindness, love, and attention. Husbands, when you are in the kitchen with your wife, a little hug with a few kind words of saying how much you appreciate your wife and that you love her pays big dividends. This is the type of foreplay that starts a holy relationship. Neither one of you needs to be aroused by lust because she responds to loving-kindness.

When you go to bed, if you embrace, hug, and kiss, it will develop into a sexual relationship that was not based on lust. It will linger into the night, and it is no more "slam, bam, thank you, ma'am," rollover and go to sleep—both of you want to hold each other. Now you have found the type of sexual relationship that is lasting and enduring as God intended it to be. I promise you will get turned on but in a whole new way that is far more fulfilling than the lustful relationships of trying to score a ten. This is the type of sexual relationship that truly creates a oneness in the marriage.

In all marriages, there are buttons that if they are pushed cause us to not act or react in love. There are certain things that irritate our mates that we do which we may not realize that we are doing. My wife had a problem with one of her feet that caused it to hurt when she wore shoes. At times, she would feel the pain and she would step out of the shoe as she was walking. It might be in a hallway, between the doorways, or in the middle of the room. I just didn't know where she was going to step out of the shoe; and then a short distance later, she would step out of the other shoe so that her legs were balanced.

I learned to check the doorway and the path into the bathroom because more than once, I tripped over her shoes to go to the bathroom during the night. About three years after Mark was born, my wife became pregnant, and neither one of us was really excited about it because the three boys had now reached the age when they were going to school, and they were old enough for us to do things as a family that everyone enjoyed. About four weeks after she discovered she was pregnant, my wife miscarried. She was bleeding quite profusely, and I told her that I needed to take her to the hospital.

After her first experience with a miscarriage, she did not want to go to the hospital. Also, her OB-GYN had died, and she did not have a new doctor. Finally, I realized that she had lost a lot of blood, and there was no choice but to take her to the hospital, so I told her I was going to take her to the hospital. She asked me to put the other three boys to bed, go to the neighbor, and ask her to babysit while I took her to the hospital. After I put the three boys to bed, I walked back into the bedroom, and my wife was gray and passed out.

I ran to the neighbor's house, rang the doorbell, and banged on the door. When the neighbor came to the door, I told her to not ask any questions but just follow me because I needed her immediately, so she did. I ran on ahead and picked up my wife. As I carried her by the neighbor woman, she said, "She is dead."

I put my wife in the car, and since we were not far from Presbyterian Hospital, I ran red lights and drove as fast as I could, praying to God for my wife on the way to the hospital. She regained consciousness on the way. I arrived at the emergency, picked up my wife, and carried her into the hospital. I told them what happened. They asked who our doctor was, and I said we did not have one, but we had been referred to a certain OB-GYN practice. They called the doctor on duty, and he came out, and he said that he would do a D and C. I told him that she had lost a very large amount of blood and was unconscious when I headed to the hospital. He did the surgery and immediately left the hospital.

The nurse came, got me, and took me into recovery. She said that she knew that I was a veterinarian and that she needed someone to change the fluid bags as they were short staffed. They were doing a C-section on a doctor's wife who was in crisis, and they needed her in surgery. She told me to change the fluids when a bag ran out. I noticed that she was very concerned about my wife, and I asked her what was wrong. She said that they were unable to get a sustainable blood pressure on my wife and that they had paged the doctor who was not returning the calls. I prayed for my wife, and she stabilized.

The nurse went into surgery, and when she came back, she told me that my wife was stable, so they would put her in a hospital room and keep her overnight. I could pick her up in the morning. I picked my wife up the next morning and took her home. When she would try to sit up in bed, she would black out and was unable to stand. I called the doctor and told him what was going on. He said that I should have her come by his office, and they would do some blood work. I told him that she couldn't even sit up in bed without blacking out, so she couldn't get to his office.

At that time there, were no veterinary labs, so we used human labs. I asked the doctor what kind of blood work he needed, and he said that he needed a CBC. I said that I would pull the blood, send it to my lab, and call him as soon as I had results. He said that would be fine. I pulled the blood, called my lab man, and told him that I needed a stat on my wife. He picked up the blood immediately, took it to the lab, and ran a CBC. He called me back and he said that he had run this blood test three times and he knew that it was accurate and gave me the results.

I called the doctor, and as I read the results to him, I could hear him shaking his head over the phone. He said to me that there was no way that my wife could be alive as she bled to death. I asked if I needed to bring her for a blood transfusion, and he said that he would rather not transfuse her because of the AIDS virus. He said her volume was stable and if I could care for her, he would rather that she built her own blood. Now I had to get up in the mornings extra early, get three boys ready for school, feed them, take care of my wife, get the boys to school, come home at lunch, get my wife lunch, and then at three o'clock pick the boys up from school. I could leave one with her and take the other two with me to my practice. I would go home at night, do the laundry, get dinner, and put the boys to bed.

This went on for six weeks before my wife was able to start doing things if I helped her. Fortunately, some of our church members and neighbors helped when they could. Now when I stumbled over a shoe, I thanked God that there was a shoe to stumble over because I might have been raising three boys without a mother. We all get upset over trivial things because we lose sight of the important major things in our lives.

During the time of the book *The Total Woman*, a Jewish man who had received Christ by the name of Zola Levitt had a radio program in which he interviewed Christians; all the rage was on the lustful sexual relationship between a man and his wife. I called Zola and said there is a better way, so he asked me to come on the program and he would interview me. My wife did not want to be interviewed, but she wanted to go and watch. When we arrived, he invited us into the studio. My wife told him that she really did not want to be interviewed, so he told her that was fine but asked her to sit beside me while he interviewed me. I shared with him what God's Word said about marriage and His Holiness that I'd just shared in this writing.

He told the people that he wished this was television so they could see this couple. He said, "The love they have for each other just radiates," and he had never seen anything like it. "Obviously, this couple has found a deeper and fuller love than I've ever seen in another couple." He finally asked my wife why this was so, and she told him that when we found a relationship that came from agape, God's love, which was without lust, our marriage took one giant leap forward and was far more fulfilling, even though we had a good marriage before that. We were thankful and satisfied with the three boys that God had given us.

That night was the first night after my wife's period, and she became pregnant. God told us that children were a gift and a blessing from him. Less than nine months later in March of 1978, our fourth son, Steven Martin, made his entrance into the world.

CHAPTER 9

Learning to Pray the Prayer of Faith

After I accepted Christ, I would sit in church and hear evangelists, missionaries, and pastors tell stories of how God spoke to them and told them to do certain things. They did those things, and they saw the miracles of God. I was totally bewildered how they were hearing from God. I felt so inadequate and was sure that I would never reach that spiritual plane. I was sure that a person called into full-time service had some special anointing and/or touch from God. I was told by many pastors that God does not speak to man anymore, except by His Word. I had a retired pastor that had been in the ministry for over fifty years tell me, "Oh Ernie, you scare me talking about God talking to you."

I thought, *What a tragedy. You have pastored all these years, and you say the only way God ever spoke to you was through His Word.* I have been blessed to have had many intimate times where God has spoken to me in various ways.

Deuteronomy 5:22–23 says:

> These words the Lord spoke unto all your assembly in the mount out of the midst of the fire, of the cloud, and of the thick darkness, with a great voice: and he added no more. And he wrote them in two tables of stone, and delivered them

unto me. And it came to pass, when you heard the voice out of the midst of the darkness,(for the mountain did burn with fire,) that you came near unto me, *even* all the heads of your tribes, and your elders.

God spoke to the people and gave them the ten commandments. They came to know that God could speak to man, and they were afraid. They wanted Moses to talk to God and relay His Word to them. God was disappointed with the people because God wants to have fellowship with man. That is what has happened in the church today. We want others to talk to God and teach us. How sad not to develop this intimate relationship with God.

There are many ways God speaks to us. He told Paul to go into Damascus, and Ananias would tell him what to do. He told Ananias to go to Damascus and tell Paul all the things he must suffer for the Lord. He told Moses he was on holy ground. God does speak to us in an audible voice. He speaks to our spirit. He speaks to us through His Word. I will illustrate how I began to hear God's voice.

John 10:27 says:

> My sheep hear my voice, and I know them, and they follow me.

The Bible tells us that if we have accepted Jesus Christ, we hear His voice, and if we are obedient, we will follow Him. I'm going to relate a true story, and I'm going to tell it first like most pastors tell the story. Then I'm going to retell it using Scripture to show you how we can have God's faith, hear the Holy Spirit in our spirit, and be used of God. Around 1:30 in the afternoon, I was home on my afternoon off when I received a phone call from Doug Johnson. I had been going to Doug for about six months to get my haircut. The first time that he cut my hair, we began to talk about the Lord. He told me how just a short time before this that he had accepted Jesus Christ as his personal Savior.

I gave him my card with my phone number on it and told him that if I could ever do anything for him or if he wanted to get together sometime to give me a call. When I answered the phone, I could hear the anguish in Doug's voice. He said, "I need you to pray for me. I am in severe pain, and the doctors cannot stop it."

God told me to go to Doug's house, pray for him, and He would heal him. So I got his address, drove over to his house, went in, laid my hands upon Doug's neck, and he was immediately healed. Now let's go back to look at what happened and how God spoke to me. When Doug called, God gave me these Scriptures in my spirit.

Mark 16:18b says

They shall lay hands on the sick, and they shall recover.

Romans 10:17 says:

So then faith comes by hearing, and hearing by the word of God.

When God spoke to me the words "They shall lay hands on the sick and they shall recover," I heard the faith because I heard God's Word in my spirit, and I knew that I could not lay hands on Doug over the phone. I needed to go to his house to lay hands on him that he might be healed. I drove to Doug's house, and as I was walking up the sidewalk to the door, God spoke to me that as Jesus stood by the grave of Lazarus, He said, "Father, I know whatever I ask you that you will do, but so they might know, Lazarus come forth."

I knew that as soon as I laid hands on Doug that he would be healed. I knocked on the door, and Doug came to the door. I have never seen a man in so much pain in my entire life. The anguish and the contortion of his face were very severe. He told me that he could not sit, lie down, or stand without severe pain. It was caused by a problem in his neck. I laid my hand upon his neck, and I said, "Father, I know that as I lay my hand upon his neck that in Jesus' name, you are going to heal him, but that he might know, I ask You, Father, in the name of Jesus Christ to heal Doug."

Immediately, Doug threw both arms up in the air, began to shout praises unto God, and to jump up and down with tears of joy rolling down his cheeks because God had healed him. Several months later, as Doug was cutting my hair, he told me that he had not told me what the problem was with his neck. He said that he was born with a deformed neck, and the vertebrae in his neck were not made the way they were supposed to be. There was nothing that the doctors could do to correct the problem surgically because of the way his vertebrae were made. He said that he had an appointment with the doctor the next day after I prayed for him.

The doctor took an X-ray of his neck, and he came out with both the X-ray that they had taken previously and the X-ray that they just finished taking. He was angry at me and said, "Where is your twin brother? Where is Doug? What kind of trick are you trying to pull on me?" Doug told the doctor that he was Doug and that he did not have a brother, let alone a twin. The doctor put the X-rays on the viewer, and he said, "This is impossible because if you look at this X-ray, you will see how all the bones are deformed, and then if you look at the other X-ray, you will see they are perfectly formed. It is a perfectly normal spine!"

Doug said that he told the doctor that God had healed him, but when he left, the doctor was still mumbling and complaining that he did not like people pulling tricks on him.

First John 5:14–15 says:

> And this is the confidence that we have in him, that, if we ask any thing according to his will, he hears us: And if we know that he hear us, whatsoever we ask, we know that we have the petitions that we desired of him.

So then faith comes by hearing and hearing by the Word of God. When God speaks to our spirit the faith through His Word, we know and have the confidence that God will perform what he has asked us to do because it is not our faith; it is His faith.

Mark 11:22 says:

> And Jesus answering said unto them, Have God's faith.

When we have God's faith, we can walk in confidence that God will perform what He said He would do. I meet a lot of people that believe they can just claim a Scripture, pray, and God will have to answer that Scripture. That is not faith; it is wishful thinking because they have not heard the faith. Mental gymnastics of taking a Scripture and praying it repeatedly will not make it happen.

James 2:20 says:

> But will you know, O vain man, that faith without works is dead? Was not Abraham our father justified by works, when he had offered Isaac his son upon the altar? See you how faith wrought with his works, and by works was faith made perfect? And the scripture was fulfilled which says, Abraham believed God, and it was imputed unto him for righteousness: and he was called the Friend of God. You see then how that by works a man is justified, and not by faith only. Likewise, also was not Rahab the harlot justified by works, when she had received the messengers, and had sent them out another way? For as the body without the spirit is dead, so faith without works is dead also.

Abraham's faith in God was made perfect when he offered Isaac upon the altar. As it says in Hebrews 11, he believed that God could raise Isaac up from the ashes. God had told Abraham that through Isaac He would build a nation that would outnumber the stars. Abraham believed that God, through Isaac, his son, would build that nation. When God asked him to offer Isaac upon the altar, Abraham, by his works of offering Isaac upon the altar, showed his faith that through Isaac, God would build a nation. The best example I know that shows that through our works we prove our faith is in Romans.

Romans 10:8–10 says:

> But what says it? The word is near you, even in your mouth, and in thy heart: that is, the word of faith, which we preach; That if you shall confess with your mouth the Lord Jesus, and shall believe in your heart that God has raised him from the dead, you shall be saved. For with the heart man believes unto righteousness; and with the mouth confession is made unto salvation.

Romans 10:13 says:

> For whosoever shall call upon the name of the Lord shall be saved.

There was a couple that would slip into the service after it had started, and just as the invitation would be given, they would leave. This went on for several weeks. I asked one of the church members to see if they could find out who they were and if we could help them. But when the couple left the church, they would not respond to anyone. They would come to church for about six to eight weeks, and then they would be gone for about three months. Then they would come back for six to eight weeks and be gone again for about three months.

This happened for about a year and a half. No one was able to talk to the couple because they would not make themselves available for us to talk to them, so we knew nothing about them. In a Wednesday night service, God spoke to me through a word of knowledge, a gift of the Spirit, and told me that there is someone here who has cancer and if that person will come forward to be prayed for, God will heal them. I knew in my heart that it was the man that God was speaking to, but he did not come forward; they left the church service.

A month later, when they came back to the church, the man's hand had been amputated. After the service, he came forward to talk to me. He said that when the invitation was given for someone here that had cancer, that was for him. He said, "I knew that you knew that I was the man, and I'm sure you wonder why I did not come forward to be prayed for."

I told him that I wondered why he did not come forward to receive God's healing. He said that he did not come forward because I was a nobody. He had been prayed for by Oral Roberts, Kathryn Kuhlman, Kenneth Hagan, Kenneth Copeland, and several other named faith healers, and he was not healed. He said, "Because you are a nobody, I did not come forward to be prayed for, and because I did not come forward, I lost my hand. Because I did not believe God, God has shown me that faith without works is dead. When I heard the faith, I did not act upon it, and thus I have suffered the consequences of losing my hand when God could've been glorified by healing me. I have learned a painful and valuable lesson not to question who God wants to use as his servant but to be obedient to Him."

CHAPTER 10

My First Funeral

The Golden Retriever Club of Dallas had several members who were clients of mine, and I received a call from one of the members, asking if I would do a funeral for one of the member's husbands. The funeral was to be for the husband of a lady who had worked for me at one time. I had to fire her because she had done some things that were not permissible in veterinary practice. Also, I had nothing but trouble and problems with her, so I copied her records and told her that I could no longer treat her dogs.

Her husband was having an affair; they were separated and were going to get a divorce. He was living with his mistress in a motel on Central Expressway, a six- lane highway in Dallas. Sometime after midnight, he walked onto the highway to commit suicide by letting a car hit him; he was hit and killed. Neither the husband nor the wife had any religious affiliation, but the member that called me asked if I would do the funeral. She was aware of the difficulties that I had in the past with the woman. She had been by to see the woman and asked her if there was anything that she could do for them and if she had someone that would do the funeral. The woman said that she did not have anyone to do the funeral, and she would like for Dr. Martin to do her husband's funeral if he would.

I told the client who called me that if the lady would call me and ask me to do the funeral, I would do it. So the lady called me and asked me if I would do the funeral. I told her I would, and I set up a time to meet with her and her mother to plan the funeral. The arrangements were made at Sparkman Funeral Home.

I had never performed a funeral, let alone one in which the person had committed suicide. All that I knew of him was that he had not led a godly life but to the contrary, an ungodly life. I called three pastors that were friends of mine and asked them how they would conduct this funeral. All three of them had the same answer, but it was not what I wanted to hear. Their answer was that they had no idea, and they were glad that it was me and not them that was doing this funeral.

I went to the Lord in prayer because several people had suggested that this would be a great time to preach a salvation message. I asked the Lord if I should preach a salvation message, and he clearly spoke to me and said, "No." He said that a funeral is for the living to comfort the living and that I would earn the right to witness to the people later about God's saving grace.

I asked the Lord how to deal with the fact that this man had committed suicide, and he told me to preach a message of comfort for one that knew Christ and that God, through the death of His Son, Jesus Christ, had made a means for the Christian to go to heaven. What the Lord was speaking to me was basically to ignore the man's life and proclaim what awaited a person that had turned their life over to Jesus Christ. I arrived at the funeral home and was met by the funeral director. He told me that we have a major problem. The two families did not get along. The husband's family was very upset and angry because she had her husband cremated. They had threatened violence, and we had the police in- house.

The husband had told her that he wanted to be cremated. They were separated and planning to divorce, but the divorce had not gone through, so she was still the legal person in charge of their lives and deaths. The funeral director told me that normally the pastor comes in from the back and leaves by way of the back when doing the service, but he wanted me to come out of the pulpit and go down the main aisle; they would direct her family to follow me down the hallway to one room. He said that they and the police would direct the husband's family to go down the hallway in the opposite direction to another room.

As I was walking to the pulpit, just before the service was to start, the funeral director handed me a note which said, "Your house is on fire." I knew that there was nothing I could do about my house, except to be there to comfort my wife later, so I asked the Lord to comfort her and to give me His anointing that I might comfort the families with the message He had laid upon my heart. I finished the service, walked down the main aisle, and they directed the wife and her family to follow me into a room. I spent some time with the wife and her family, and they thanked me for doing the service. They said that it was a great comfort to them.

The funeral director had told me not to meet with his family, but I felt impressed of the Lord that I should go and meet his mother, dad, brothers, and sisters, and offer my condolences in the loss of their son. So I went down the hall and into the room where his family had been taken. I met with his mother and dad and offered my condolences. They told me that the service was very comforting. They were so glad that I had preached the message that I had preached and that I had come by to meet them after the service. I then excused myself and went to our house.

The fire department and the police had blocked off our street. I parked the car, slipped through the alley, and was able to get to our house. Fortunately for us, it was not our house that was on fire but the next-door neighbor's house which completely burned. The neighbors had saved our house by getting on the roof with hoses and watering down the wood shingles. I had a storage building that I built right next to the eve of our house. The rafters in the building were completely charred, but the fire had not burnt the wood shingles on top of the rafters or it would have gone into the eve of the house and burned our house. The swimming pool was full of soot and ashes that ended up staining the plaster, but that was minor because our house was saved. Later I heard from several Golden Retriever Club members who were Christians and they said that they did not think that there could have been a more perfect funeral message under the circumstance.

CHAPTER 11

Teen Challenge

Being a member of the Assemblies of God and with my history of working with hippies, drug addicts, and alcoholics, I was involved with Dallas Teen Challenge when it was formed. I became a good friend of the director, Lyle Noah. Teen Challenge was started by David Wilkerson as a minister to the gangs in New York City. He had a place where the gang members could come to stay after they had received Jesus Christ as their Savior and when they needed a place to get their lives together. The North Texas district saw the need in the DFW area, so they purchased a building in Dallas and started a Teen Challenge ministry.

I worked closely with the ministry and Lyle Noah during the time he was director. Paul Ecker was hired to be the new director, and some of my church members met him at Lakewood Assembly of God. The next night, we were having a church social at our home, and they invited Paul and his wife, Linda, to come. Linda had arrived in town that day, and they came to our home. Paul and Linda had a son and daughter that were the ages of my boys, and we became friends. The night of the social, I did not have much time to visit with Paul as I was socializing with the church members, so Paul and I agreed to have lunch on Monday.

Paul came by the animal hospital and picked me up to go eat. I did not know Paul, and he did not know me as we had just met. When we arrived at the restaurant and were seated, Paul told the waiter that he had picked me up at Huntsville prison and this was my first day out, so they needed to watch me closely because he didn't know how I was going to react to my freedom. What do you say to a comment like this? Nothing? The waiter took our orders, served us, and you could tell that he was very nervous.

When it came time to pay the check, Paul and I were disagreeing as to who was going to pay the bill. One would never expect this to happen in over a thousand years that a waiter would ask you what you had been in prison for, but the waiter came to the table with the check, looked at me, and asked what I was in prison for. I told him that I had killed the last waiter that did not give me the check. He handed me the check and hurried off.

Paul's face turned as red as a beet because he had met someone that could go toe to toe with him. I paid the check, and we left the restaurant. This was the start of a great friendship. I consider Paul to be my best friend, and I cannot count the number of times that he has been there when I needed a friend and some help. This was to be the first time Paul had worked with drug addicts and alcoholics, so we spent a lot of time together talking about how to minister to these types of people.

On Sundays, Teen Challenge would take the young men in the program to different churches, and they would share testimonies and sing. Because my church was not far from the building that the guys lived in, on Wednesday nights, they would bring them to my church for the Wednesday night service. I got to know the young men in the program and had many opportunities to lead them to Christ.

Paul Ecker asked me if they could have copies of our messages that we had recorded on cassette tapes, so we always made an extra copy of each message to give to Paul. He had his staff members listen to the tapes and categorize them according to topics so when a man in the program was struggling in an area of his life, they would give him the tape on that topic to listen to. Our church was not a large church. We had from twenty-five to a hundred people in a service. I did not know that when missionaries from all around the world would come to see Paul Ecker, they would ask him if he had tapes of sermons that he could loan to them or give them that they might take back with them to use in ministry. Paul was duplicating the tapes that we gave him and was handing them out by the boxful to the missionaries from around the world. Little did I know that I was preaching all over Africa, the Far East, South America, and around the world.

One day, when Paul and I were going to lunch, he brought me a box that was a two-foot cube, and it was full of letters. He told me that he had been giving my tapes with the Teen Challenge address on the label to missionaries, and these letters were written by people all over the world that had either accepted Jesus Christ because of the tapes or were ministered to, and they were writing, asking if it would be possible for someone to send more tapes to them. Many of these letters came from prisoners that were in prison in foreign countries. I have continued to work with Dallas Teen Life Challenge (renamed Adult and Teen Challenge Dallas), and even today, I teach the men for two hours a week.

CHAPTER 12

From Show to Brokenness

I had been ordained for about three years. On the first Monday of the month, the North Dallas section of pastors met for lunch, and they would have a speaker. Our church at this time was very small, and my wife and I had to give sacrificially to the church for it to make it financially; this was putting a strain upon our finances. I would have to stop at the store and buy a gallon of milk every evening because I could not afford to buy two gallons.

When I would arrive at the pastor's meeting, the first thing I would be asked by other pastors was how many people got saved on Sunday and how many people you baptized. Then they would proceed to tell me how many people had gotten saved and baptized in their large churches. I needed someone that would talk with me and encourage me as we were struggling to stay afloat. I would try to talk to some of the older pastors and told them that I was struggling. They would tell me, "Whatever you do, don't let your congregation know that you are struggling emotionally, financially, or spiritually. Put on a good front because a pastor must have it together and never let the church know that he is struggling in any form."

I finally laid it before the Lord that I couldn't take it anymore and that I needed help. God told me that I needed to go before my congregation to let them know that I was struggling and that some of them had hurt me with their attitude toward me and my family. So I went to church that Sunday morning, and when it was time to preach,

I stepped out of the pulpit and stood down on the floor in front of the congregation. I poured out my heart unto the congregation and then told them I needed them to come and pray for me. I knelt across the altar, and they came and prayed for me.

After they prayed for me, then one by one, each person began to confess the things that they were struggling with and asked for prayer. We would pray for that person, and then another one would confess, and we prayed for them also. Almost everyone in the church lay down their façade, spoke their true heart, and became open and vulnerable to each other. This was the most incredible thing that could have ever happened in the church because there were no more masquerades and façades in the body of the church. Now everyone was open and honest.

Out of it grew a deep, deep love for each other. Jesus said that he did not come for the righteous and those that were well, but he came for those that were sick and hurting. What we learned was that the church needs to be a spiritual hospital where the sick, tired, and hurting can come and be healed. But this cannot and does not happen when the church is wearing a façade that when you enter the church door, you put on a smile and pretend that you are spiritual and everything is going great. Then you leave the church with all your pain and your hurts because you are too proud to ask God and his body for help.

The church began to grow, and lives began to be truly changed. The members looked for ways to help one another. One couple gave my wife and me a twenty- fifth anniversary trip to Paris and Switzerland. Others helped take care of our children while we were gone on that trip. Even today, when any previous member has a problem, immediately someone is on the phone, and the message is relayed to the previous members, and they reach out to the one in need physically, emotionally, and financially. God says that He's looking for a broken and contrite heart that He might heal and renew the soul and spirit.

CHAPTER 13

Leaving the Assemblies of God

One day, as I was praying, God spoke to me and said that I needed to withdraw our church from the Assemblies of God and become an independent church. I knew that if we withdrew from the Assemblies of God that I would have to resign my ordination because they do not let the Assembly of God pastors continue to pastor churches that are not Assembly of God. The next day, Lyle Noah called me and said, "Ernie, don't tell anyone where you heard this, but I just came from a meeting with the North Texas District Council. They are planning to sell your church property and assign you to a different church because the property where your church is located is very valuable. They want to take the money and put it in what they consider a more productive ministry."

Now no one from the North Texas District or North Texas Section had ever attended my church. Our church had supported both the section and the district and, as a formative church, should have received support from both. I told the Lord that I wanted confirmation from him that we were to leave the Assemblies of God. On Sunday morning, we went to the church, and I normally taught the adult Sunday school class. I went into the class, and I told them that my wife and I were going to the office, and we were going to pray. I wanted them to go to the altars and pray until God spoke to them, and when it was 100 percent unanimous, they were to come and get us. I gave them no hint of what they were to be praying about. My wife and I went to the office, closed the door, and prayed.

In about forty-five minutes, one of the members came and said we don't fully understand this, but God has spoken to us, and it is 100 percent unanimous that we are to withdraw the church from the Assemblies of God. The district council had called me on Friday and told me that the superintendent and the assistant superintendent were going to be in our church service on Sunday morning.

A few minutes after the members told us what God had told them, the phone rang, and it was the superintendent. He informed me that some things had come up and they would not be coming, but they would come next Sunday. I told him that there was no need for them to come next Sunday because our church had just voted to withdraw from the Assemblies of God and that I would be sending the information they needed on our withdrawal. I would also be resigning my ordination with the Assemblies of God. He told me that I could not withdraw the church because it belonged to the Assemblies of God. I told him that he was mistaken because we had our own nonprofit church corporation with the state and that the members owned the church. When we came into the Assemblies of God, it was agreed that the corporation would remain intact.

He told me that I would have to meet with the Assemblies of God leadership, and I told him that I had no problem meeting with them. We mailed the information to the assemblies along with my resignation, and a meeting was set up in which I would meet with the leadership. I met with the leadership, and it was evident very quickly that it was going to be a hostile meeting. I asked God to give me the grace and peace to be loving and kind, and God granted me that grace and peace. One of the pastors said that we could not withdraw the church. He did not care that we had our own corporation and said that they owned our church and would take us to court to retain ownership. I said, "Sir, you have never had ownership of our church."

One of the other pastors informed him that there had been many cases taken to court, and the church always won because the courts have always maintained that the membership owns the church. Then he said to me that I was a rebel, and they had no place in their association for rebels. They wanted to strip me of my ordination instead of accepting my resignation. I said, "Sir, if you are calling me a rebel because I follow the leadership of the Holy Spirit, I am honored, and if you are calling me a rebel for any other reason, I forgive you."

All but one of the men agreed that they would not accept my resignation but chose to have a trial in which it was already predetermined that they would strip me of my ordination. Finally, one of the pastors spoke up and said, "Gentlemen, as I have sat here and listened to this conversation, I am convicted of God that we have failed this man and his church. This man and his church have supported the section and the district, and we of the leadership that should have taken the lead have done absolutely nothing to support this pastor and his church."

And he turned to me and said, "I have never been in your church. I have never met with you, which we are supposed to have done. I am asking for your forgiveness for my part of being a failure and not supporting you the way that I should have and the way that is required. I don't know what the rest of this committee will do, but I for my part seek and desire your forgiveness."

I told him, "Not only do I forgive you, I forgive the others also, even though they have not asked for it."

Nine months later, I received a letter from the district saying that they had accepted my resignation of my ordination.

The church revised our corporate structure by changing the name back to Mount Zion Fellowship and including provisions for ordination. If a pastor was ordained in any another denomination and was not stripped of his ordination by the other denomination but had resigned it in good standing, the pastor would be interviewed. If the candidate was deemed to meet the qualifications of a pastor, we would recognize their ordination and would grant ordination. And then provisions were made to ordain young men that were called of God that met the qualifications in Timothy and Titus.

Even though we left the Assemblies of God and became an independent church, we continued to support Dan and Vi Lund, missionaries in Malawi, Africa. We also continued to support Dallas Teen Life Challenge and to minister to the young men when they came to Wednesday night services.

CHAPTER 14

God Shrinks and Purifies the Body

We had a couple that joined our church. The husband was originally from Colombia in South America, and after two or three years of being members of the church, they felt the call to go to Colombia as missionaries. The church ordained the husband, and we counseled them that they were to go to Colombia and live a modest lifestyle as they planted a church in Columbia. The only support that they were going to have would come from our church, so we stressed to them that they needed to be on a strict budget because we were a small church without large resources. Unfortunately, outside of the church, they were receiving the prosperity gospel. They were caught up in the event and believed that because they were missionaries, God should abundantly provide for them.

After four or five months, they ran out of money and were forced to come home. They came back to the church, and the husband was very broken and discouraged. We did not need an associate pastor, but the church decided to encourage this young man by giving him the position of associate pastor.

God had spoken to me and told me that He was going to shrink and purify the body. He did not tell me how He was going to do it. The associate pastor and his wife began to go to the people in the church and tell them that I was too busy and that I did not have time to take care of the needs of the church, but they had the time and were better equipped to take the needs of the church. They wanted the people to come to them so they would minister to the members and their needs. They were like David's son Absalom that stole the hearts of the people by telling them the lie that I did not have time to minister to the needs of the church.

The deacons and I called the couple in and talked to them about what they were doing. We told them that they either needed to support me and the church and stop undermining the church or we would have to dismiss him as an associate pastor. They immediately went to the people whose hearts they had stolen and told them that they were being treated unfairly and that he should be made pastor instead of me. We called them in and told them that he had an opportunity to resign as associate pastor and that they would need to leave the church quietly. We would give them a going away party, but that they needed to leave the members of the church alone.

They agreed that they would do this, and we gave them a very nice going away party with lots of nice gifts and then expected them to leave quietly. Within an hour after the party was over, they were calling the members, telling them that they needed to come to them and start a new ministry. Many times, my wife and I had personally given sacrificially to help this couple with their finances. We gave of our time and love to them, and they stabbed us in our backs with their response.

I went to God and asked him why and how this happened. God told me that it was His doing and that He had told me He was going to shrink and purify the church. Paul, in his writings, said they were not of us or they would have remained with us. When I realized that God was behind this, it was much easier to forgive and move on. Through the next six months, there was a large drop in attendance, but God, in His wisdom, unified the body with a love that I had never seen in any other body that I had been associated with.

CHAPTER 15

God's Protection

I picked up the newspaper the first thing in the morning, and I read that this was the last day to remove signs that had been grandfathered. It listed the types of signs that had been grandfathered, and they needed to be taken down by five o'clock that day. My animal hospital sign was one of those signs, but I had not received the notice that my sign was not in compliance with city code. The notice had been sent to the owner of the property, and for devious reasons, he had not notified me.

I had decided that, if necessary, I would go home and get my acetylene torch and cut the sign down. If the sign was destroyed, it was just destroyed. On my way to my house, I saw a man driving a truck with a crane that had a sign logo on the side of the truck. I rolled down the window, honked the horn, and got his attention. He pulled over to the side, and I asked him if he would like to make $100 cash. When he asked me how, I told him that I had a sign that needed to come down. He said that he would follow me to the sign and then give me an answer.

He followed me back to my animal hospital, looked at the sign, and said that it would be easy to cut the pipe at the bottom, remove the sign, and set it in front of my hospital. The only problem was that there was a three-foot base made from concrete. He said that he couldn't remove that base, but he could cut the sign down and move it for the hundred dollars, so he did.

After going home and getting some sledgehammers, I was pounding on the concrete, trying to break it up. I was not getting very far when my very best friend, Paul Ecker, the director of Dallas Teen Challenge, drove up. He asked what I was doing, and I told him that we had to remove the base because of the sign ordinance. He got out of his vehicle, took off his sports coat and his tie, and within minutes had broken up the base with the sledgehammer. This is a man that helped us move several times, and I saw him pick up a washing machine, carry it out of the house, and set it in the back of a two-ton moving truck. My wife told him that he could have been Paul Bunyan.

We cleaned up the concrete mess. I got my acetylene torch and cut the rest of the pipe off at the base, and we filled in the hole. The sign was completely removed by five o'clock. The next day, an agent from the company that I was leasing from showed up and told me that I was evicted and had thirty days to vacate the property. I asked him on what basis was I evicted. He told me that I had a sign that did not meet the sign ordinance, and thus I had broken my lease and was evicted. I asked him to show me the sign.

He said, "Follow me, and I will show you the sign." He went outside and discovered that the sign had been removed. He got very red-faced and started to hem and haw around. Then he took the eviction papers with him and left. A few weeks later, another agent representing the company came to me and told me that he was authorized to pay me $5,000 for my lease as the company was going to tear the building down to build a new shopping center. I looked at him and I told him that if he thought he could buy my lease for $5,000, he was a lot crazier than I thought he was. He told me that if I thought I was going to get $25,000 for the lease that I was the one that was crazy because the corporation had taken Kentucky Fried Chicken to the Supreme Court and had won. Kentucky Fried Chicken lost on a very small technicality and had to vacate the premises without any compensation.

Now it became clear why the corporation had not given me the notice on the sign because, to be honest, they were a bunch of crooks. I had a ten-year lease. We had been there approximately four years, so I had six years left on my lease. I had a client that was a lawyer that just happened to be there when the agent was trying to buy my lease.

The lawyer overheard the conversation and knew who the corporation was. After the agent left, he told me that he would represent me at no charge because with an extremely minor technicality, he had lost a case against this corporation which was very unscrupulous in their dealing with their tenants. He asked me to give him a copy of my lease and he would give me advice. He said, "If we must go to court, I will not charge you any fees because from my understanding, you have done nothing to break your lease. If it's a standard lease, they either must pay you a fair price for your improvements and the time left on your lease or they must always keep your building intact and accessible for you to maintain your business."

On Thursday, which was my day off, I told my wife, "Let's go to the corporate headquarters to talk to the man who owns this building and work out some type of an agreement."

Joe Chaffin, the man that I had leased from, had passed away with cancer. He was an honest man, but the people that were left were not honest. My wife and I arrived shortly after 8:00 a.m. I went to the receptionist and told her that I needed to meet with the owner of the corporation. Her answer was that he doesn't meet with anyone and people must meet with someone working for him. She informed us that we didn't have an appointment and that we couldn't get one. So I told her that she could inform him that I was going to stay in his office until either he asked me himself to leave or he meet with me because my way of doing business was to sit down with the person and talk face-to-face as I did when I had leased the property.

At three o'clock, when they saw that I was not leaving, a secretary came out and told me that the man would meet with me when he finished his meeting. The man came out at about 3:30 and told me to come into his office. As soon as we entered his office, he looked at me and said, "You are very foolish if you think you can win this case because we have taken Kentucky Fried Chicken to the Supreme Court, and we won. You do not have the finances to take us on, so why don't you just accept our offer and go on your way?"

I looked at him and told him that my way of doing business was to sit down face-to-face and work out a fair and equitable agreement for both people.

He said, "We don't operate that way, so why don't you just leave?"

I said, "Sir, if you want to go that route, I have an attorney that has agreed to take this case and represent me at no charge to me because he wants you."

He asked me who the attorney was, and I gave him the attorney's name. Then he was ready to sit down and talk. He said that he would send me a letter in three days with an offer. I told him that if he thought $25,000 would even come close not to bother and that we would go to court. In three days, I received a letter offering me $50,000, six weeks to vacate, and three days to respond. The attorney had given me some of his paper with his letterhead on it, and he told me that I could use it but to just be sure to send him a copy when I used his paper. I did some calculating and came up with a figure of $175,000 because the remodeling that I had done in the building probably at that time would cost $100,000. Also, I needed some money to make a move as well as some compensation for the lease that was left.

I sent him a letter stating that the $175,000 was not negotiable and that he had three days to accept it or we would see him in court. On the third day, the representative that I had met with called and asked for more time. I told him that he gave me three days to respond to his offer, and I had given him the same amount of time. I expressed that he would not have given me one minute more and that I had talked to the attorney who said this was a fair offer and that we were ready to go to court; however, I would give him until 9:30 in the morning to respond. So he agreed to have me an answer by 9:30 the next morning.

At 9:30, he called me and said that they would accept my offer. I would have six weeks to vacate. They would pay me one half up front and the other half when I vacated. If this was agreeable, he would have a courier carry over the papers. I said that it was agreeable, but I would want the attorney to read the papers to be sure that it was exactly what we were agreeing to. He responded that it would be fine. When I received the papers, the attorney said that they were in order, to sign them, and return them.

Now I had six weeks to find a new location and to move, which basically was impossible. I found a house on Buena Vista that had a small warehouse in the back. I called the real estate agent who notified me that there was a contract on the property, but that he would write a backup contract if I was interested. I told him that I would like to write a backup contract and that I needed it as soon as possible.

I went to North Park National Bank where the president of the bank was a client of mine. We had bought a house in foreclosure from him through the bank. I met with the president, gave him a copy of the real estate contract, and asked him to process a loan application because time was very short. He recommended a ninety-day loan for the total amount, and then after the deal closed, if it closed, we would work out long-term financing. I was unable to find any other location.

One month later, the real estate agent called me and said that the contract had fallen through and wondered if I still wanted to purchase the property. I told him, "Yes." We were able to close the purchase of the property in three days because the bank had already approved the loan. Then I immediately started moving my things.

We sent out notices to my clients that we would be moving immediately. Even though I needed to do some remodeling, the house was such that I could practice in it while I remodeled, so we made the move of the practice. The next day, I went to the back door of my animal hospital and noticed that it had been pried open. I saw an inch and a half pipe that was three feet long, so I picked it up and walked through the kennel and then walked up into the waiting room. There were two men in the waiting room that had guns in their waistbands. I raised the pipe over the head of the one that was facing away from me, and I told them both to hit the floor with their hands out front or I would bust his skull with the pipe. The men hit the floor. I grabbed the phone, called 911, and told the police that I had two armed men lying on the floor that had broken into my property. I asked the police to get there as soon as possible.

They arrived in three to five minutes, came in, and cuffed the two men who proceeded to squeal like pigs that they were hired by the owner of the corporation to break into the property. The police wanted to know who the owner was and his address, so I told them. A squad car was dispatched to arrest the owner of the corporation. I called the corporate headquarters and asked to speak to the owner of the corporation. His secretary said, "You know he doesn't talk to you or anyone else."

I replied, "Ma'am, I think he had better talk to me."

At that moment, the police entered the corporate office, demanded to see the owner, told him to put his hands behind his back, and they were ready to cuff him. The police asked me if I wanted them to arrest him, but I asked to talk to him. He got on the phone with all kinds of apologies and made an agreement that they would take everything I needed out of the old building and move it to my new location as well as do anything else that I needed if I would not press charges against him. I talked to the police who told me that we could still press charges later if he did not live up to his agreement, so I told them not to arrest him. They did take the two men that had broken into the animal hospital to jail because they had outstanding warrants. These men, for lack of a better description, were goons. That afternoon, they had a crew removing the things that I needed from my old practice, and by the next day, it all had been moved to my new practice.

I had moved into my new property, started to practice, and then applied for a building permit. We were getting denied a permit because the lower echelon of inspectors said that we did not have enough parking places. My wife's cousin had drawn the blueprints and researched the building permits back to the original permit. He told me that there was something about a river that God continues to speak to me. I asked him if it was the beginning or end of a river, and he thought that was what it was. I replied that it would it be the Delta, and he said, "I think that's it."

Finally, I took the blueprints to the office that issued the building permits and insisted on meeting with the supervisors of each department. I took the blueprints to each supervisor and went over them with the supervisors. The supervisors were people that had worked as plumbers, electricians, carpenters, and heat and air specialists. As they got older, they weren't physically able to do the work, so they had gone to work for the city as inspectors and then moved up into supervisor roles. These men knew what it was to build the building where most of the young inspectors had never built a building but just made up rules that didn't make sense.

Each supervisor approved their section and signed the blueprint so that I knew if we did what was on the blueprint, we would get a certificate of occupancy. I then went to the man in charge of the parking, and I asked him if there was something about a Delta that would apply to my parking. He stood up and began to shout, stomp his feet, and almost scream. I asked him, "What's the problem? I just asked you about the Delta." He said that the problem was that there is a Delta theory which was two paragraphs long, but no one knows what it means or how to interpret it. He found the book, opened it to the Delta theory, and handed it to me. I read it, and it was the most ambiguous thing that I had ever read in my life.

He said to me, "Now do you know why I got all emotional?" I could understand, but I needed the parking so that I could get a building permit and eventually a certificate of occupancy. So we sat down, and as best we could, we reread the paragraphs, looked at the blueprint, and finally he said, "I think you qualify for the Delta theory."

I asked him to write that on the blueprint and sign it. He was glad to do that so that when it came back across his desk, he would know that he had already approved the parking and would not have to look at the Delta theory again. I remodeled the building, continued my practice, and pastored the church all at the same time. We got our certificate of occupancy.

CHAPTER 16

The High Priest of the Church of Satan of the Southwest District

A young lady and her three-year-old daughter had started coming to the church services. After a few weeks, she came forward and received Jesus Christ as her Lord and Savior. After they continued to come to church for several weeks, she told me that she had a major problem because her husband was the high priest of the Church of Satan of the Southwest District. Her life was in danger because she had received Jesus Christ as her Lord and Savior, and in his position, they were not allowed to leave the Church of Satan. He would have his family killed.

I asked her where he was that I might go see him. She said that it won't do any good, and I told her that God didn't bring her to a saving knowledge of Jesus Christ to get her killed. Greater was He that was in her than he that was in the world.

Ephesians 6:12 says:

> For we wrestle not against flesh and blood, but against principalities, against powers, against the rulers of the darkness of this world, against spiritual wickedness in high places. Wherefore take unto you the whole armor of God, that you may be able to withstand in the evil day, and having done all, to stand.

She said that her husband was in the minimum-security prison in Seagoville, and I asked her to make arrangements for me to be on the list of his visitors so I could go see him. After she made the arrangements, I called and got an appointment to see her husband. Being a minimum-security prison, they had a waiting room where we could sit and visit. When he walked into the room, he did not have any handcuffs on.

I introduced myself, and we sat down. He looked at me and he told me that I was the real thing because Satan had told him that he would be dealing with the Spirit of God. He said, "You don't know how many pastors and religious people through the years have tried to talk with me, and they were a joke. But Satan tells me that you are a child of the Most High God, and because you are, I will listen to what you have to say."

Over the next two hours, I had probably the deepest theological discussion that I'd ever had in my life. I was not able to convince him that he needed to come to Jesus Christ as his personal Savior. He told me that he knew who he was serving and he was content to continue to serve Satan. I said, "Then let's talk about your wife and your daughter. You know that your wife has given her life to Jesus Christ, has received Him as her personal Savior, and has made Him Lord of her life."

He was aware of that and said that she knew the consequences. I looked him straight in the eyes and said, "This is your daughter, and she is your flesh and blood. I do not care about your spiritual walk and your beliefs in this situation, but I am appealing to you as a father and a man that she is part of you. To take either or both of their lives would be a great travesty. I am appealing to you in a humanitarian effort to get you to grant them their lives."

God, through the power of the Holy Spirit, ministered to this man's humanity, and with tears in his eyes, he said, "I will grant them their lives, and you can tell them they do not have to fear for their lives." I thanked him. He looked at me and said to me once again, "You are the real thing. I realize that I have not dealt with you alone but with the Spirit of God."

I went back and shared with his wife that she was safe, and so was her daughter. We thanked God that He had intervened on their behalf. She continued at the church for about six months. Then she went back to her home which was either in Illinois or Indiana to live with her parents until she could get her feet on the ground and support her daughter.

CHAPTER 17

The Changing Demographics of Oak Lawn

O ak Lawn at one time had been one of the more elite neighborhoods and at times had been referred to as downtown; I don't know how it got the downtown designation because it was north and west of downtown Dallas. The Oak Lawn area had begun to deteriorate, and most people had moved to the new developing suburbs. The homosexual community found that they could buy the homes and refurbish them at a very reasonable price, so they were taking over the area.

Homosexual nightclubs were developing. The prostitutes were leaving the area, and the adult theaters and the homosexuals were redeveloping the business community. They built the Metropolitan Community Church in the area. The AIDS epidemic had hit the homosexual community very hard. The symptoms of AIDS are described throughout the twenty-eighth chapter of Deuteronomy. We welcomed the homosexuals to come to our services. We had several that had developed AIDS, and we ministered to them. Some of the homosexuals that had developed AIDS were led to Christ.

After much prayer and seeking God, I felt led of God to preach on Romans 1. Bryan Stuckey, a member of our church, wrote a tract about AIDS as God's judgment while explaining God's grace. We mailed thirty-four thousand tracts to the 75219 zip code which included the

Oak Lawn area. We had a telephone answering service for our church, and I received a call from them asking me, "What in the world have you done?" They were receiving hate calls and threats, one right after another, and they were being cursed out. I told them that they did not need to answer our phone and that we had sent out the tract that talked about AIDS as God's judgment while explaining God's grace for those that would turn from their sin and receive Jesus Christ as Lord and Savior.

They said that they would continue to answer the phone, but now they knew what had caused such uproar. We received well over a twenty-four-by-twenty- four-inch box of letters threatening our lives and our building. We were informed that they were going to come to disrupt our service and make an example of us.

The next Sunday, we arrived at the church early. I told the members as they came in what had happened and the response that we had received by telephone and letter. I asked them to be on their best behavior with God's love, to love them, and not let them draw us into hate. We wanted to be sure that they understood that we love the sinner and hate the sin and that their sin is no different than any other sin. A normal married couple came that Sunday because they had received the tract.

I received a phone message from Don Baker, the president of the Dallas Gay Alliance. He wanted me to return the call, and after playing phone tag for a couple weeks, we finally connected. I told Don that I would meet him at the church and take him to lunch. I took one of the other church members with me, and we took him to El Fenix Mexican restaurant on Lemon Avenue. When we sat down to eat, Don told me why he was a homosexual and the struggles that he had being a homosexual in society. Don had been a school teacher, and when they found out that he was a homosexual, he was let go. Don's grandfather was an Assembly of God pastor, and his dad was an Assembly of God deacon. Don told me that the tract we had sent out had deeply offended him and the homosexual community.

When he asked me why we sent the tract, I told him that Ezekiel 33 told us that we needed to warn the wicked or the blood would be upon our hands, so we had sent the tract in obedience to God's Word.

I told him also that if he would read the tract carefully that he would find grace and love rather than judgment. Then I looked at Don and I said, "Don, you and I are diametrically opposed to each other. Unless you receive Jesus Christ as your Lord and Savior, we will remain that way. Don, I would defend to my death your right to proclaim your homosexuality, and I would think if you thought about it, you would defend to your death my right to send the tract." Also I said, "I receive mail on a regular basis that offends me, and I throw it in file 13. I am offended, but they have the right to send it to me because of our freedom of speech. I have the right to throw it in the trash, which is what I do." I said, "Don, I'm sorry that you were offended, but I have the right to send it, and you have the right to throw it in the trash."

After I made that statement, Don reached into his briefcase and pulled out a lawsuit that they were going to file against me and the church. He told me that this was a lawsuit that he was going to serve me with today but that I was right; I did have the right to send the tract out. At that moment, he tore up the lawsuit, put it back in his briefcase, and said, "We will not be suing you."

I paid the check, and we went to the car. As we started to drive back to the church, I told Don that I loved him and was going to continue to pray for him. He looked at me with tears flowing down his cheeks and told me that I was the first pastor that he had ever met that he believed genuinely loved him, and he asked me to please pray for him. He then told me that he had been to no less than twelve pastors offices, and they told him that he was going to hell and to get out of their office. But he said, "I really sense and feel your love and want your prayers."

Don died of AIDS, but before his death, he was reconciled with his family. I do not know if he turned from his sin and received God's love and grace.

I received a telephone call from the *Dallas Morning News* requesting to interview me for an article that they were going to write on homosexuality. It was to be a front-page main story in the Sunday paper. I told them that I would let them interview me, so a time was set for me to meet the reporter at the church. I told the church that I was going to be interviewed, and I asked that they fast and pray for me that

God would give me the wisdom and the right words to say. The church members fasted and prayed for me.

When I met the reporter, it was obvious from the very beginning that she wanted to pit me and our church against the Metropolitan Community Church and the homosexual community. The reporter asked me why the Presbyterian Church in the area had a homosexual music leader, and I told her that she was asking the wrong person because I did not know why they had a homosexual music leader. Then she tried to put words in my mouth, and she asked if it was wrong to have a homosexual music leader. I responded to her that I did not know why they had a homosexual music leader, so I could not sit in judgment. Then she asked me if I would have a homosexual music leader, and I told her that we would not have a homosexual music leader.

Next she asked me if homosexuals came to our church, and I said, "Yes, they do come to the church, and they are made welcome." She asked if a homosexual could join our church. I replied that if a homosexual repents of his sin, turns from his homosexuality, and receives Jesus Christ as his Lord and Savior, he can become a member of the church, just as any other person who repents of their sin and receives Jesus Christ as their Lord and Savior can become a member of the church. To become a member of the church, a person must repent of their sins, receive Jesus Christ as their Lord and Savior, and become a new person in Christ by not living in their past sins.

When the reporter could not pit me against the Metropolitan Community Church and the homosexual community, the front-page article in the Sunday paper now became a mid-page article in a Thursday paper. It continues to amaze me how God can take an ordinary man that looks to God to accomplish His will. God said in His Word that when you're brought before judges to take no thought what you're going to say, but He would give you the words to speak. Because the members had prayed and fasted for me, God gave me words of love instead of words of conflict that the reporter was trying to stir up between us and the homosexual community.

CHAPTER 18

The Closing of Mount Zion Fellowship

Because of the changing demographics of the Oak Lawn area, most of the members had moved to the suburbs to raise their families in a more family- friendly atmosphere. They continued to come back on Sundays and Wednesdays for services. In 1995, God spoke to me that it was time to close the church because the members needed to establish relationships in the communities where they lived. They all knew and understood this, but they had formed such a tremendous bond of love and fellowship with each other that they did not want to close the church. However, they knew that this was God's will, and they wanted to be in God's will. So after much prayer, it was decided to close the church and to give the building to Dallas Teen Life Challenge.

Arriving at a date to close the church was very difficult since the members wanted to put it off, and I had the same feelings. God spoke to me after I had preached a sermon on Sunday morning that I needed to tell the church that this was the last service, but I didn't do it. The next Sunday, as I got up to preach, there was no anointing. Within a few minutes, I realized there was no anointing and that God had said it was time to close the church. I stopped preaching and told the congregation, "It is over. God has said we need to move on. There is no anointing to preach another message, so let's have some fellowship and say our goodbyes."

The body has remained very tight-knit. If someone is ill or going through a real struggle, they are on the phone to other members who still pray and minister to each other.

CHAPTER 19

Selling My Practice and Home in Dallas

God spoke to me one night as I was praying and said that it was time to sell our house and move. We started looking for acreage in the McKinney area. We were not having much luck finding a new place to live. My wife kept telling me that I would not want to drive into Dallas to practice. Then God spoke to me that I should sell my practice. I said to God, "I am willing to sell my practice, but I am so busy that I do not have time to sell my practice. If you want me to sell the practice, bring a veterinarian to buy it."

A couple weeks later, I met a veterinarian who asked me if he could come and spend the mornings with me in my practice for one to two weeks. I told him that would be fine. He had been running the emergency clinic which was open at night and on the weekends. He had recently remarried, and they had a young child. He knew the emergency practice was not conducive to good family life, but he had been out of a normal practice for years and wanted to know what it was like to run a normal practice. He would come in the mornings when we opened the practice.

We would go to lunch and talk about the practice. Then he started coming on Monday and on Friday. Soon he told me that he wanted to buy my practice. I replied that the practice was not for sale. He said that all practices are for sale for the right amount of money. I asked him to make me an offer, so he came to me later with an offer that was not nearly enough to buy the practice. I told my wife what he had offered, and we discussed the offer, but we did not discuss what we would need for the practice to sell it.

We went to bed that night as usual, and after my wife fell asleep, I got up to have my quiet time with the Lord. God spoke to me and gave me an amount that I needed for the practice. The next morning, my wife got up and said, "You are going to offer to sell the practice to the veterinarian." She gave me an amount that was exactly what God had told me in my quiet time. This was confirmation that God wanted us to sell the practice to this veterinarian.

So I called him after I got to work and told him that I would sell him the practice for that amount of money. He said that he needed a few days to talk to his banker to see if financing could be arranged. He called me back a few days later and said that he would buy the practice for that amount. He wanted us to get an attorney to write a contract, but I told him that attorneys were expensive and that I would not pay an attorney to write a contract until I knew that he could get the money to buy the practice. He thought this was going to be impossible because he was applying for a small business loan from the government which would need a contract. I told him that my word was my word; we had shaken hands on it, and he could have his banker contact the president of my bank.

His banker said that he did not see any way to get the loan through the government without a contract, but he would call my banker and talk to him. My banker told him, "If Dr. Martin has given his word, it is far better than a contract written on paper because his word is his word."

After his banker talked to my banker, his banker wanted to come by to see the animal hospital and meet with me. I told him to come on as I had nothing to hide, and I was very open about the sale of the hospital. He came to the animal hospital, and we visited for about forty-five minutes. Then he said that he would see what he could do to get this through the government loan process.

A short time later, the veterinarian called me and told me that the loan was approved, and as far as his banker knew, it was the only time that something like this had ever been approved. We then went to the lawyer, got the contract written, and set up a closing date.

I had sold the animal hospital, and our house was on the market. On my day off, my wife and I met different real-estate agents in the McKinney area to look at property. We had spent the day with one agent, and I told him that I wanted to go back by the three different properties that he had shown me to try to decide concerning the properties. We were driving down Custer Road when we saw a ranch-style house for sale on ten acres. We took down the number, called about the property, and got the information.

The real-estate agent that was selling our house contacted the real-estate agent handling the ranch-style house and the property. After viewing the property, we made a cash offer for the asking price. The lady that owned the property had lost her husband, and she wanted to sell the property. She did not want to haggle with people over the price. There were three other people trying to buy the property, but they were offering less than the asking price, so when our offer came in for the asking price, she accepted it right away.

An attorney had made an offer on our house, and he wanted to do several inspections. Most of them were the normal inspections, but then he brought out a plumber to do an inspection on the drainage of the house. The house had cast- iron plumbing which should not be pressure tested because it is sealed with lead. It is not like PVC pipe that is glued. Also, the draining system on a house is not under pressure, but it depends upon gravity. They did this test without permission and they damaged some of the pipes.

I called our real-estate agent, and she called the attorney's agent to set up a meeting. I explained that his plumber had damaged some of the plumbing, so he had two choices. Because his people had damaged the plumbing, he would either pay for the repair of the plumbing or sign a waiver on the plumbing and take the house as is with no recourse on the plumbing. He had a conference with his agent, and she informed him that he had better take the offer because of the danger of lawsuits that we could file against him to recover the damage that his plumber had done to the house. And because the plumber that he had hired had damaged the plumbing, he could make him fix it at their expense. He agreed to sign the waiver and close the sale of the house.

Now the house and the practice were both sold. We had to move out of our home, and we did not have a new house to move in to. It was going to be five days before we could move into the property where we were going to build a new animal hospital. We loaded our household furniture and belongings onto large U-Haul trucks, parked them in my father-in-law's driveway, and we went to San Antonio for five days.

When we came back from San Antonio, we moved our furniture and belongings into the house where we were building an animal hospital, and we crammed it all in one end of the house so that I could remodel the other end into exam rooms and a surgery room. I had some clients that lived in Plano, and it was closer for them to come to McKinney than to go to Dallas. It was agreed when we sold the practice in Dallas that these clients in Plano could be contacted by me at my new location without interfering with our restrictive agreement in the sale. These clients wanted me to see them during the remodeling phase, so I went ahead and saw them while I was building a kennel and remodeling the inside of the house. This took about two months.

We knew that we were going to have to find a house. We located a three- bedroom house on two acres in McKinney that had a four-car garage and a workshop on the end of the garage. This appeared to be our ideal home since the three older boys were out of the house, and we had one son that was finishing up high school. We were able to buy the house, move our furniture into the house, and then finish the remodeling of the hospital. The kennel could hold just over a hundred dogs, and we were able to open the hospital officially before Thanksgiving. The hospital was filled with borders during the Thanksgiving holidays.

My wife and I and our youngest son, Steven, did most of the work. There were two men from Teen Life Challenge that did not have a place to go during the holidays, so they stayed in the hospital and helped us with all the borders. It did not take long for the hospital to grow into a thriving practice.

Jan was working as my receptionist, doing whatever was necessary to help me and keeping the books for the practice. Because we were so busy, we needed help, so we hired our oldest son, James, who had a degree in accounting and business information systems to be the hospital administrator.

CHAPTER 20

The Move to the Country

While we were living in Dallas, Jan's mother and dad moved to Dallas and lived about a mile north of where we lived on Glennox Lane. When we moved to a new house on Hillview, they lived about a mile south of us. They continued to live in Dallas when we moved to McKinney. When I was in Dallas, I would stop by to see how they were doing. Their driveway was beside the house, and the garage was in the back. Many times, I would just pull up to the back and stay in the car. They were usually outside because they loved to work in their large garden, so they would come over to visit with me while I was sitting in the car.

One day I pulled up, and Jan's dad, who was one of the gentlest and sweetest men that you would ever meet, came to the car. He said in a very raised voice, "Get out and come into the house."

I was shocked and concerned that there was something seriously wrong for him to act that way. I went into the house and sat down on a chair in the kitchen beside her dad. He looked at me and said, "I want you to make me a promise that you will not put me or my wife in a nursing home." They were both very healthy for their age and were quite capable at this stage of their life to take care of themselves.

I sat there for a couple minutes to gather my thoughts and then I answered him, "We will do everything possible not to put either of you in a nursing home. However, if one of you should reach the stage of dementia in which it is impossible to care for you in a home, we may have to go to a secure facility that cares for patients with dementia."

He was satisfied with my answer, and then we visited about other things. About six months later, my wife received a phone call around five o'clock from her mother, and she told Jan that she thought her dad was dead. It takes us about forty-five minutes to get to their place, so we drove to Dallas. When we arrived, the next-door neighbors and the police were at the house. Her dad was sitting in the recliner and looked like he was asleep, but he was dead. He had been out working in the garden that morning when he told the neighbor across the fence, "Thank God that He gave me another day." Then about one o'clock after lunch, he sat down in his recliner as usual and just went to sleep.

His wife, knowing that this was what he did most afternoons, continued to work in the garden and do other things, so she did not check on him until around five. She was unable to rouse him and realized he had died. One of the first things that she told me was, "You promised that you would not put us in a nursing home, but I cannot live alone." We decided that we would not make rash decisions.

My wife and I were happy in the home that we had bought in McKinney, but there was no way that her mother could live with us in the house that we were in. I am the proverb that you can take a country boy out of the country, but you can't take the country out of the country boy. I had always wanted to buy some land where I could feed a few steers for our own meat. Homegrown beef without antibiotics or hormones that has been fattened to prime is just much better eating.

I loved good steaks and hamburgers, so we started looking for acreage that we could either build a house or buy a house that was already built that would accommodate her mother. We looked for almost a year and had almost given up that we were going to find what we could afford. I told my wife that our son Charlie and I were going to take one last look on a Sunday afternoon. We started to drive, going up every little county road that we saw, and in reality, we were lost when we found this beautiful property. I called the number on the sign, and I talked to a man who said that there were twenty-two acres. There was not a road on the property which was raw native pastureland. He told me that I sounded like an honest man, so he gave me the code to the key box so we could go in and look at the property.

We unlocked the gate and went in to look at the long narrow piece of property that, on the west side, was bordered with a railroad track and on the east side by a creek. The property had many large pecan trees that you could not wrap your arms around as well as lots of big oak trees and lots of juniper cedar trees. It was set up so that houses could be built back behind the trees, and no one would be able to see the houses from the road. The property had electricity but no water, and it was located on a white rock road.

Charlie called his mother and said, "You have to come and see this property now."

My wife and her sister who was visiting from New Orleans came right away, and all of us went to see the property. We were able to purchase the property with Charlie. Then my wife and I had to design a house that would accommodate her mother. The first thing that I did was purchase an unassembled Quonset building from a company that was in bankruptcy in Toronto, Canada. I had it shipped to the property, and we found someone to help us build the barn which was fifty-by-one-hundred feet. I left thirty feet open to the south where the cattle could be fed and cared for and put in a concrete floor in the rest of the building which was enclosed.

My wife designed a house that had our house on one end, and it connected to her mother's house. There was a spare bedroom so that if you closed one door, it became part of her house, and if you closed the other door, it became part of our house. In this way, if her mother ever needed full-time care, the caregiver could stay in the spare bedroom. Otherwise, it was a guest bedroom for us.

Her mother had a kitchen, utility room, and a large bedroom with a fireplace, and we made her house all handicap accessible. We sold our house and bought a bumper pull thirty-foot RV which my wife and I were going to live in it while we built our house. But Charlie got married, and he and his wife wanted to live in the RV while we were building our houses. So my wife and I rented a one- bedroom house near the animal hospital where we lived for a year.

We stored as much as we could in the barn and packed the one-bedroom house with most of our furniture until our house was finished. I had a friend that had a Caterpillar, and I borrowed a tractor with a front-end loader with a box blade. He and I built a road into the property. This same friend helped me set oil well pipe for fence corner posts.

Some guys from Dallas Teen Life Challenge came out and helped me build the fence so that I could buy some steers and feed them out. It took ten months to build the house, and after we finished building our house, Charlie and his wife built their house on the same property. Jan's mother wanted to garden, so I bought a tractor with a Rototiller and plowed up a space for a large garden. The first year, we froze a thousand ears of sweet corn, canned jars of pickles from the cucumbers, had acorn squash, as well as lots of beets and tomatoes. I bought two steers, fed them corn, and had them butchered—so we were living the life.

In the spring of the next year, I bought eight steers that weighed about six hundred pounds each. I let them graze the pasture during the summer while feeding them a little corn once a day so that they would come to the barn, knowing that they were going to get fed when I called them. This way, I could check on them daily, and if for any reason I needed to get them to the barn, I could call them, and they would come. We did not have to have a horse or a group of people to go out and drive them to the barn. In September, I started to feed them a lot more corn so that I could fatten them up. I would sell beef to my clients that wanted corn-fed beef with no antibiotics or hormones in their system. It was nice to have a ready market for my steers since I had more clients that wanted beef than I could supply. I would feed the steers corn until the end of February or first of March and then have them butchered. In April, I would buy eight more steers and repeat the process.

CHAPTER 21

Neck Surgeries

I began having severe pain in my neck and both of my arms. The pain became so severe that it was debilitating. I called one of my clients who was an orthopedic surgeon. I had seen his dog on an emergency when it had been hit by a car. The dog survived and did well. The doctor got me right in and took an X- ray of my neck which revealed I had a herniated disc at C4 and C5 as well as a large bone spur in my neck. He did not do neck surgery, so he referred me to Dr. Kevin Gill. He called in a favor from Dr. Gill who agreed to see me that day, and he sent me for an MRI. After he read the MRI, he told me that I needed surgery as soon as possible to remove the disc, fuse the vertebrae, and remove the bone spur. But he told me that this might not solve all my problems because I had stenosis of the spinal canal that would require a different surgery.

We scheduled the surgery to do the fusion, remove the bone spur, and see how I would do. The bone spur was removed, and my neck was fused. I was hospitalized overnight. The next morning, when the doctor came in, I was pain- free. I was given a neck brace to wear when I was in a vehicle for protection, but because they had put a titanium plate with four screws in my neck, I did not need to wear the brace, except in the vehicle. When I left the hospital, I went to work at my animal hospital. My only restrictions were for some time, I was not to lift more than ten pounds; so I had the other people that worked for me lift the animals. They took a piece of bone from my right pelvis to fuse my neck. The area where they took the bone became severely infected because of a contaminated suture which was used to tie off vessels and close the area.

Dr. Gill had me washing the area twice a day with soap and water, but it was not getting any better. I had one of my RN's re-sterilize a long thumb forceps and stitch scissors before I removed the contaminated sutures. Then I took twenty-five ml of hydrogen peroxide shot into the wound and flushed it out. The next morning, it stopped draining and healed up. Dr. Gill was not thrilled that I had used hydrogen peroxide to clear up the infection, but I told him his soap and water did not work. It was healing, and he could not argue with results. I did well for several months, and then the pain returned with a vengeance.

Dr. Gill referred me to Dr. Ballista at Southwestern Medical School. Dr. Ballista ordered an MRI and then followed it with a myelogram of my neck. It was confirmed that I had stenosis of the spinal canal in my neck and that a laminoplasty of C2 through C7 was needed. Dr. Ballista said that I would be in the hospital at least ten days, but I would not be able to go back to work for at least thirty days nor do surgery for at least six weeks. I was told that the pain from the surgery itself could last one and a half years.

I had the eight-hour surgery on Tuesday. I do not remember anything in recovery. I just remember being rolled down the hall to my room; I had a neck brace on and was in excruciating pain. They had me on a morphine pump; and at 2:30 in the morning, I broke out with hives from the morphine, so I quit taking it. Dr. Ballista came in the next morning at 6:30, and I said, "I guess you will get me up today." He replied that the physical therapist would get me up. Even though there were pumps on my legs to prevent blood clots, I told Dr. Ballista I was ready to get up right then. He said that the physical therapist would get me up, but I told him, "You did this to me. Now get me up."

So Dr. Ballista took the wraps off my legs, and he got on one side of me with my wife on the other side of me. They helped me sit up on the edge of the bed. Immediately the room was swirling around my head. I sat there for a few minutes until it stopped and I got my bearings. Then I said, "I want to stand up."

He replied that the physical therapist would get me up, but I insisted that I wanted to stand up now. He got on one side with my wife on the other side, and they helped me stand up, but again the room was swirling around me. After a couple minutes, I had my bearings and was able to stand. I stood for a few minutes, and then I sat back down on the edge of the bed. He asked me if I was ready to lie back down, but I told him that I would like to sit up because they would be bringing breakfast at seven.

After I ate breakfast around seven, I laid back down. The wraps were put back on my legs. Around nine, the physical therapist came in and asked me if I was ready to go for a walk. I told her that I was. She was a very small attractive young lady who put this belt around my waist to steady me. There was no way if I began to fall that she was big enough to hold me up. We started to the door when I realized I was not ready to go for a walk, so she had me sit in a straight back chair and told me that she would be back for me in twenty minutes. When she came back, I was just about screaming in pain because sitting in a straight back chair was one of the most painful things one can do after neck surgery.

She said, "Let's go for a walk." She was on my right side to help secure me. When we went through the door, there was a railing on my left side. I took the railing with my left hand, and by the time we had walked past two rooms, I had my bearings, and my feet were under me. I knew that I could walk without any trouble. She insisted that we needed to turn around and go back to the room, but I told her that the only way I was going to be able to get out of the hospital was to walk and get my strength back. I kept on walking while she kept insisting that we needed to turn around because I had to get back to the room.

When I told her that it was her problem, she said, "How are you going to get back to the room? I can't carry you back." I knew that she would not have to carry me back because now I had my strength to walk, so I walked around the entire floor of the hospital. When we came back to the door to my room, she insisted that I must go in and lie down, but I walked around one more time while she protested. Then, when she said, "That's enough," I went in and lay down. She told me I was amazing because she had not had a single patient that had this surgery that was able to walk more than two rooms for at least ten days. She put the wraps back on my legs and she told me not to get up without help. My wife had spent the night in the hospital with me, so she didn't get much sleep. After lunch, she fell asleep; and shortly, I needed to use the restroom. I punched the nurse's button several times, and no one came. I did not want to wake up my wife, so I managed to get the wraps off my legs, got up, and went to the bathroom. Now, since I was up, I decided that I just may as well go for a walk, so I walked around the hospital floor two times. The nurses were giving me the thumbs up. Then I went back to lie down, and I put the wraps back on my legs.

My wife woke up around three, and we walked around the hospital two more times. At four o'clock, the physical therapist came in and she said, "I heard about you. You don't need me, and I'm leaving."

Dr. Ballista came in the next morning, which was Thursday. He said, "I don't think we can do anymore for you in the hospital, so if you would like, you can go home." Dr. Ballista is a spirit-filled Christian and is an incredible man; he always has a smile on his face, incredible bedside manner, and concern for his patients.

I don't like hospital food, and my wife is an extremely good cook, so we said we would go home. He stayed until they checked me out, and he went with us to the car. After I was in the car, he motioned for me to roll the window down, and he said, "If you are climbing the walls on Monday, you can go back to work. You are just not to lift anything for six weeks."

My wife drove me to work on Monday, and I worked for about six hours. I was on no pain medication, so the pain was excruciating. My neck was swollen at least double in size, so working took my mind off the pain. If I had time between patients, I could lie down on the large sofa in my office until the next patient. On Tuesday, I went back to work full-time and drove myself to work.

We had bought the property where we were going to build our house. Charlie and his wife were living in the RV on the property. Two weeks after the surgery, they needed some dirt moved by the RV next to the barn. So I said that I would go to the property with them to tell Charlie how to move the dirt with the tractor and the front-end loader.

Charlie had never driven a tractor nor scooped, moved, and leveled dirt. So I got on the tractor, moved the dirt, and leveled the dirt, but it needed one more scoop of dirt. There was a slight slope to drive on to dump the dirt. I had the scoop loaded and up in the air so that I could see under the scoop to know where to dump the dirt. I had driven on the slope for several loads with no problems, but this time, the rear wheel hit a sinkhole, and the tractor started to tip over. If I had not had the brace on my neck, I would have just pushed both levers to dump the scoop and lower the scoop. More than likely, the tractor would have tipped slightly and then righted itself.

The tractor had a roll bar, but I was concerned that because of my neck, I might not be able to hang on as the tractor tipped if it should rollover. So I decided the safest thing was to let the tractor tip over with the scoop up so that the tractor could not rollover.

I positioned myself on the side of the tractor with my back to the ground and was hanging on to the steering wheel until the tractor was almost tipped over. Then I jumped back and cleared the tractor. My left index finger caught in the steering wheel when I jumped; I broke the metacarpal bone in my hand. My first thoughts were that in jumping off the tractor, I might have done something to my neck to cause the severe pain in my hand. The pain wouldn't let up, so we went to my animal hospital and took an X-ray of my hand. The metacarpal bone was broken. I called the orthopedic surgeon and told him that I had broken my hand. He told me to meet him at his office where he put a cast on my hand.

When I had the brace on my neck, everyone felt sorry for me and wanted to know how I was doing. Now that I had the brace on my neck and a cast on my hand, which I was supposed to hold up to keep it from swelling, everyone was laughing at me instead of giving sympathy.

When it was time to go back to see Dr. Ballista for my final checkup, my wife insisted on going with me because she wanted to know what I could do and what I wasn't supposed to do. Dr. Ballista did a complete neurological exam, and when he finished, he said that everything was in good shape and that I could return to a normal life, doing all the things that I had in the past. My wife immediately objected to his statement that I could do anything that I had done in the past. She told him, "Dr. Ballista, you do not understand. He will be digging post holes, driving post, and doing all types of work on the property, including cutting wood with a chainsaw."

Dr. Ballista replied that he had no problem with any of those things. I still had the cast on my hand. I looked at Dr. Ballista with a straight face and said to him, "Some friends of mine said they would pay my entry fee to ride bulls at the Mesquite rodeo this weekend. Is that okay?"

He got a complete look of horror on his face that I had never seen on any man, and I could just see him thinking, *I spent eight hours fixing this man's neck, and now he wants to ride bulls.*

I told him that I had never ridden bulls, but I just wanted to know what the limits of what I could do were. He either didn't hear me or was still taken back by my statement that I wanted to ride bulls. Dr. Ballista was never at a loss for words and would always answer my questions, but he stammered and stuttered, "I think you need to talk to the orthopedic surgeon to see if you can ride with a broken hand." We thanked him for his good care and for fixing my neck before we left, but this bull-riding question was going to take a whole new turn later.

CHAPTER 22

Thoughts of Retirement

I never intended to retire from practice. I have a major problem, which is I am a perfectionist with a very strong work ethic that was instilled in me as a young boy and a young man. My dad taught me that you gave a full hour of work for an hour of pay; and if it was necessary to get the job done and do it right, you gave a little extra. Since the practice grew at a very rapid rate, my intentions were to hire veterinarians to work for me, and as I got older to let them carry the load so that I could take more time off. Then my wife and I would do the things that we were not able to do when I carried the load of the practice. I took my own emergencies so that in my practice, we gave 24-7 service.

When I hired a new veterinarian to work for me, I gave them a full day off. We set up the emergencies on a fifty-fifty basis, and we each took every other weekend on call. The problem that I had was that many times on their nights and weekends, they did not answer their pager. Then the telephone secretary would call me and tell me that they could not reach the doctor on call, so I would end up taking the calls. When I asked them why they did not respond to the calls, their answer was usually that they were busy doing something else and couldn't be bothered. I also found that new doctors had only done one surgery on a live animal while they were in school. As a result, I had to stand over their shoulder, watch them do surgery, and direct them through the surgery which took them three times longer than I could do the surgery. So instead of relieving the load of the practice, it added to the load.

More than once, after a doctor had said they could spay an animal on their own, they would get in trouble; the RN would come running to the exam room and motion with a frantic motion that I was needed in surgery. I would excuse myself from the client and rush back to surgery. To give you an example, one time I arrived in the surgery room and found blood was gushing out a cat's abdomen. The veterinarian was just sitting there, frozen, and not knowing what to do. The RN handed me a pair of gloves which I put on rapidly. I picked up a scalpel, opened the incision longer, reached in and clamped the stump of the uterus with a hemostat, and stopped the bleeding. Then I told the veterinarian to ligate the stump of the uterus.

While he was ligating the uterus, I looked at what he had removed and asked him, "Where are the ovaries?" Even though he insisted that the ovaries were on the horns of the uterus, I said, "They are not." So now I had to extend the incision farther forward and look into the abdomen to find the ovaries which were now much more difficult to locate because I no longer had the uterus to follow to the ovaries. I located the ovaries, removed them, and showed him that he had not removed the ovaries. The cat recovered fine but just had a much longer incision than necessary to spay a cat.

Another problem that I had was the inability of a young veterinarian to diagnose what an animal had, and when they didn't know, I had them come for advice or counsel. Many times, my kennel staff would come to me and say that a veterinarian was treating an animal, it was getting sicker, and it was about to die. I would tell them to bring me the chart with the animal. Then I would call the doctor over and ask what he was treating the animal for and why the animal was getting worse instead of improving. The response was usually, "I don't think that's what it has." And I hadn't even told him what I thought it had.

I would ask him, "What do you think it has?"

The response might be that he did not know but was trying to find out. I would tell him if he would look at the history, look at the physical exam, and to look at the blood work, then the diagnosis would stare him in the face. And the usual response was that he did not believe that's what that animal had, and if I thought that's what it was, I could take the case over. So I would take the case over and treat it. Usually, in three to five days, the animal would have recovered enough to send it home. I would talk to the doctor and go over the case with him because I wanted him to learn; but instead he would get a chip on his shoulder and wouldn't talk to me for two weeks.

We constantly had to deal with employee problems. We had sixteen employees, and when you have that many employees, there seems to be a problem with some of them getting along. Also, with continuing new state and federal regulations, it was an overwhelming burden just to try to keep up. I was told years ago that if what you were doing was no longer fun, it was time to get out. I would tell my wife that this twenty-year-old man kept looking in the mirror, but this old man kept looking back at him. People were always asking me if I was going to retire, and I told them, "No! They will take me out of the practice in a box." Then, one day, as I looked in the mirror, I felt like the old man that was looking back at me.

I realized that if I was burning the candle at both ends while running the practice, I was going to go out of that practice in a box much sooner than I needed to. God spoke to me and told me to sell the practice. I told Him that I was too busy to sell the practice and that if He wanted me to sell the practice, He needed to bring someone to buy it.

Within two weeks, I received a letter from a husband and wife that were both veterinarians. They wanted to know if I wanted to sell my practice. I threw the letter in the wastebasket. God told me to take it out, so I did. I put it on my desk in July but did not see the letter for several months because it was covered with other things that I needed to look at but just didn't have time to do.

I had scheduled a continuing education seminar in Boston. My wife and I would take two weeks to go to the seminars so that we could vacation on the way to the seminar and on the way back. On the third day after we left, I received a phone call that one of our best employees had quit because she could not get along with another employee. We went to the seminar in Boston, then drove to Maine to go to Acadia National Park, went into Canada, and came back through Wisconsin to see the Wisconsin Dells. We were due back on Monday, but on Friday, I received a phone call that one of the RNs had come back from lunch, drunk. I said, "You fired her, didn't you?"

The reply was that they sent her home and told her to come back to see me on Monday. Our employee manual stated very clearly that if an employee came to work with alcohol on their breath, they would be immediately terminated. The liability of being an employee that had been drinking was too great to even allow alcohol on the breath. Anytime I am gone from the practice for just a few days, when I get back, I'm overwhelmed with people that want to just see me. Clients that had seen another veterinarian in the practice while I was away also wanted to see me to be sure that the treatment was correct. So, on Monday, I called in the RN that came to work drunk and I terminated her employment. My intentions were to talk to the other employee, but by the time I got through seeing my last patient and taking care of some other business, that employee had gone home. I felt like I could talk to that employee the next morning, but we were overwhelmed.

During the day, that employee had done something in front of me that was not acceptable. I was hoping to talk to her that evening, but again, we were overwhelmed, and she had gone home before I could talk to her. The next day, first thing in the morning, I called her in to the office and confronted her about the situation that I had seen on Tuesday. Even though I told her what I had seen, she still denied it. Then I confronted her about the employee that had quit, and she denied any part in that situation also. So I told her that I could no longer use her and I let her go. When I went back to my desk, lying in the middle of my desk was the letter from the two doctors that had written, wanting to know if my practice was for sale. I had not seen that letter since I had placed it on my desk in July, but there it was, lying in plain view on my desk.

I called the doctors, talked to one of them, and asked if they were still interested in buying a practice. The response was, "If you would have called in July, we would have told you no." They had been working on a deal closer to them, but it fell through. They were very much interested in looking at my practice. They asked for directions and said that they would drive by that night. If they were interested, they would call me the next morning.

I received a call first thing the next morning to let me know that they wanted to come out and see the practice. I told them that they would have to come after eight in the evening so that no one knew why they were there. That was fine with them because they needed time to close their practice and then come to look at mine. They came the next evening and toured the practice. Then we sat down, did some visiting, and talked about prices concerning what the practice was worth.

I told them that I did not want a big, long, lengthy drawn-out contract and that I had sold my Dallas practice with a handshake and a one-page contract. They sent me a twenty-eight-page contract. My first thought of a response to them was that this type of contract was not acceptable, and I wouldn't even look at it; but my wife said that we needed to take it to a lawyer to have him look at it. The attorney looked at it and told us that 85 percent of it could be eliminated very quickly but that this was a common contract for a business. The wife wanted to come out to spend a few days a week for a month in the practice to see how I practiced and to see if my practice would be a fit for them. I agreed to it, and she came out for a month.

Meanwhile, the lawyers were working on the contract. After several months, I realized that the lawyers were doing their lawyer thing of going back and forth, little by little, on the contract while running up a huge bill. So I talked to my two lawyers and told them that we would meet in their office on Friday morning at eight o'clock with the husband and wife veterinarians and their lawyer. We would go over the contract with everyone present and then either come to an agreement or take it off the table. The veterinarians told me that their lawyer could not come on Friday, so I told them that the deal was off the table. Their response was, "No way! We will have him there."

We met at eight o'clock, went over the contract, and came to an agreement by 11:30. I told the attorneys that my wife, the other two doctors, and I were going to lunch at a certain restaurant; and if they had the contract done, they could join us. At 1:30, they had not come, so we went back to the lawyer's office where they were still working on the contract. We went to the courthouse and made the changes that were needed to finalize name changes and ownerships. At 3:30, the lawyers said that the contract was ready, and we could come to sign it. Their attorney, on the half that he had been working on, put back in the things that we all had agreed to take out. I was upset and said, "The deal is off."

The husband and wife said, "No, no, we agreed to the contract." They reprimanded their attorney for what he had done and it was agreed to rewrite that half of the contract. At 5:30, they called us to say that the contract was ready to sign. On May 1, we signed the contract to sell the practice, and I retired. I agreed to stay on to work for them through June until the veterinarian that they had hired could come into the practice.

CHAPTER 23

Retirement

Proverbs 16:9 says:
> A man's heart devises his way: but the Lord directs his steps.

Our plans are not always the same as the Lord's. I had hoped that my wife and I could spend our time traveling and seeing many sights that we had not seen. We did some traveling, but I started having a lot of pain in my legs. I went to see Dr. Ballista, and he ordered an MRI of the thoracic disc of my back which showed that I had a congenital defect at T5 and T6. He was going to try to use a scope to repair the defect. Before he could coordinate the surgery with a thoracic surgeon and the others that were necessary to do the surgery, I lost the use of both legs from mid-thigh down; and yet, somehow, I was able to walk. I did fall several times, and because the condition had worsened, it was decided that it would be necessary to cut an eight-inch incision between my ribs, starting in the back and coming around toward the front.

The next year, after Dr. Ballista had operated on my neck, we went to the State Fair of Texas where they had a stuffed bucking bull. I had my picture taken on the bull, and my son used Photoshop on the picture, so it looked real. He printed an eight-by-ten which I took to Dr. Ballista as a joke because I had asked him after the neck surgery if it was okay for me to ride bulls. When I gave him the picture, I told him that it was a fake, but he did not hear me, so he thought it was real.

There were five teams of doctors that were going to operate on me, and as they all came in before the surgery to explain what they were going to do and to get me to sign releases for the surgery, they asked me if I had any other questions.

I replied, "The only question I have is when I can get back to riding bulls." I did not know that the night before the doctors had met at Dr. Ballista's office to coordinate the surgery with each other, Dr. Ballista had shown them the picture of me on the bucking bull. After the surgery was over, Dr. Ballista told me that it was the most interesting surgery that he had ever done because all the doctors were talking about this man who, especially after having major neck surgery, still wanted to go back to riding bucking bulls. And now after a major thoracic back surgery, a man that was in his early sixties still wanted to keep riding bulls. I think that they thought I was probably the craziest man that they had ever operated on and beyond help.

I told Dr. Ballista that I had told him when I gave him the picture that it was a fake. He said that he guessed he missed that part but that it sure made an interesting surgery. I was staying in the hospital about a week as I had tubes in my chest to remove the air and keep the lungs inflated. When the first tube was removed, the doctor jerked it out and poked a hole in my lung which caused more air to leak and one lung to partially collapse. The other tube had to be left in for a longer period of time to get the air out and to inflate my lung. It was extremely painful to sneeze, cough, and to laugh. This pain would last for over a year.

When I was released from the hospital, the doctors thought that the others would give me instructions on what I could and could not do, so none of them gave me my limitations. Dr. Ballista told me that after ten days I could do what I felt like I could do. My wife said that even though I had never ridden bulls, I had a bull rider's mentality, so that was the wrong thing for him to tell me.

Ten days after I left the hospital, I drove to the animal hospital that we had sold and to the bank to make a deposit. When I leaned out the window to push a button to get a teller, something tore in my chest, and I was in excruciating pain. By the time I got home, the pain was beyond description. I backed up to the recliner, gritted my teeth, and fell back into the recliner. For the next six weeks, I only got out of the recliner to go to the bathroom, and my wife would have to get a hold of my hands to help pull me up. I would grit my teeth to keep from screaming. Then I would go back to the recliner, grit my teeth, and fall back into the recliner. She gave me my meals sitting in the recliner. That's where I slept and lived for six weeks, and then either the pain became bearable or I got used to it.

When I went back to see the thoracic surgeon and told him what happened, he said that I was not supposed to be driving for at least six weeks and probably closer to three months. I told him that no one had given me those instructions when I left the hospital, but he said that someone should have given me those instructions. There seems to be a misnomer, and this story goes around amongst my children and grandchildren, that I do not obey doctors' orders, but that is not true. I obey the orders that are given to me, but if the doctors failed to tell me that I'm not supposed to be doing something, I haven't disobeyed an order if I do it.

I did recover and got the use of my legs back. I returned to normal activity which did not include bull-riding. It took a year and a half before I could sneeze or laugh without pain in my chest. I became extremely weak, had no endurance, and found it to be very difficult to walk two-tenths of a mile from our house to the road and back to pick up the newspaper. I started to walk that distance every day, and after two weeks, I began walking up the hill on the road. Every two days, I would add a distance between telephone poles to my walk. I was eventually walking one and a half miles, and when I was able to walk that distance, I started to jog a short distance, then walk, and then jog. I got to the point that I could jog twice as far as I walked. Also, during this time, I was taking pictures of the many birds that were on our property, and I got some incredible photographs of many types of birds, including my favorite, the cardinals.

Taking photographs and walking became the therapy to regain my health and strength. Physically and emotionally, this was a very difficult period in my life. I did find comfort and strength in God to carry me through this ordeal. I found that God was ever merciful and gracious in this time of need.

I had taken some photos that I wanted enlarged and printed on canvas and framed. My wife, our son Mark, and I went to a frame shop on the square in downtown McKinney. While we were picking out frames, the owner of the shop had a photo on which he was trying to make some adjustments on his computer, but he was not having success. Mark asked the owner to let him try, and Mark was able to do it.

The owner was impressed, and they got to talking about reproducing artist's paintings. They decided to form a business in which my son would reproduce the paintings, and they would print them for the artists. Mark worked with him for three months and had developed a professional relationship with the artists, but he was not being paid for his share of the work that he was doing. I was the one that put up the money for the partnership. I gave the owner three days to pay Mark his share or I told him that we would dissolve the partnership. He did not pay Mark in three days, so we dissolved the partnership.

The artists wanted Mark to continue to do their work. We found a building on North Kentucky Street in downtown McKinney that we could rent, and we started a business called Imaging on the Square in which Mark reproduced artist paintings and printed people's photos on canvas. We did not intend to get into the picture-framing business, but the people that he printed for wanted a finished product. I had experience doing woodwork and had built three animal hospitals, so I took on the job of framing pictures. North Kentucky was not a good location for traffic for people who came to do business downtown, and we needed more room, so we moved to a building on South Tennessee. We started to take portraits in studio and on-site for people that wanted portraits taken.

Our son Steven and his wife, Jenniffer, went to Scotland for Steven to go to veterinary school in Glasgow. My wife and I were able to go to Scotland during the summer after his first year in school. We spent seven days in Aberfeldy, which is in the middle of Scotland. Steven loaned us his tom-tom so we could travel and find our way around Scotland. Because Scotland is a small country, we thought that we could see all of Scotland in one week. It is very deceiving in that there is one main road that runs from the north and bifurcates going south to Glasgow and Edinburgh.

On the main highway, one can travel seventy miles an hour, but after leaving that main highway, the roads become very narrow, and one can go fifty miles an hour for short distances. Then the roads become narrower, and many of them become one-lane roads where travel might be ten to fifteen miles an hour. Every so often for a very short distance, there were places where the road was wide enough so that cars could pass.

We did not get to see as much of Scotland as we had hoped to see; but because it rains every day, what we saw was so lush and green, and the terrain and scenery were extremely beautiful. We had an incredible time traveling around Scotland and spending time with Steven and Jenniffer. We spent a week in Aberfeldy, and then we returned to Glasgow for three days. I was always told that my ancestry was primarily Scotch Irish. When we got to Scotland, my wife said, "You look exactly like these people."

I even had a lady come up to me and say, "I hope you don't mind me asking, but I just must ask if you are my uncle that disappeared twenty years ago because you look like him." When I opened my mouth to speak, she immediately knew that I was not him because of my American accent, and I assured her that I was not him. I was told that there was no Irish in my heritage because if I were Irish, I would have been told that I was Irish. The people of Scotland could not immigrate to the United States from Scotland, so they would go to Ireland to establish citizenship before going to the United States. Thus they were known as Scotch Irish; so I was told that I was Scottish. We had an incredible time touring Scotland, especially the old castles, as well as taking incredible photographs. We greatly enjoyed the time that we had with our son and his wife.

One evening, Jan's mother was complaining about chest pain, so we called 911. The fire department came with two trucks and an ambulance. They checked her out, said that she was having a heart attack, and they wanted to take her to a local hospital in McKinney. She told them that she wanted to go to Baylor on Gaston Avenue in Dallas, and they said that they could not take her to Dallas. She would not go to McKinney, so they got her stable and helped to get her in our car. The paramedics told me to drive her to Dallas, but if her condition should worsen to stop at any hospital that was close and take her into the emergency room to have her treated.

We made it to Dallas, and at first, she was told that she had not had a heart attack. She was kept in the hospital overnight to run some more tests. The next day, they determined that she had a mild heart attack and discovered that she had diabetes. They started to treat the diabetes and her heart.

My daughter-in-law, Cory, wanted me and my wife to go to family night out with her and the grandchildren. The fire department had all the different types of fire trucks there for the public to see. One of the firemen told me that I needed to come out and become a volunteer firefighter. I told him that I was sixty-two years old and didn't think they could use an old man. He kept insisting that they had a job for me. So I finally agreed to go to a Monday night training to see what they had. I went with the firemen as they did the checks on each apparatus. Then they had a meeting, and I asked the chief if he could use an old man. He said, "Yes, I have a job for you. We are getting a new three- thousand-gallon tender, and I need someone with maturity and experience driving large trucks to drive my tender."

The number one cause of death for firefighters is heart attacks, and the number two cause of death is turning the tender over, so he needed someone that was mature and experienced to get the tender to the fire. He said, "I need you, and I want you to join the department to be my tender driver and operator. My wife asked me why I wanted to be a fireman, and I told her that all little boys want to grow up to be firemen.

She said, "Does that mean you have grown up?"

I said, "No, now the fire department pays for my toys."

My wife could not object to me becoming a firefighter because of the way they had responded when her mother had the heart attack. The volunteer fire department is dependent upon volunteers to come when there is a call. Sometimes only four may show up, and the rules are that two go into the fire and there must be two outside; otherwise, if there are not four firefighters, they cannot fight the fire. I told the chief that I needed to be trained to fight fires because if one of the firemen got in trouble, I was going in; but I did not want to go in unless I was trained.

He said that the county would pay for the training at Collin County Community College. They had a program that met at nights and on Saturdays that would give the same training as for those enrolled in the daytime program. So I signed up and went to firefighter school.

I was able to do everything that was required, and there were many in their twenties and thirties that could not do it. The full bunker gear with air tank weighs fifty pounds. During training, we needed to climb to the top of a thirty- five-foot ladder while fully bunked out and carrying an ax, and then do a leg lock while discharging a one and one-half-inch line. Next we were to shut down the line and come down. I wasn't sure that I could do this because, at my age, I did not have the sense of balance that I did when I was younger. When I was in high school, my dad and I would climb to the top of windmills, and while standing on an eighteen-inch platform, we repaired them. The instructor told me to try the exercise, and he told me how to do it. He said if I was not able, he would still pass me through, but I was able to do it.

They had three mazes that were in rooms that had absolutely no light, so we were in total darkness while fully bunked out. I had to feel a rope and go through the maze that had drop-off holes, elevations, and wires hanging down that would cause one to hang up; and this had to be done with one tank of air. I did all three mazes that morning and still had a half a tank of air left. That afternoon, they had a firefighter pretending to be incapacitated somewhere in the maze. This time we had a partner, and we had to locate the firefighter and bring him out of the maze. This was done in two different mazes.

I did both mazes and rescued the firefighter, plus the three mazes in the morning on one tank of air. There were many firefighters that could not do one maze on a tank of air. The chief and I had agreed that I would not go into an actual fire, but after this, he said, "We may need to redo our thinking because you are in better shape than most of the firemen that are a lot younger." But we agreed that I would go into training fires but not actual fires unless it was an emergency.

The chief sent me to advanced pumping school to learn how to pump water in complicated situations when a hydrant was not readily available. The other firemen wanted me to drive the engine and pump the water when we arrived at the fire because they said that when I was pumping, they knew they would have water. The chief also sent me to advanced driving school because he wanted me to train the new firemen how to drive the fire trucks. I did not teach my boys how to drive because it made me too nervous, and I would make them too nervous. So my wife taught them to drive.

Now I was in much larger vehicles that were much more difficult and dangerous to drive. I would have some fun with the firefighters while teaching those to drive who had never driven a truck of any kind. When they got in, I would take them for a ride to demonstrate how to drive the different apparatuses, especially the tender. I would ask them if their insurance was paid up, and they would ask me, "Why?"

I would tell them that the number one cause of death in firefighters was heart attacks, and I was in my sixties; and the number two cause of death was turning the tender over. I said, "I'm going to have a heart attack and turn the tender over, so I hope your insurance is paid up."

No one got out, but I think some may have been a little nervous. There is nothing that will give you that adrenaline rush quite like driving the fire engine while running code with the lights flashing and the siren blaring. It is just a real blast.

After I retired, I started to teach at Dallas Teen Life Challenge on Thursdays from 12:30 to 3:00 each week. The men in the program are there either voluntarily or probated from the courts as they have drug or alcohol addiction problems. The program is on the honor system, and the men are not in lockdown, but are free to come and go if they desire. But if they want to remain in the program, they are not allowed to leave without permission. The program is a Christ-centered approach to addiction that through God's Word and bringing the men to a salvation experience by accepting Jesus Christ as their Lord and Savior, they will be set free from drugs.

Second Corinthians 5:17 says:

> Therefore if any man be in Christ, he is a new creature:
> old things are passed away; behold, all things are become new.

The emphasis is upon bringing these young men to accept Christ as their Lord and Savior and to disciple them with God's Word. The biggest key to the success of the program is to get the men to realize that they are accountable for their past and for their addiction; and they must take responsibility for their sins. If they turn from their sin and accept Jesus Christ, they will find in Him the strength through His Word and Spirit to live for Christ.

Romans 8:3 says:

> For what the law could not do, in that it was weak through the flesh, God sending his own Son in the likeness of sinful flesh, and for sin, condemned sin in the flesh.

When these young men through the grace of God find in Christ the strength to overcome their addiction, and when they begin to mature in the Word, they usually reach a point by at least nine months when they are moved into the reentry program where they are allowed to get a job and work. During reentry, they stay at the facility for another nine months or whatever time is necessary for them to return to a normal society. I teach the Word of God, but my main emphasis is to teach them to find answers to their everyday questions and how to live their life for Christ by His Word. Many times, they will ask me, "Dr. Martin, what do you think about this?"

And I will say that it doesn't make any difference what I think. Together we search the Scriptures to find out what God says about it. I receive so much more than I give as I get to watch the power of God through His Spirit and by His Word change these men's lives.

I took a job at Cedar Valley Community College, teaching veterinary technicians two nights a week. The class started with thirty students. Most of the students were working for veterinarians, and they wanted to become certified veterinary technicians. There would be one final exam at the end of the semester. As I taught them each week, I stressed to them the things that they needed to learn and emphasized that these things would be on the final exam. The week before the final exam, I went over every question that would be on the final exam, and I told them that if they knew these things, they would make a perfect score on the exam. I gave the final exam and was absolutely shocked by the results. I had one student that made a 94 another student that made a 78, and one made 70 being a passing score. The rest of the class scored below 50 points. I did not reapply for the teaching position because I deemed it a waste of my time since my time could be better spent with people that were motivated and wanted to learn.

The day before Katrina hit New Orleans, we received a call from Jan's sister, Nieta, asking if she, her husband, their son, and their daughter-in-law as well as two dogs could come to stay with us. They all stayed with us during Katrina. My wife's brother-in-law, Cliff Nunn, who was pastor of First Presbyterian Church, went back after about two weeks and surveyed the situation. The church and their home were flooded, and there was no electricity. A month later, Cliff and Nieta decided to go back to New Orleans. We helped Jan's mother buy a thirty- five-foot RV for them to live in, and I took it to New Orleans. The only place to set it up was on the yard of First Presbyterian Church of New Orleans where Cliff was the pastor. I stayed and connected the RV into the sewer system, got the generator to run the electricity, and then I helped them to start cleaning out their house.

The stench was overwhelming from the mold and all things rotting because of the flooding and no electricity. I stayed for five days and nights before returning home. Cliff and Nieta worked tirelessly, cleaning up the mess, and supervised the rebuilding of First Presbyterian Church of New Orleans, and they rebuilt their house. Then they sold the RV.

I was on my way to teach at Dallas Teen Life Challenge, and I had just ordered a meal at El Chico when my wife called me and said that her mother had died. She did not know what to do, so I told her to wait until I got home. Then I called the fire chief to ask him what to do. He called EMS and the coroner, and they came to the house.

Jan's mother's doctor, Dr. Madeley, said that he would sign the death certificate, so we did not need an autopsy. Her mother had already made funeral arrangements with one of her relatives to take care of the funeral. So we called the funeral home, and they made the arrangements for the funeral service locally and the burial in Oklahoma. Cliff and I did the service.

Jan received a phone call from her sister Nieta that her husband, Cliff, had collapsed while they were walking, and he was in the hospital in critical shape. The next morning, she called to let us know that Cliff had passed away. Jan and I immediately packed things and drove to

New Orleans. We spent the first two nights with Nieta at her home, and then when her daughter, son, and families came, Jan and I went to a motel. We stayed for a couple days afterward to be there for her sister.

After Katrina, Nieta's daughter-in-law, Cathy, stayed with us until she found a job in Dallas, but her husband, Bruce, had gone back to New Orleans and continued to work until he sold his house which had not flooded. Then he got a job and moved to a house they bought in Allen. Nieta did not want to continue to live in New Orleans, so she sold her house and moved in with us until she could find a house. She bought a house in Allen, and it has been good for her and my wife, Jan, to spend time together.

I developed severe pain in my lower back, so I went to Dr. Ballista who, after an MRI and a myelogram, discovered that I had a chip off of a disc, and I needed surgery. Dr. Ballista said that it would be a day surgery that would be done microscopically and should take about forty-five minutes. The surgery took five and a half hours, and they had the cut me open. There was severe hemorrhaging, even though my clotting time was normal. They were finally able to remove the chip and do a laminectomy at L5 and L6.

I was hospitalized overnight, went home the next day, and the pain was gone. Almost a year later to the day, I was in severe back pain again. I went back to Dr. Ballista, and after an MRI and a myelogram, they found that at L4 and L5, there was another chip which would require surgery. Dr. Ballista told me that because of the last surgery with all the hemorrhage, there would be a lot of scar tissue, and there would be complications with this surgery. That was okay because complications happened to the other guy.

I woke up three and a half hours later, and my left leg was completely paralyzed. I was told that I would never walk again without a walker. I had to pick my leg up with my hands to get it in or out of bed. I had to pull myself up to the walker to stand before trying to walk. This is not how life was supposed to be; I expected after the surgery was complete that there might be a small amount of pain to deal with, and then I would be well.

One is told before surgery that there is a chance of waking up paralyzed, but I thought God wouldn't let that happen to me because after all, I have been faithful to God and have served Him. He doesn't let bad things happen to good people. Dr. Ballista came in to talk to me about my paralysis, and I could tell that he was hurting probably more than I was. I told him, "I know it's not your fault, and I forgive you."

As I lay in the bed that night, there was a peace from God that flowed upon my heart and soul that I cannot understand nor explain. It was not that I will walk again someday and be normal but rather He would walk with me because He is my God. In God, I would find the strength to go through this new crisis in my life.

Over the next three days, I laid in that bed with a newfound joy in the Lord that I had never experienced, and I was able to praise and worship Him. The physical therapist came in the next morning and told me what my life would be like. I told her that I was not going home with that walker, but she told me that if I did not use the walker, I would go home in a wheelchair. I told her, "No way."

And she said, "How do you propose to walk?"

I asked her to bring me a cane, and she informed me that with a paralyzed leg, I could not walk with a cane. We argued for twenty minutes, and finally, out of frustration, she said, "I'll bring you a cane tomorrow, and when you fall on your face, don't blame me."

The next morning, she brought me a cane, and within five minutes, I was walking around the hospital. Even though there was no back pain, I had severe headaches. Also, my bladder quit working, and I had to go back into surgery three days later for a spinal leak which took three and a half hours to repair.

Before going into surgery, Dr. Ballista asked if I would like for him to pray. I said, "Yes." He prayed as tears ran down my face, and I knew the peace of God was going with us into surgery. Because of the previous surgery a year before, the dura had become so friable that only with God's help was Dr. Ballista able to piece it back together again and seal up the leak. I left the hospital with a catheter, a severe bladder infection, and a cane. That weekend, the catheter was driving me nuts, so on Monday, I went to see my urologist. He removed the catheter and continued the antibiotics.

During the surgery, I had lost more than half of my blood, but they chose not to transfuse me. I had scheduled a continuing education seminar in Ashleigh, North Carolina, two weeks after the surgery. The doctor released me to go to the seminar. My wife and I had scheduled to spend a week in the Smoky Mountains, and while we were there, we climbed the highest mountain in the Smoky Mountains on a hiking path. My biggest problem going up was getting out of breath because I did not have enough blood to maintain my oxygen level. I had to keep sitting on the sissy benches and resting to catch my breath to make it up the mountain.

My wife and I had done a fair amount of hiking, and while I would be taking pictures, she would sit on a bench along the trail or on a rock to rest. I started calling the benches "sissy benches." She knew that it was just good-natured teasing. We made it to the top of the mountain. What I didn't know was that walking up with the paralyzed leg was not a real problem but walking down was a very major problem because a paralyzed leg and foot has no ability to grip the ground. I thought that I was going to have to roll down the mountain. I finally figured out a way by using my cane that I could walk down sideways, so I was able to make it back down the mountain.

For the next year and a half, I went to physical therapy but was making very little progress. I went back to see Dr. Ballista, and he suggested that I change the physical therapy to Dr. Ross Query at Southwestern Medical School. In six weeks, the improvement was dramatic, and I was able to walk without a cane. He gave me exercises to do at LA Fitness, and with his instructions, I built the leg up to where it was stronger than my right leg, and I could leg press 240 pounds with either leg. Even though the left leg is a third smaller than my right leg, I built it up to the same strength. I do have a drop foot and am unable to lift my toes. The nerves that go to the muscles in the bottom of my foot never came back, so I have no muscle in the bottom of my foot, and I walk on bone.

If I have been on my foot very long, the pain in the foot seems to go way past ten. The pain can get very severe at about 2:30 in the morning when the tendons and the joint capsules contract in the foot. The result is the foot is pulled downward into a severe arch, and the only way to stop the pain is to stand on the foot, stretch it out, and then walk around for five to ten minutes to loosen it back up.

At that time, I was not taking pain medicine because all it does is dull the senses, and it really doesn't stop the pain. My way of dealing with the pain is just get up and do the things that I need to do. By keeping occupied, my mind pushes the pain to the back, and I almost forget that I have the pain until I sit down; then the pain in the foot can be very severe. I can walk in a way that most people do not know there's anything wrong with me.

My left foot feels like it is a wooden foot, and most of the time, it feels like it is in an ice bath. I just go on living as normal a life as I can. I can no longer run, but I can get around normally. I've had several people ask me why I have not sued the doctor, and I've told them that I have forgiven him. He was an extremely good and competent doctor, and he hurts almost as much as I do. I will not tell you that it has been easy to not be able to function in the same capacity that I could before the surgery, but I've had to learn to be thankful that I am able to walk and do the important things in life.

I have always been physically strong with great endurance, so this has been an adjustment that I've had to make. I could not have made it if I did not know Jesus Christ as my comforter and my strength. As the old saying goes, if the world gives you a lemon, add some sugar and make lemonade; that sugar is Jesus Christ.

My wife had been giving the granddaughters horseback-riding lessons, and she and the granddaughters were pressing Grandpa to buy horses. I had put it off for several years because I knew the expense of raising horses and the work that was involved in caring for horses. But Grandpa finally gave in and bought two mares; one was a brown and white paint, and the other one was a dune quarter horse. The three older granddaughters enjoyed riding the horses. I then bought a bay Arabian gelding who was fifteen years old but still wanted to run. The oldest granddaughter could handle him, so she rode him.

One day they were riding, and the quarter horse threw the granddaughter that was riding her. I sold that dune quarter horse mare because I would not keep a horse that is not trustworthy for someone to ride. My daughter-in-law in Scotland called my wife and said that she had a three-year-old black and white paint gelding that was starving to death because where he was, there were too many horses. She wanted to know if we would take him. He was not broke to ride. We took him, and I found a man in Oklahoma to break him.

After the trainer had him about two months, I went to Oklahoma and rode him in the round pen. A week later, I rode him in the larger arena. The next week, we took him out on eighty acres where he got his feet tangled in wire and was jumping and twisting all over the place; but I managed to stay on him. Then we went through a gate and the dog went under the fence. When he saw the dog, he jumped sideways about six feet. I managed to stay on him, but when we were coming back, for no reason at all, he did a 180-degree turn in the air and then began to buck. I was able to stay on him, and the rest of the way back, he behaved, and things went well.

I continued to go up once or twice a week and ride him on the eighty acres. He was the smoothest riding horse that I had ever ridden. His trot didn't even jar me, and when he was in a full lope, it was like sitting in a rocking chair. The trainer had a ten-year-old gray roan Hancock bread quarter horse gelding that they wanted to sell, so I took my grandchildren to Oklahoma to ride him. My five-year-old granddaughter rode him, and he just came down to her level. My grandson rode him, and he came to his level. He was able to ride him out of the round pen. This horse would come to the level of the experience and the ability of the rider.

When I got on him, he would really get up and go. He had been used in team roping, calf roping, working cattle, and training wild mustangs to break them to lead. We decided it was time to bring Dreamer, the name my daughter-in-law had given the horse, home, so we were going up one last time. I saddled up Dreamer and told my wife that I was going to take him out and ride him, then they would saddle up Big Gray, and she could come out and join me. We would ride back together. I rode Dreamer, and he was doing great when my wife came out to join me. Then, suddenly, Dreamer reared straight up and began to buck as hard as he could. I was able to ride him, get his head up, stop him from bucking, and then rode him back to the barn.

We still decided to have the trainer bring both horses to our place on the next day. The trainer and his wife would ride Dreamer and Big Gray, and my wife and I would ride our horses, Tracy and Blaze. Then the trainer would ride Big Gray, and I would ride Dreamer through our pastures, and all went well. The trainer told me that I needed to ride Dreamer almost every day but that I should start him in the round pen before I rode him in the pasture.

The next day, I saddled Dreamer and rode him in the round pen. I was just ready to take him out on the pasture but decided to lope him one more time around the round pen. He began to buck, so I rode him hard in the round pen but did not ride him in the pasture. On the next day, I saddled him, and the same thing happened in the round pen, but when I started to get off, my left foot, which is my bad foot, just barely caught his ribs. He jumped sideways, dragging me for about two feet before I could get my foot out of the stirrup. At that point, I decided that he was too dangerous and not trustworthy enough for a seventy-year-old man to ride.

We were attending a spirit-filled church. I had been talking to the pastor about praying the prayer of faith, and he wanted to know more. We agreed to meet for lunch, but when the pastor came to pick me up, he told me that plans had changed. He had received an urgent phone call, asking him to go to the hospital to pray for a man that had liver cancer. On the way to the hospital, I began sharing.

Romans 10:17 says:

> So then faith comes by hearing, and hearing by the word of God.

I explained to him that when Jesus prayed for someone, that person was always healed. But Jesus said that He only did the works of His Father that His Father may be glorified. I told him that we needed to have the mind of Christ to pray the prayer of faith. Either the person that we were praying for or one of us needed to hear faith or we could not pray the prayer of faith; it would be just wishful thinking. He said to me, "It is in your hands. When we get to the hospital, you are going to take the lead. I'm just going to watch and observe that I might learn how to pray the prayer of faith."

The man had been in a coma all night, but he came out of the coma long enough to ask his sister to call the pastor and ask him to come and anoint him with oil according to James 5:14–15 that he might be healed. The man had been diagnosed with terminal cancer of the liver; his liver tests were off the chart. The doctor had told his sister when he arrived at the hospital in a coma that he just had hours to live. After the man's sister had called the pastor, he slipped back into a coma. When we came into the room, the man came out of the coma. I asked him, "Do you believe if we anoint you with oil and pray for you that God will heal you?"

In a very emphatic voice, he said, "I would not have called you if God had not told me that if you anoint me with oil and pray for me, I will be healed."

We anointed the man with oil and prayed for him. Within minutes, the jaundice disappeared; the man became completely coherent and visited with us for about twenty minutes. The doctors repeated the entire liver test and did another CAT scan—everything was normal. The next day, they sent him home completely healed of cancer. The pastor was very impressed, and he asked me to spend time with him that he might come to understand how to pray the prayer of faith for people in need.

When we bought the property for our houses, it was going to cost over ten thousand dollars to bring water to the front of the property, and then we would have to bring it to our houses, so we decided to put in a water well. The well had to be dug to 1,100 feet to reach water. The water level rose to four hundred feet, and they put a pump in at five hundred feet. The water continued to bring up a lot of sand, and thus the pumps did not last long. One of the old pumps which weighed about a hundred pounds was lying beside the well. I needed to move the pump, so I picked it up, and when I did, I felt a pop in my back and severe pain. I went in the house, put a heating pad on my back, and was able to sleep that night.

The next morning, as my wife and I went down to feed the horses, I reached down to pick up a bale of hay. The pain in my back became so severe that I could not stand up straight, and my left leg needed to be flexed to stand the pain. I managed to make it back to the house. I called Dr. Ballista's office, but he was not available for three days. I had met Dr. William Bruck at the Carrell Clinic when he had seen my third son, Mark. I called his office and was told they would work me in that day. Dr. Bruck gave me an injection to relieve the pain and sent me for an MRI which showed I had ruptured a disc at L3 and L4. Because the previous surgeries on my back were so extensive, he did not want to operate.

I was sent to Dr. Lloyd to do a spinal injection, but it did not help at all. He wanted to repeat the injection in two weeks, but I told him that it was time for surgery. They did a myelogram and scheduled surgery. Dr. Bruck did not want to do surgery because of the damage from the scar tissue on the spinal cord, and he said that with the problems I had with my last surgery, this was an extremely risky surgery. Being a veterinarian, I knew the only thing that would relieve my pain would be to do surgery to remove the material that was pressing on the spinal cord and open the spinal canal with a laminectomy. I told Dr. Bruck he might not understand this, but we were praying people. "God has assured me that this surgery will go well, and I have no fear of going through the surgery."

He replied that he prayed before every surgery to ask God to guide and help him be his instrument to do the surgery to get people well. He gave God the praise and the glory. Before we went into surgery, I asked Dr. Bruck if it was all right if I prayed, and he said, "By all means."

We thanked God for what he was going to do. They did a laminectomy at L3 and L4 and removed the disc material that was in the spine. I was hospitalized overnight and went home the next day. I was not to lift more than five pounds, not to bend or twist, and I was to walk five minutes four times a day for the first two weeks. I saw Dr. Bruck in two weeks when my weight limit was raised to ten pounds, and my walking was to increase slowly.

I saw Dr. Bruck again in six weeks when he started me in physical therapy. It was recommended that I walk in the pool and do some swimming. Dr. Bruck told me that my spine was worn out and that I should never lift more than twenty-five pounds for the rest of my life. He allowed me to drive my tractor and to ride a horse if the horse only walked. Once again, God was faithful in bringing me back to health, but I did not get the prognosis that I wanted to hear that I could return to a normal way of life of lifting fifty-pound bags of horse feed and carrying bales of hay. Instead, I was told that if I wanted to keep walking, I needed to change my lifestyle; and for me, it was extremely difficult to wrap my mind around my physical limitations.

I would not be honest if I did not say that I still wrestle with wrapping my mind around these physical limitations because one of the reasons I bought the property where we live was to keep me young, strong, and healthy by cutting firewood with the chainsaw and doing physical work. I much prefer physical work over working out in a gym. When I cut a stack of firewood, not only do I feel good because I have done the physical work but also because I see the results; there is a stack of firewood that we can enjoy in the fireplace on those cold nasty nights.

God and I have had more than one conversation about this situation. God has shown me that my goals and qualities of worth are far different than his goals and qualities of worth. Our qualities of worth and goals are on a horizontal plane, and God's qualities of worth is to mold us into the image of His Son, Jesus Christ.

Romans 8:28 says:

> And we know that all things work together for good to them that love God, to them who are the called according to his purpose.

When reading Romans 8:28, one should not stop there without going on and reading in context what the next few verses say.

Romans 8:29–31 says:

> For whom he did foreknow, he also did predestinate to be conformed to the image of his Son, that he might be the firstborn among many brethren. Moreover whom he did predestinate, them he also called: and whom he called, them he also justified: and whom he justified, them he also glorified. What shall we then say to these things? If God be for us, who can be against us?

God's goals and purpose for our lives is to mold us into the image of Jesus Christ, and for this to happen, we must stop listening and looking on the horizontal plane and get a heavenly vision from the vertical plane as we look to Jesus Christ, the Author and the Finisher of our faith.

We had five acres behind the animal hospital on Custer Road that we had not been able to sell. When we got a contract on the property, we decided to reinvest the money in a building and to move the business of Imaging on the Square to the new location. In the new building, we put in a classroom where artists could teach classes and workshops and added a large portrait studio with a green screen. There is a large new area for an art gallery in which different artists are featured every month. The new building is at 1799 North Graves Street in McKinney, Texas. The name was changed to The Martin Place. The building also has a large parking lot and a fair amount of land.

I was seeing Dr. Bruck on three-to-six-month intervals to check on my back. About a year after the surgery, I was having severe pain again, and he asked me if I was ready for another surgery. They did an MRI and a myelogram which showed that the disc at L2 and L3 was bulging. Because of the number of laminectomies, the structure of the back was changing. The vertebrae had moved in such a way that they were beginning to cut the spinal cord, so a fusion of the back was recommended from L2 to S1 in which they would put in two titanium rods and ten screws.

We had a trip planned for the entire family to go to Kauai, and since it had been planned for a year, I asked if it would be possible to make the trip and then do the surgery. Dr. Bruck said that if I was extremely careful, we should be able to make the trip. We were due to get back from Kauai on Sunday afternoon, and I scheduled the surgery for Tuesday, June 23, 2015. Dr. Bruck and his PA told me that I would be in the hospital four to six days, and then in a rehab facility for two weeks. For the first six weeks, maximum pain medication would probably not control the pain, but then it would start getting better. By four to six months, I should be almost pain-free. I talked to three other people that had the same surgery, and they told me that was what they experienced.

Between March when I saw Dr. Bruck and June when we made the trip to Kauai, I had many episodes of severe back pain when I would spend three to five days sitting in the recliner because it was too painful to walk or do anything else. I told the family as we were planning the trip to Kauai that I wanted each family to pick out the things that they wanted to do as a family and to schedule those activities. We would try to do at least a couple days of all the families together doing the same thing and would probably eat most of the evening meals together. We budgeted a little extra and flew everyone first-class because we knew there was no way that I could fly coach. We boarded the plane, not knowing how my back would react to the flight and the activities once we arrived in Kauai, but my back was doing fine after the flight.

The whole family drove through Waimea Canyon, attended the Luau Kalamaki, took a train ride through Kilohana Plantation, and took a sunset cruise. James, Mark, and I hired a private helicopter to tour the island, and it took us by many waterfalls so that we could take photographs. One of the highlights for me was riding in an open cockpit biplane with my second son, Charlie; it was a real blast. Some of the other activities were driving up the North Coast, playing in the ocean, making leis, kayaking, and helicopter tours. My back held up, and I was able to do most of the things that I really wanted to do. The flight back was uneventful. We arrived Sunday afternoon, and on Tuesday, I was at the hospital at 5:00 a.m. for my back surgery.

Dr. Bruck came in to talk to Jan and me before the surgery and said that we should expect about eight and a half hours of surgery time. When I woke up from the surgery, I felt less pain than when I went into surgery; so, at first, I was wondering if I was dreaming or if I had died and gone to heaven. Then I thought it might have been because they had used hydromorphone during the surgery; and the medication might be what was keeping me from having the anticipated severe pain. The nurses told me that I was on a hydromorphone pump, and to start with, I should pump it every three minutes so the pain would not get ahead of me. I pushed the button three times and then decided to wait and see if I was going to have pain. If the pain started, then I would use the pump.

I did not have pain during the night, so I did not use the pump. I got very little sleep because about every hour, a nurse was doing something to me or checking to see if I was all right. The next morning, I was told that I needed to use the pump consistently for at least thirty minutes before I would be fitted with my back brace and before I got up for a walk. I pushed the button three times, and I was having no pain, so I quit pushing the button. They came around 9:30 and fitted me with my back brace, then the physical therapist got me up to go for a very short walk. Even though I felt I could walk farther, she said that we needed to go back because I needed to take it slow. I did not have to wear the back brace in bed, so they took it off, and I lay back down.

The physical therapist came back that afternoon and allowed me to walk a little further. She said that she would see me in the morning to go for another walk, and if I did well the next day, they would release me to go directly home without rehab. The occupational therapist said that with help from my wife, she would release me to go home the next day.

The next morning, the physical therapist went with me for a walk, allowed me to walk the length of the hospital and back, and said she would release me to go home the following day. Dr. Bruck released me to go home with arrangements for in-home therapy for two weeks that I was confined to the house. I was to walk five minutes four times a day until my doctor visit two weeks after the surgery. I was sent home from the hospital with a walker, but after three days, I did not need the walker to walk normally.

My wife was not happy that I wanted to walk without the walker, so we agreed to wait one more day when the in-home physical therapist would come to the house, and we would ask him if I could walk without the walker. When he came the next day, he watched me walk across the room. He said that his purpose was to get me where I could walk normally without the walker, and I was walking normally. After the surgery, I was limited to lifting only five pounds, no bending, and no twisting. My back was very rigid and stiff, and with the back brace, there was no way that I could bend. I had to be more careful how I walked because I did not realize how much my balance was affected when the lower back is stiff above the hips.

When I went back to see Dr. Bruck after two weeks, they took an X-ray; he said that everything was healing well. Dr. Bruck asked me if I thought I could drive, and I told him that I could. He told me, "We normally do not release people to drive for at least six weeks, but you are doing so well that I have no problem with you driving if you so desire. He also released me to go out for short periods of time, such as going out to eat.

Four weeks after the surgery, I received a phone call that my bone stimulator was being delivered. They brought it out and told me that I either needed to wear it over the top of my brace or to take my brace off and lay on it for four hours a day. The time could be broken up into two-hour segments. It is amazing how well God knows me because He told me that He wanted me to write this book, and He knew the only way that it would get done was for me to be forced to lie down for four hours a day because I could always find something else that I would rather do.

Writing a book is not my thing, so I am using Dragon Naturally Speaking speech recognition software with the computer. Dragon sure seems to have trouble understanding what I am saying, but I do not type, so it would not have gotten done if it wasn't for this software. My oldest son, James, has been reading what I have written, and since I don't always go back to proof what I've spoken, he said at times he has no idea what I have said; but at other times, it is very humorous. An example is when I asked Jan's dad if I could marry his daughter. Dragon said that I asked her dad if I could bury his daughter. My son thought it might be more interesting to leave it the way Dragon recorded it.

Once again, God's grace and mercy are almost without description, and I cannot find the words to describe the incredible miracle that God performed in this type of surgery. I did not take any pain medication following the surgery because I did not need it. Nine months following the surgery, the doctor told me that the fusion had taken and healed well. The lower part of my back from L2 to S1 was stable, but he told me that the rest of my spine was basically worn out. I was going to have to make a choice if I wanted to keep walking; I would have to change my lifestyle because he was not sure he could fix me next time if other parts of my back broke down.

CHAPTER 24

My Ordinary Life

I was teaching one day at Dallas Teen Life Challenge when one of the men spoke up and said that he did not think it was fair that some people are more privileged than other people; it seems that God shows favoritism to some people over other people because they have had an easier life. Those people seem to be God's "teacher's pet." I looked at the person and said to him, "Are you referring to me? It's okay. Let's be honest that you believe that somehow, I am more special to God than you are."

He said, "Yes." God's Word says that he is no respecter of persons, and it is not His will that any should perish, but all should come to a saving knowledge of Jesus Christ. So if someone is a special person, then God is not telling the truth in His Word. I said, "Let me tell you about my life."

My parents worked hard to provide for our family. We raised chickens, milked cows, raised beef, and my mother always had a garden, but my parents did not have any extra money. The first house I lived in was back in the hills, and in the winter, if it snowed, the only way out was to walk two miles to the main road. We did not have electricity or running water in the house. When I was two or three, we moved to a house on the main road next to Trenton, North Dakota. At five years of age, I was given my first chore; it was to water the chickens.

I was six years old when we got electricity and running water. We were on a septic system, so we had to be very careful how much water we used or it would plug up the septic system. Saturday night was bath night. My two younger sisters took their bath together first and saved the water. Then my brother and I added some warm water and took our bath together. We milked cows, and at eight years of age, I was milking cows and carrying five-gallon milking machines full of milk and emptying them into ten-gallon milk cans.

Every year on the first day of February, we would get hundred-day-old baby chickens. When these chickens got big enough to go outside to eat, we got another hundred baby chickens. It was my job every morning to catch six chickens and cut their heads off. My mother would dress and clean the chickens to eat. When I turned eight, I started to drive the tractor and rake hay or work summer fallow with a flex tiller or a chisel plow. I would come home with a quarter inch of dust covering me. My mother would take the broom and sweep me off. Then I could wash my face and hands. Jeans were usually bought at JCPenney, and they were always bought too big, so we had to roll up the cuffs. This was so that we would not outgrow them before they were worn out.

Before the year was up, the knees had been patched at least twice. I was the minority in my class at school. Most of my class was part Indian and part white; their parents lived on welfare and what they could steal. These children were not motivated to get good grades because they had no incentive from their homes to improve their lifestyle. One family lived in a cave that had a cow hide for the door and had dirt floors. This is where the children were raised. There were several families that made homes from railroad ties. They also had several old cars where the children slept.

The children did not have clothes until they were six years old, so they ran around naked for the first six years of their lives. These children were very jealous of those of us in the class whose parents were farmers and hard workers, so they tended to pick on us starting in about the third grade. They did not like the fact that we were motivated to get good grades, and they had no desire to better themselves. It was not uncommon for them to pick fights with us and try to beat us up. I have a scar on my right arm where one of them cut me with a knife. No one would tell the principal or the teachers because they didn't seem to do anything about it, and no one would tell their parents because if they went to the principal, it made things worse because these kids became more determined to make your life miserable. They just kept on doing what they were doing. They called us names, and the name that they called me was so vulgar and degrading I do not feel that I can even write it.

Now the interesting thing was that in the wintertime, they were our best friends because we had sleds, and they didn't. They would offer to pull our sled up the hill if they could ride down with us. We had a fifteen-minute recess in the morning, a fifteen-minute recess in the afternoon, and a thirty-minute lunch break. If we hurried, we could get up the hill at recess, get one ride down the hill, and get back to the school in time for class. At lunch, if we stuffed our lunch down real fast, we could get two rides.

I had severe asthma when I was a child, and the cold weather irritated my asthma, so I had trouble getting up the hill. I had the longest sled that could carry three or four people, so they would offer to pull me up the hill if they could ride on my sled, and the more people we had on the sled, the faster it went. During the winter, they would be our best friends, but as soon as the snow melted, it was back to the same old taunting, name-calling, ganging up, and beating on you that went on.

So when people say that I do not understand what it is to be a minority, they do not understand what I went through. My parents taught us that we were not to fight. We were to gut it up and, if at all possible, stay out of the fight and out of trouble. I only fought back to protect myself. Because our school was a small rural school, we had to take state exams in the seventh and eighth grade to get an eighth-grade diploma.

The last week of school was exam week, and each exam would take one to two hours, and then we would have thirty-minute breaks before taking the next exam. When I was in the eighth grade, the exams would be on my last three days in the Trenton school system because we were going to high school in Williston. After we finished the first exam, one of the boys that was six feet tall came up to me and started calling me a nickname, mocking and making fun of me; I was only about five feet tall. I asked him to stop, but he sucker punched me in the nose, and my nose began to bleed. This made me angry, and because I had a very hot temper, one did not want to make me angry.

When he punched me in the nose, I stepped up, and with my right hand, I hit him in the stomach. When he doubled over, I caught his chin with my left fist and knocked him over backward. I do not know if it was the blow to his chin or the fact that he hit his head on the concrete that knocked him out cold. I had a standard that I would not hit a person that was down, but I was out of control with my anger that had built up over the past years, so I reached down, picked him up, held him up, and then knocked him down again. In so doing, I knocked out his upper two front teeth, and I was ready to pick him up again.

It took six guys to pull me off him and keep me from beating him to a pulp. He came to after a few minutes. We went our separate ways and cleaned ourselves up. I am not proud of this incident, but it stopped the name-calling and the harassment by all the other boys. They were now afraid of me because they realized even though I was small, I was extremely strong, and if I was pushed to the limit, I would fight back to win.

During haying season, we hired high school boys in the neighborhood to help haul hay. The boy that I had knocked his teeth out worked for us, and he told me that he was not holding a grudge because he knew that he had it coming.

His only comment was, "Why did you wait so long before you whipped up on us?"

I told him that I did not like to fight, and we were instructed by my parents not to get into fights but to try to solve things peaceably. But when he sucker punched me with no warning and bloodied my nose, I reacted to it the way I did.

Despite the problems, I continued to study hard and work towards the goal of getting a good education. My dad said that a good education is something that no one can take away from you, and even if it is at great cost, it is worth pursuing. My parents had to pay tuition for us to go to high school so that we could get a good education to prepare us for college. I studied hard and made good grades to earn as many scholarships as I could. Since my parents were paying tuition for us to go to high school, there would not be money to pay for a college education.

I went to North Dakota State University, which was at that time known as North Dakota Agriculture College. When I enrolled in pre-vet, I went to the veterinary science department and asked if they had a job opening, and they said, "No." I had looked around and saw a room full of dirty test tubes and petri dishes. I asked if these needed to be cleaned, and they replied that no one wanted to do that. I went in the room and found a small electric motor and put a test tube brush in the motor. I would grab a handful of test tubes and run the brush into them to clean them, then I cleaned the petri dishes.

When I finished, I went out to find someone to find out what they wanted done with the clean glassware. A technician went in and looked at what I had done. She got a doctor to show him what I had done. I got hired, so I had a job working to help pay for as much of my education as possible. I got up early in the mornings, worked before class, worked after class, and worked all day Saturday.

I was accepted into the College of Veterinary Medicine at Oklahoma State University, and while I was in college there, at times I had five part-time jobs to try to earn as much as I could. Then I borrowed the rest of the money that I needed to go to veterinary school. I came out of college with debt that had to be paid, and I worked to pay that debt. As you can see, I was not born with a silver spoon in my mouth, but everything that I have has come through sacrifice and hard work. I was never granted any special favors, nor did I ask for them. I put my nose to the grindstone, and with perseverance and hard work, I am what I am today. I am just an ordinary man that believed in an hour's worth of work and a little extra if needed for an hour's pay.

When I accepted Jesus Christ as my Lord and Savior, I was born as a babe in Christ, just like everyone else.

First Peter 2:2 says:

> As newborn babes, desire the sincere milk of the word,
> that you may grow thereby.

I thirsted after the Word of God, and I spent two to five hours a day studying the Word of God that I might get to know God in His nature, His personality, His character, and His Majesty that I might fall in love with Him. So you see, I was not born physically or spiritually with a silver spoon in my mouth, but by the grace of God and through hard work and dedication to God. I have and am what I am today because of His amazing grace. As I have said before, I am an ordinary man with an extraordinary God.

CHAPTER 25

Dark Times Reveal God is God

This is a difficult chapter to write because it tells of a very dark time in our lives which we would rather not reveal nor discuss. However, through it was the time when I came to know that God was God.

Second Corinthians 1:8–10 says:

> For we would not, brethren, have you ignorant of our trouble which came to us in Asia, that we were pressed out of measure, above strength, insomuch that we despaired even of life: But we had the sentence of death in ourselves, that we should not trust in ourselves, but in God which raises the dead: Who delivered us from so great a death, and does deliver: in whom we trust that he will yet deliver us.

The house that we had bought on Hillview in Dallas had a fifteen-year note that was divided into five-year segments. At the end of each five years, the note had to be renewed with the current interest rate. The note came up for renewal, and in the meantime, the bank had been sold. The president of the bank who had authorized the note was no longer with the bank. We went to see the man that had been given the oversight of our bank loan, and he immediately told us, "Before I renew this note, I'm going to check you out like you've never been checked out before."

Eventually we were told that we did not qualify to renew the note, even though we had made every payment on time for five years. We had moved to the animal hospital on Buena Vista which had a large note, and we had the responsibility of the church. This was also during the time when God was shaking the church and shrinking it. Many of the people for whom we had sacrificed and poured ourselves into were now the ones that were causing problems in the church and stabbing us in the back.

I was working long hours at my animal hospital, still taking my own emergency calls at night and on the weekends, and carrying the load of the church as its pastor. This became a time in our lives of great financial stress, physical draining, and overwhelming emotional stress. Also, Jan was on the PTA board at the elementary school and the junior high and was the computer volunteer chairman at the elementary school. She taught the women in Sunday school and then led children's church. In addition, Jan kept books for the church and the animal hospital and worked at the animal hospital on Saturday. All of this began to take a toll upon my wife. I thought she was sleeping okay, but she was not going into the phase four of sleep, the dream phase, that she needed to rest her brain. I noticed that she was having difficulties sorting things out, and imaginations were beginning to replace her ability to reason.

Second Corinthians 10:5 says:

> Casting down imaginations, and every high thing that exalts itself against the knowledge of God, and bringing into captivity every thought to the obedience of Christ.

In the charismatic circles, many people do not believe in mental illness but that this illness is an oppression of Satan that causes people to not be able to function mentally. The Scripture that I just quoted indicates that there is a spiritual battle. You need to cast down imaginations and Satan's attempt to mess up your mind.

My wife reached the point that if you said something to her, it became fact in her mind. She began to believe that people were spying on us. It got to the point that I could no longer reason with her at all, and she reached the point where basically she could not function. She did realize that she needed help, but we did not know where to turn. Finally, I called the doctor that was my personal physician as well as a friend since our children were friends and went to school together. I asked him to come by the house and talk to Jan to see if we could get her to go to the hospital so that we might get her help.

The doctor had known Jan for years, and when he came in and visited with her, he said that she needed treatment by a psychiatrist. Jan agreed to go with him and me to the hospital. When we arrived at the hospital, he called a psychiatrist to come see Jan, and he said that she had a mental condition which was probably caused by sleep deprivation and exhaustion. At this point, Jan could not sign papers to authorize treatment. The doctor filled out the papers for me to get authority to have her treated. I had to go to the county and commit her for treatment.

When the doctor hospitalized her, he told me that in ten days, she would begin to recover and to be able to reason. I told the doctor that I did not believe in psychiatry, but in this case, I had no choice but to put my trust in God that together they could get my wife well. He was not offended by my lack of faith in psychiatry because I had seen so many psychiatrists and psychologists make people dependent upon them and upon medication. The doctor told me that I needed to understand that the brain was a biological organ and that sometimes the chemistry in the brain gets out of sync. It needs medication to help it to return to normal function.

If a person's pancreas produces too much insulin or not enough insulin, the body is out of sync, so the insulin must be regulated to control the blood sugar. Diabetics need insulin to live, and with proper diet and insulin, the person can live a normal life. He told me the brain needed certain chemicals to function properly, and sometimes it needed a supplement. He told me that if he could give her the right medications and the right type of counseling, she would return to a normal sleep pattern. Then her brain would begin to function normally, the paranoia and the inability to reason would disappear, and she could live a normal life. If there were any times when she might be having trouble reasoning through a problem, the problem could be solved with counseling if it was caught early. If not, she might need to return to medication.

I went to see Jan at lunch every day and in the evening before I went home at night. Our anniversary was during the time that she was hospitalized. The hospital allowed me to have a very nice meal catered, and they gave us a room to ourselves for an hour. On the tenth day, my wife was able to sign the papers for treatment and thus avoided a court appearance where a judge would have made the decision for her care. At this time, she was given one-hour passes to leave the hospital and go outside with me to walk around the grounds. Soon she was given a three-hour pass to go home and spend time with me at the house, and then she returned to the hospital.

The trip home went well, and she was released to go home on the fourteenth day. For the next six months, it seemed like we were walking on eggshells because neither one of us knew what to expect. During the time that she was hospitalized, I did not know if she would ever get well and I would have my wife back or if she would remain in a mental state where she could not function outside of the hospital. I had never dealt with a person that had a mental condition before, and I had no idea what to expect or how to cope with this illness.

I reached the point in my life that I was totally physically exhausted. I was physically bankrupt, emotionally bankrupt, and at this point, spiritually bankrupt with no ability to believe or have faith. I could no longer pray. I told God that He knew what I would pray, but I had no faith to pray the prayer. I said, "God, our lives are in your hands, and God, you are going to have to carry the entire load in this situation." It was during this time that I truly came to know the sovereignty of God. That God is God! Being pressed out of measure so that there was nothing left made me feel like I had the sentence of death; the only place to turn was to God.

That is when God is at His best with His grace, His mercy, and His love. Paul said that his deliverance came through all the majesty of a majestic God. And, truly, God does deliver and continues to deliver. However, we have both been conscious of times when she was extremely tired and stressed about a certain situation. With God's help, we talked about that situation until she could reason through it and let it go. My wife made a complete recovery and has not had to go back on medication.

Jan said there were several things that added to her recovery. First was the love she felt from me because I visited her twice a day, brought her gifts, and expressed my desire for her to be well. Her parents were very supportive, visited every day, took care of our youngest son, and loaned us the money to pay off the note on our house. In addition to praying for her, the church members helped in various ways.

When Jan returned home, she listened to the Bible on tapes several hours a day, and God restored her mind. She also took better care of herself physically and did not take on so many responsibilities. Our personal doctor said that this experience with Jan totally changed his attitude toward mental illness. He knew her well before, saw her during the few months of recovery, and has seen her complete recovery to a normal and productive life.

Many pastors and Christians do not understand mental illness. Some people that appear to be mentally ill are demon-possessed and need to be delivered. Having ministered to many of these people, I have seen God's deliverance. But my brothers and sisters, you need the discernment of the Holy Spirit in dealing with people that are showing symptoms of mental illness. Only by the Spirit can we know if it is demon powers or a biological dysfunction of the brain. A person that is mentally ill from a biological abnormality in the brain needs to be sent to a psychiatrist that can get the brain functioning properly before they are ministered to with the Word of God because in that mental state, the person cannot reason. The Word of God may become a tool that is detrimental rather than helpful.

I have ministered to many people who are mentally ill. The first thing I do when I recognize that it is not a demon spirit but rather is a biological problem, which results in a chemical imbalance in the brain, is to get medical help as soon as possible to protect them and those around them since they cannot reason properly.

Most depression is just simply "I didn't get my way, I didn't get what I wanted," and many times, it is "I did not get the attention that I thought I deserved." So the person becomes depressed. This type of depression is self- centeredness and is physically and spiritually harmful. It needs to be dealt with as the sin that it is. However, there is another depression which is a mental illness in which the biological function of the brain is out of symmetry. This type of depression needs to be treated by a psychiatrist that is medically trained to get the brain back in symmetry.

Clinical depression and mental illness are both very difficult to treat because each person's brain is biologically different from other people's brains. It is difficult to arrive at the proper medication to reestablish symmetry in the brain. Clinical depression produces a darkness and despair that a normal person cannot understand, and there is a tendency to tell these people just to snap out of it and start functioning like a normal person.

Let me tell you that they would love to snap out of it and start functioning as a normal person would function, but they just simply can't. In this state of depression, many people are in so much pain that the only answer that seems to make sense to them is suicide. It is extremely taxing and overwhelming to minister to these people, and it will sap every ounce of energy that you can muster. They need professional help, but they also desperately need to know that you love them, that they are loved by others, and that their life has purpose and meaning.

Sometimes, even with medical and professional intervention and all the love you can give, it is not enough; these people will take their own lives. Mental illness is extremely difficult to understand, and one cannot take the blame if someone else took their own life. I had a father say to me that he will never understand why his fifteen-year-old son blew his brains out. I told him that you will never understand it, but you must and will come to accept it.

CHAPTER 26

God Where Are You?

J ob 23:8–9 says:
Behold, I go forward, but he is not there; and backward, but I cannot perceive him: On the left hand, where he does work, but I cannot behold him: he hides himself on the right hand, that I cannot see him.

Job was in incredible pain and wished he could die. He sought God with all his heart, and he could not get an answer. There seemed to be a steel plate between God and Job, and his prayers could not get through to God. It was as if God had forsaken Job, cut him off, and did not care. Let's face it; this has happened to all of us far more times than we can remember. We just do not understand why a loving God would treat us this way.

Job 42:5 says:

I have heard of you by the hearing of the ear: but now my
eye sees you.

As Job discovered at the end of his trial, he previously knew about God, but now he knows God. O, for the day we will see God face-to-face and bow down to worship him. It will be worth it all, and these fiery trials will be forgotten when we enter His glory.
Psalm 22:1–2 says:

> My God, my God, why have you forsaken me? Why are you so far from helping me, and from the words of my roaring? O my God, I cry in the daytime, but you hear not; and in the night season, and am not silent.

Jesus cried out to God just before He was crucified and asked why His Father had forsaken Him in His greatest need. It was necessary for God to withdraw Himself from Jesus because, in His Holiness, God is a consuming fire. Jesus as the son of man was going to pay the price for sin, the wage of which is death. Death is the separation from God forever after having bowed a knee and confessed Him as Lord.

Philippians 2:10–11 says:

> That at the name of Jesus every knee should bow, of things in heaven, and things in earth, and things under the earth; And that every tongue should confess that Jesus Christ is Lord, to the glory of God the Father.

It was necessary for God to forsake Jesus. Otherwise, when as the son of man He took the sin of the world on his flesh and became your and my sin, the Father would not consume Jesus. Jesus would pay our debt by dying and going to hell in our place so that we might have eternal life. How did Jesus accomplish this horrendous task? He had perfect faith that His Father could and would keep Him. He did not need the presence of the Holy Spirit to know that God was faithful to fulfill His promise to raise Jesus from the dead and exalt Him above all men in heaven.

Hebrews 5:8 says:

> And there shall come forth a rod out of the stem of Jesse, and a Branch shall grow out of his roots: And the spirit of the Lord shall rest upon him, the spirit of wisdom and understanding, the spirit of counsel and might, the spirit of knowledge and of the fear of the Lord; And shall make him of quick understanding in the fear of the Lord: and he shall not judge after the sight of his eyes, neither reprove after the hearing of his ears.

Though he was a Son, yet learned he obedience by the things which he suffered.

Proverbs 8:13 says:

> The fear of the Lord is to hate evil: pride, and arrogancy, and the evil way, and the froward mouth, do I hate.

Hebrews 12:2–7 says:

> Looking unto Jesus the author and finisher of our faith; who for the joy that was set before him endured the cross, despising the shame, and is set down at the right hand of the throne of God. For consider him that endured such contradiction of sinners against himself, lest you are wearied and faint in your minds. You have not yet resisted unto blood, striving against sin. And you have forgotten the exhortation which speaks unto you as unto children, My son, despise not you the chastening of the Lord, nor faint when you are rebuked of him: For whom the Lord loves he chastens, and scourges every son whom he receives. If you endure chastening, God deals with you as with sons; for what son is he whom the father chastens not?

Jesus looked beyond the cross to the joy that was set before Him. He had learned through suffering that He could trust His Father to keep His Word. Jesus knew that He would not be left in hell but would be resurrected and return to heaven to be exalted.

Mark 1:9–13 says:

> And it came to pass in those days, that Jesus came from Nazareth of Galilee, and was baptized of John in Jordan. And straightway coming up out of the water, he saw the heavens opened, and the Spirit like a dove descending upon him: And there came a voice from heaven, saying, You are my beloved Son, in whom I am well pleased. And immediately the Spirit drives him into the wilderness. And he was there in the wilderness forty days, tempted of Satan; and was with the wild beasts; and the angels ministered unto him.

Right after Jesus was baptized, He was taken into the wilderness and tempted by Satan for forty days and nights without food, water, or rest. When Satan tempted Him by quoting scriptures, Jesus did not yield to the temptation but quoted God's Word. One thing that we forget is that Jesus knew what His purpose was from the beginning: that was to go to the cross and pay the debt for sin for all mankind. When Satan offered Jesus a shortcut, it had to be very tempting. But Isaiah says, "God made Him of a quick understanding of the fear of the Lord." Jesus learned obedience by suffering before He started to minister to the people. Not learning obedience to the Lord is one of the greatest mistakes made by Christians and pastors today. They do not hate sin, nor do they fear God. One of the reasons we do not fear God is He does not always judge our sins immediately. I asked God why He did not judge my sin with chastisement, and He told me that He would rather love me into the kingdom. However, if necessary, He would give me a good spanking. I asked God why I keep sinning when I know it is wrong, and He said that I love my sin. If I hated sin, I would not do it. Thus, I did not fear God so there would probably be a lot of suffering because of His deep love for me.

1 Peter 1:5–9 says:

> Who are kept by the power of God through faith unto salvation ready to be revealed in the last time. Wherein you greatly rejoice, though now for a season, if need be, you are in heaviness through manifold temptations: That the trial of your faith, being much more precious than of gold that perishes, though it be tried with fire, might be found unto praise and honor and glory at the appearing of Jesus Christ: Whom having not seen, you love; in whom, though now you see him not, yet believing, you rejoice with joy unspeakable and full of glory: Receiving the end of your faith, even the salvation of your souls.

I came to realize that my faith had to be tried by fire for it to be purified to bring me to the day of redemption. During that purifying of my faith by fire, many times I was not going to sense God's presence. I was going to feel like I was in a vacuum and that God did not care, but He was carrying me. I had His Word to keep me, and I needed to trust in His Word instead of feelings. I had to learn through fiery trials that God was there with me. It was God who was bringing me through the fire and teaching me to stop walking in the flesh and by feelings but rather trust in His Word by faith. By putting one foot in front of the other to keep walking and enduring one step at a time, one can get out of the flesh and feelings, and then walk in His Word by faith.

Romans 8:17 says:

> And if children, then heirs; heirs of God, and joint-heirs with Christ; if so be that we suffer with him, that we may be also glorified together.

If I will endure to the end, there will be an abundant entrance into heaven when I have finished my work here on this earth, and I will spend eternity in the presence of God the Father, Jesus the Son, and the Holy Spirit. That will be the greatest reward any ordinary man could hope for from an extraordinary God.

CHAPTER 27

Incredible Saving Love

I received Jesus Christ as my Lord and Savior on August 23, 1970. At the time of this writing, it has been almost forty-eight years ago. Little did I dream what an incredible walk it would be for a little country boy born in North Dakota who eventually lived in the big city of Dallas, Texas. As I approach the later years of my life, I find myself crying out like the apostle Paul that I might know Him and the power of His resurrection. I long for the day that I might see my Lord and Savior, Jesus Christ, and when I am able to fall at his feet and thank Him for saving me, a wretched sinner. I thank God for the intimacy that we have had while I have been a stranger upon the earth. I long for the time when my faith shall become sight and I will be able to embrace Him in person.

Hebrews 2:1–18 describes Jesus becoming the Son of Man with particular emphasis on verse 14.

Hebrews 2:14 says:

> Forasmuch then as the children are partakers of flesh and blood, he also himself likewise took part of the same; that through death he might destroy him that had the power of death, that is, the devil.

Jesus Christ, the Son of God, became the Son of Man, and as the Scripture says, He became fully man in flesh and blood. When Jesus became the Son of Man, He put His being the Son of God in a blind trust which He gave to His Father to be executor of the trust. Jesus Christ did this so that He might be totally man and could completely identify with us in our flesh.

Philippians 2:5–8 says:

> Let this mind be in you, which was also in Christ Jesus: Who, being in the form of God, thought it not robbery to be equal with God: But made himself of no reputation, and took upon him the form of a servant, and was made in the likeness of men: And being found in fashion as a man, he humbled himself, and became obedient unto death, even the death of the cross.

Hebrews 5:8–9 says:

> Though he were a Son, yet learned he obedience by the things which he suffered; And being made perfect, he became the author of eternal salvation unto all them that obey him.

Before you brand me as a heretic, please hear me out because what I am about to write becomes vital to understand what a great price God the Father and the Son paid for our salvation. There are two ways to get to heaven; the only way for you and I to make it to heaven is through repentance of our sin and receiving Jesus Christ as our Lord and Savior. The other way to make it to heaven is to keep the law, and if it were not for this way, we would not have salvation.

But when Jesus Christ came to the earth and became the Son of Man, he became a partaker of flesh and blood with all its strengths, weaknesses, and desires. He became fully man with the same flesh and blood that you and I live in. Adam and Eve were created in perfection without sin, but they were not able to maintain that perfection. When they were tempted, they fell. We, likewise when we were tempted, sinned. Jesus as the Son of Man had the same desires and temptations in the flesh that you and I experience. He suffered against these temptations, remained obedient, and was able to present his body without spot and without blemish as the perfect sacrifice for our sins.

Matthew 5:17 says:

Think not that I am come to destroy the law, or the prophets: I am not come to destroy, but to fulfil.

Romans 6:23a says:

For the wages of sin is death.

We must understand that the consequences of sin required a judgment which was death and that death was eternal judgment in hell. And God being a just God needed someone to pay that price for you and me. He required a perfect lamb without spot and without blemish to be sacrificed, and the blood must be shed to cover the sins. Jesus did not come to destroy the law but to fulfill the law in perfect love; and He became the sacrificial lamb without spot and without blemish. He took upon him the sins of the world and his sinless flesh became sinful flesh. When this happened, God had to turn His back on His Son and withdrew the Spirit. Jesus had to take our punishment, which was death. Jesus fulfilled the law with love and perfect faith in that He believed the Father that if He kept the law, God would resurrect Him from hell and raise Him to sit at the Father's right hand.

Isaiah 53:1–12 says:

Who has believed our report? and to whom is the arm of the Lord revealed? For he shall grow up before him as a tender plant, and as a root out of a dry ground: he has no form nor comeliness; and when we shall see him, there is no beauty that we should desire him. He is despised and rejected of men; a man of sorrows, and acquainted with grief: and we hid as it were our faces from him; he was despised, and we esteemed him not. Surely he has borne our griefs, and carried our sorrows: yet we did esteem him stricken, smitten of God, and afflicted. But he was wounded for our transgressions, he was bruised for our iniquities: the chastisement of our peace was upon him; and with his stripes we are healed. All we like sheep have gone astray; we have turned every one to his own way; and the Lord has laid on him the iniquity of us all. He was oppressed, and he was afflicted, yet he opened not his mouth: he is brought as a lamb to the slaughter, and as a sheep before her shearers is dumb, so he opened not his mouth. He was taken from prison and from judgment: and who shall declare his generation? for he was cut off out of the land of the living: for the transgression of my people was he stricken. And he made his grave with the wicked, and with the rich in his death; because he had done no violence, neither was any deceit in his mouth. Yet it pleased the Lord to bruise him; he has put him to grief: when you shall make his soul an offering for sin, he shall see his seed, he shall prolong his days, and the pleasure of the Lord shall prosper in his hand. He shall see of the travail of his soul, and shall be satisfied: by his knowledge shall my righteous servant justify many; for he shall bear their iniquities. Therefore will I divide him a portion with the great, and he shall divide the spoil with the strong; because he has poured out his soul unto death: and he was numbered with the transgressors; and he bare the sin of many, and made intercession for the transgressors.

Psalm 18:1–50 says:

{To the chief Musician, A Psalm of David, the servant of the Lord, who spoke unto the Lord the words of this song in the day that the Lord delivered him from the hand of all his enemies, and from the hand of Saul: And he said} I will love thee, O Lord, my strength. The Lord is my rock, and my fortress, and my deliverer; my God, my strength, in whom I will trust; my buckler, and the horn of my salvation, and my high tower. I will call upon the Lord, who is worthy to be praised: so shall I be saved from mine enemies. The sorrows of death compassed me, and the floods of ungodly men made me afraid. The sorrows of hell compassed me about: the snares of death prevented me. In my distress I called upon the Lord, and cried unto my God: he heard my voice out of his temple, and my cry came before him, even into his ears. Then the earth shook and trembled; the foundations also of the hills moved and were shaken, because he was wroth. There went up a smoke out of his nostrils, and fire out of his mouth devoured: coals were kindled by it. He bowed the heavens also, and came down: and darkness was under his feet. And he rode upon a cherub, and did fly: yea, he did fly upon the wings of the wind. He made darkness his secret place; his pavilion round about him were dark waters and thick clouds of the skies. At the brightness that was before him his thick clouds passed, hail stones and coals of fire. The Lord also thundered in the heavens, and the Highest gave his voice; hail stones and coals of fire. Yea, he sent out his arrows, and scattered them; and he shot out lightnings, and discomfited them. Then the channels of waters were seen, and the foundations of the world were discovered at your rebuke, O Lord, at the blast of the breath of your nostrils. He sent from above, he took me, he drew me out of many waters. He delivered me from my strong enemy, and from them which hated me: for they were too strong for me. They prevented me in the day of my calamity: but the Lord was my stay. He brought me forth also into a large place; he delivered me, because he delighted in me. The Lord rewarded me according to my righteousness; according to the cleanness of my hands has he recompensed me. For I have kept the ways of the Lord, and have not wickedly departed from my God. For all his judgments were before me, and I did not put away his statutes from me. I was also upright before him, and I kept myself from mine iniquity. Therefore has the Lord recompensed me according to my righteousness, according to the cleanness of my hands in his eyesight. With the merciful you will show yourself merciful; with an upright man you will show yourself upright; With the pure you will show yourself pure; and with the froward you will show yourself froward. For you will save the afflicted people; but will bring down high looks. For you will light my candle: the Lord my God will enlighten my darkness. For by you I have run through a troop; and by my God have I leaped over a wall. As for God, his way is perfect: the word of the Lord is tried: he is a buckler to all those that trust in him. For who is God save the Lord? or who is a rock save our God? It is God that girds me with strength, and makes my way perfect. He makes my feet like hinds' feet, and sets me upon my high places. He teaches my hands to war, so that a bow of steel is broken by mine arms. You have also given me the shield of your salvation: and your right hand has held me up, and your gentleness has made me great. You have enlarged my steps under me, that my feet did not slip. I have pursued mine enemies, and overtaken them: neither did I turn again till they were consumed. I have wounded them that they were not able to rise: they are fallen under my feet. For you have girded me with strength unto the battle: you have subdued under me those that rose up against me. You have also given me the necks of mine enemies; that I might destroy them that hate me. They cried, but there was none to save them: even unto the Lord, but he answered them not. Then did I beat them small as the dust before the wind: I did cast them out as the dirt in the streets. You have delivered me from the strivings of the people; and you have made me the head of the heathen: a people whom I have not known shall serve me. As soon as they hear of me, they shall obey me: the strangers shall submit themselves unto me. The strangers shall fade away, and be afraid out of their close places. The Lord lives; and blessed be my rock; and let the God of my salvation be exalted. It is God that avenges me, and subdues the people under me. He delivers me from mine enemies: yea, you lift me up above those that rise up against me: you have delivered me from the violent man. Therefore will I give thanks unto thee, O Lord, among the heathen, and sing praises unto your name. Great deliverance gives he to his king; and shows mercy to his anointed, to David, and to his seed for evermore.

When I see the incredible price that God the Father paid in sacrificing of His Son, Jesus Christ, and that His Son, Jesus Christ, willingly made that sacrifice, I am so humbled and broken that in my feeble attempt to serve such an incredible God, I do not feel worthy to be counted as one of His children. God's grace so overwhelms me that an ordinary man can be so blessed to have such an extraordinary God who loved me and bought me with a price that I am totally incapable of repaying. The one and only true God is beyond description, and all that I can do is fall upon my face, worship Him, and praise Him for His incredible love.

CHAPTER 28

The End-Time Church

On the day of Pentecost, God baptized the disciples with the Holy Spirit, and Peter stood up and spoke to the crowd. Acts 2:14–16 says:

> But Peter, standing up with the eleven, lifted up his voice, and said unto them, You men of Judaea, and all you that dwell at Jerusalem, be this known unto you, and hearken to my words: For these are not drunken, as you suppose, seeing it is but the third hour of the day. But this is that which was spoken by the prophet Joel (Joel 2:28–32); And it shall come to pass in the last days, says God, I will pour out of my Spirit upon all flesh: and your sons and your daughters shall prophesy, and your young men shall see visions, and your old men shall dream dreams: And on my servants and on my handmaidens I will pour out in those days of my Spirit; and they shall prophesy: And I will show wonders in heaven above, and signs in the earth beneath; blood, and fire, and vapor of smoke: The sun shall be turned into darkness, and the moon into blood, before that great and notable day of the Lord come: And it shall come to pass, that whosoever shall call on the name of the Lord shall be saved.

The day of Pentecost was the beginning of the end-time church. When most people think of the end-time church, they think of the time just before Jesus returns the second time. The reality is that the end-time church started on the day of Pentecost. As we are nearing the end of this stage, Jesus told his disciples what to expect.

Matthew 24:1–31 says:

> And Jesus went out, and departed from the temple: and his disciples came to him for to show him the buildings of the temple. And Jesus said unto them, See you not all these things? verily I say unto you, There shall not be left here one stone upon another, that shall not be thrown down. And as he sat upon the mount of Olives, the disciples came unto him privately, saying, Tell us, when shall these things be? and what shall be the sign of your coming, and of the end of the world? And Jesus answered and said unto them, Take heed that no man deceive you. For many shall come in my name, saying, I am Christ; and shall deceive many. And you shall hear of wars and rumors of wars: see that you be not troubled: for all these things must come to pass, but the end is not yet. For nation shall rise against nation, and kingdom against kingdom: and there shall be famines, and pestilences, and earthquakes, in divers places. All these are the beginning of sorrows. Then shall they deliver you up to be afflicted, and shall kill you: and you shall be hated of all nations for my name's sake. And then shall many be offended, and shall betray one another, and shall hate one another. And many false prophets shall rise, and shall deceive many. And because iniquity shall abound, the love of many shall wax cold. But he that shall endure unto the end, the same shall be saved. And this gospel of the kingdom shall be preached in all the world for a witness unto all nations; and then shall the end come. When you therefore shall see the abomination of desolation, spoken of by Daniel the prophet, stand in the holy place, (whoso reads, let him understand:) Then let them which be in Judaea flee into the mountains: Let him which is on the housetop not come down to take any thing out of his house: Neither let him which is in the field return back to take his clothes. And woe unto them

that are with child, and to them that give suck in those days! But pray you that your flight be not in the winter, neither on the sabbath day: For then shall be great tribulation, such as was not since the beginning of the world to this time, no, nor ever shall be. And except those days should be shortened, there should no flesh be saved: but for the elect's sake those days shall be shortened. Then if any man shall say unto you, Lo, here is Christ, or there; believe it not. For there shall arise false Christs, and false prophets, and shall show great signs and wonders; insomuch that, if it were possible, they shall deceive the very elect. Behold, I have told you before. Wherefore if they shall say unto you, Behold, he is in the desert; go not forth: behold, he is in the secret chambers; believe it not. For as the lightning cometh out of the east, and shines even unto the west; so shall also the coming of the Son of man be. For wheresoever the carcass is, there will the eagles be gathered together. Immediately after the tribulation of those days shall the sun be darkened, and the moon shall not give her light, and the stars shall fall from heaven, and the powers of the heavens shall be shaken: And then shall appear the sign of the Son of man in heaven: and then shall all the tribes of the earth mourn, and they shall see the Son of man coming in the clouds of heaven with power and great glory. And he shall send his angels with a great sound of a trumpet, and they shall gather together his elect from the four winds, from one end of heaven to the other.

Matthew 24:32–39 says:

Now learn a parable of the fig tree; When his branch is yet tender, and puts forth leaves, you know that summer is nigh: So likewise you, when you shall see all these things, know that it is near, even at the doors. Verily I say unto you, This generation shall not pass, till all these things be fulfilled. Heaven and earth shall pass away, but my words shall not pass away. But of that day and hour knows no man, no, not the angels of heaven, but my Father only. But as the days of

Noah were, so shall also the coming of the Son of man be. For as in the days that were before the flood they were eating and drinking, marrying and giving in marriage, until the day that Noah entered into the ark, And knew not until the flood came, and took them all away; so shall also the coming of the Son of man be.

The disciples came to Jesus and asked Him to tell them how they would know when He was coming back the second time. Jesus told them that there would be wars, earthquakes, and floods. There would be great tribulation, and it would be like the times of Noah before He came back. Some people in every generation have believed that Jesus was coming back during their generation. One thing that we miss before the return of the Lord is that in the time of Noah, the world had become so wicked. It took Noah a hundred years to build the ark; and during that time, he did not have one single convert.

God told Abraham that if there were ten righteous men in Sodom and Gomorrah, He would not destroy the cities. God says that He has no pleasure in the death of the wicked but that it is His will that all should repent and be saved. God's nature is not to destroy but to save. The church has fallen asleep, and it has become desensitized to unrighteousness. Many churches have fallen into the lie brought by Satan that God is all love and tolerance.

I never thought that I would see the day when evil is called good and good is called evil, but we have seen it. If one takes a stand against homosexuality, that person is called evil, unloving, and homophobic. If one takes a stand for homosexuality, that person is called loving and accepting. The sad thing in this lie that has been perpetuated is that it is damning people to hell. God's Word states very clearly that no homosexual will be found in the kingdom of God, and God's Word is the same yesterday, today, and forever. It changes not. The world must understand that in Ezekiel 33, God told the righteous to warn the wicked that they might turn from their wickedness and be saved. We as Christians must come to understand that we are the messengers that God has placed in this world to speak His truths from His Word, regardless of the consequences which may be persecution.

Second Timothy 4:3–4 says:

> For the time will come when they will not endure sound doctrine; but after their own lusts shall they heap to themselves teachers, having itching ears; And they shall turn away their ears from the truth, and shall be turned unto fables.

Second Peter 2:5 says:

> And spared not the old world, but saved Noah the eighth person, a preacher of righteousness in the flood upon the world of the ungodly.

Both John the Baptist and Jesus went preaching repentance. They did not go preaching to say a prayer so you could go to heaven. Only eight people were saved from the flood. Millions of people died in the flood. Today we have a cheap gospel preached that is leading people straight into hell.

Mark 12:30–31 says:

> And you shall love the Lord your God with all your heart, and with all your soul, and with all your mind, and with all your strength; this is the first commandment. And the second is like namely this, You shall love your neighbor as yourself. There is none other commandment greater than these.

I will use an illustration.

A man and women decide to get married. They are at the church. The bride walks down the aisle and meets her husband to be. The pastor asks them to repeat the wedding vows and then to give each other rings and then pronounces them man and wife. The husband then whispers in the wife's ear, "I will meet you here next week for an hour."

How long do you think this relationship will last? That is what probably 95 percent of the people that have prayed a sinner's prayer are doing. They don't read their Bibles or develop a relationship with God. There are many people like the five foolish virgins that have no oil in their lamps or like the man that was with those that had been bid to marriage supper but did not have on the wedding garment.

Matthew 22:1–14 says:

And Jesus answered and spoke unto them again by parables, and said, The kingdom of heaven is like unto a certain king, which made a marriage for his son, And sent forth his servants to call them that were bidden to the wedding: and they would not come. Again, he sent forth other servants, saying, Tell them which are bidden, Behold, I have prepared my dinner: my oxen and my fatlings are killed, and all things *are* ready: come unto the marriage. But they made light of *it*, and went their ways, one to his farm, another to his merchandise: And the remnant took his servants, and entreated *them* spitefully, and slew *them*. But when the king heard *thereof*, he was wroth: and he sent forth his armies, and destroyed those murders, and burned up their city. Then said he to his servants, The wedding is ready, but they which were bidden were not worthy. Go you therefore into the highways, and as many as you shall find, bid to the marriage. So those servants went out into the highways, and gathered together all as many as they found, both bad and good: and the wedding was furnished with guests. And when the king came in to see the guests, he saw there a man which had not on a wedding garment: And he said to him, Friend, how came you in hither not having a wedding garment? And he was speechless. Then said the king to the servants, Bind him hand and foot, and take him away, and cast *him* into outer darkness; there shall be weeping and gnashing of teeth. For many are called, but few *are* chosen.

Matthew 25:1–13 says:

Then shall the kingdom of heaven be likened unto ten virgins, which took their lamps, and went forth to meet the bridegroom. And five of them were wise, and five *were* foolish. They that *were* foolish took their lamps, and took no oil with them: But the wise took oil in their vessels with their lamps. While the bridegroom tarried, they all slumbered and slept. And at midnight there was a cry made, Behold, the bridegroom comes; go you out to meet him. Then all those virgins arouse, and trimmed their lamps. And the foolish said unto the wise, Give us of your oil; for our lamps are gone out. But the wise answered, saying, *Not so*; lest there be not enough for us and you: but go you rather to them that sell, and buy for yourselves. And while they went to buy, the bridegroom came; and they that were ready went in with him to the marriage: and the door was shut. Afterward came also the other virgins, saying, Lord, Lord, open to us. But he answered and said, Verily I say unto you, I know you not. Watch therefore, for you know neither the day nor the hour wherein the Son of man comes.

Malachi is the last book in the Old Testament, and it is both prophetic and a warning to the New Testament church.

Malachi 1:8 Christ as my Lord and Savior on August says:

And if you offer the blind for sacrifice, is it not evil? and if you offer the lame and sick, is it not evil? offer it now unto your governor; will he be pleased with you, or accept your person? says the Lord of hosts.

God said to the priest that they dishonored His name by bringing sacrifices that were blind, lame, and imperfect. Then they expected Him to be pleased with their offering. We do the same thing when we do not give our first and best unto God. If we have anything left over, we will give it to God and think and believe that he should be pleased. God is not pleased if all we do is go to church on Sunday and maybe read the Bible for a few minutes once or twice a week. In the second chapter of Malachi, God said that the priest had become partial in the Word; in other words, they had picked out what they like in the Word and ignored or rejected whatever did not make them feel good or convicted them.

God said that no lie went out of the lips of Levi. What He was saying was that we cannot change God's Word to satisfy humanity, even if it is for the overwhelming majority of the people. God's Word does not change. Many times, Moses stood alone when he led the children of Israel out of Egypt, but he refused to compromise God's Word. God also states in the book of Malachi about His hatred of divorce and that a refiner's fire will come to purify the shepherds. God said to the church that if you will return unto God, then He will return unto the church.

I find that when people including myself read the Word of God, they are influenced by doctrines and traditions that they were taught. People often miss what the Word really says and means. To be open to new revelations from God, each time a person reads the Bible, they should read it as if this was the first time. We tend to gloss over areas that we believe we understand and have been taught. A good example of this is: how many animals did Noah take into the ark? The answer I always receive is that he took a pair of each of the animals into the ark. I get this same answer from pastors as well as other Christians.

Genesis 7:2 says:

> [O]f every clean beast you shall take to you by sevens, the male and his female: and of the beast that are not clean by two, the male and his female.

We teach our children from a very early age that Noah took one pair of all animals into the ark. This is not what the Word of God says, but when I bring it up to pastors, they tell me that I am nitpicking and that it is not important. I find that God's Word is very clear that we are not to take away from His Word or to add on to His Word. This is just a small but very clear example that shows we are influenced by what we are taught. Many times, we miss a very important fact in the Bible because we gloss over the words that we think we understand. We forget that God's Word says what it says.

When I accepted Jesus Christ as my Lord and Savior, God told me that I needed to forget every doctrine that I was taught and every tradition that I had learned; He would teach me His doctrines from His Word. If we set out to study the Word of God to make it line up with a doctrine or tradition that we have been taught, we are not open to what God's Word is really saying. We must be able to admit that our understanding of the Word of God could be in error and that we might be wrong. We need to have an open mind so that we can accept the Word of God for what it says and not what we want it to say.

I have seen many people, when they were confronted with a Scripture, that did not agree with their doctrine and who tried to explain it away. If they could not explain it away, they said that the scripture had to be in error; they chose to ignore the truth rather than to examine their doctrine and admit that they were wrong. I learned a long time ago not to argue doctrine with fellow Christians but rather to agree to disagree in love until we could grow up into the full stature of Jesus Christ.

Ephesians 4:11–16 says:

> And he gave some, apostles; and some, prophets; and some, evangelists; and some, pastors and teachers; For the perfecting of the saints, for the work of the ministry, for the edifying of the body of Christ: Till we all come in the unity of the faith, and of the knowledge of the Son of God, unto a perfect man, unto the measure of the stature of the fullness of Christ: That we henceforth be no more children, tossed to and fro, and carried about with every wind of doctrine, by the sleight of men, and cunning craftiness, whereby they lie in wait to deceive; But speaking the truth in love, may grow up into him in all things, which is the head, even Christ: From whom the whole body fitly joined together and compacted by that which every joint supplies, according to the effectual working in the measure of every part, makes increase of the body unto the edifying of itself in love.

In Matthew 13:1–58, Jesus tells several parables. They are a picture of His relationship with the church; and when taken together, they will give us an understanding of the church. In the first parable, He speaks of the sower sowing the Word of God.

Matthew 13:1–23 says:

> The same day went Jesus out of the house, and sat by the sea side. And great multitudes were gathered together unto him, so that he went into a ship, and sat; and the whole

multitude stood on the shore. And he spoke many things unto them in parables, saying, Behold, a sower went forth to sow; And when he sowed, some seeds fell by the way side, and the fowls came and devoured them up: Some fell upon stony places, where they had not much earth: and forthwith they sprung up, because they had no deepness of earth: And when the sun was up, they were scorched; and because they had no root, they withered away. And some fell among thorns; and the thorns sprung up, and choked them: But other fell into good ground, and brought forth fruit, some an hundredfold, some sixtyfold, some thirtyfold. Who has ears to hear, let him hear. And the disciples came, and said unto him, Why speak you unto them in parables? He answered and said unto them, Because it is given unto you to know the mysteries of the kingdom of heaven, but to them it is not given. For whosoever has, to him shall be given, and he shall have more abundance: but whosoever has not, from him shall be taken away even that he hath. Therefore speak I to them in parables: because they seeing see not; and hearing they hear not, neither do they understand. And in them is fulfilled the prophecy of Esaias, which says, By hearing you shall hear, and shall not understand; and seeing you shall see, and shall not perceive: For this people's heart is waxed gross, and their ears are dull of hearing, and their eyes they have closed; lest at any time they should see with their eyes, and hear with their ears, and should understand with their heart, and should be converted, and I should heal them. But blessed are your eyes, for they see: and your ears, for they hear. For verily I say unto you, That many prophets and righteous men have desired to see those things which you see, and have not seen them; and to hear those things which you hear, and have not heard them. Hear you therefore the parable of the sower. When any one hears the word of the kingdom, and understands it not, then comes the wicked one, and catches away that which was sown in his heart. This is he which received seed by the way side. But he that received the seed into stony places, the same is he that hears the word, and anon with joy receives it; Yet has he not root in himself, but endures for a while: for when tribulation or persecution arises because of the word, by and by he is offended. He also that received seed among the thorns is he that hears the word; and the care of this world, and the deceitfulness of riches, choke the word, and he becomes unfruitful. But he that received seed into the good ground is he that hears the word, and understands it; which also bears fruit, and brings forth, some an hundredfold, some sixty, some thirty.

In the parable where some of the Word fell by the wayside, the people that hear the Word of God think it sounds good, but they are not drawn by God, and they have not been seeking God. Satan comes and takes the Word from them so they will live their lives without any change. Then for some, the Word is sown on stony ground. These are the people that received Jesus Christ, but they had no idea that there must be a commitment and that there is a cost to pay. So when the Word offended them, they rejected it; and they go back to live their old ways in the world.

Probably the largest group of people is those sown among thorns, thistles, and weeds. These people start out with the desire to serve God and walk with him; but then they become overwhelmed making a living, raising a family, climbing the corporate ladder, buying a bigger and newer house, and having fancier cars. They are overcome keeping up with the Joneses and living the social life so that the Word is completely choked out and becomes unproductive and unfruitful with their walk with God. Then there are those that are sown on the good ground that bear fruit thirty, sixty, and a hundredfold. These are the people that have counted the cost of taking up their cross daily, denying themselves and following God. This parable describes the types of people in the church, and there are only a few that are really committed and carry the load of the church.

Numbers 11:4 says:

And the mixt multitude that was among them fell a lusting: and the children of Israel also wept again, and said, Who shall give us flesh to eat?

When Moses brought the children of Israel out of Egypt, many Egyptians came out with the Hebrew children because they saw the hand of God and his protection on the Hebrew children. They had no commitment to the nation of Israel or to their God. They just wanted the benefits and the safety of the God of Israel without any commitment. So when things got unpleasant, they began to murmur and complain that they were better off in Egypt. This had a negative effect upon the Hebrew children. We find the same thing in the church where we have those that were sown by the wayside, those sown on stony ground, and those sown among thorns and weeds. These people influence the Christian church members, and they become a burden to those that are committed. Their murmuring and complaining tear down the church and make it more difficult for the committed Christian to walk with God.

Matthew 13:24–30 says:

Another parable put he forth unto them, saying, The kingdom of heaven is likened unto a man which sowed good seed in his field: But while men slept, his enemy came and sowed tares among the wheat, and went his way. But when the blade was sprung up, and brought forth fruit, then appeared the tares also. So the servants of the householder came and said unto him, Sir, did not you sow good seed in your field? from whence then has it tares? He said unto them, An enemy hath done this. The servants said unto him, Will you then that we go and gather them up? But he said, Nay; lest while you gather up the tares, you root up also the wheat with them. Let both grow together until the harvest: and in the time of harvest I will say to the reapers, Gather you together first the tares, and bind them in bundles to burn them: but gather the wheat into my barn.

Matthew 13:37–43 says:

> He answered and said unto them, He that sows the good seed is the Son of man; The field is the world; the good seed are the children of the kingdom; but the tares are the children of the wicked one; The enemy that sowed them is the devil; the harvest is the end of the world; and the reapers are the angels. As therefore the tares are gathered and burned in the fire; so shall it be in the end of this world. The Son of man shall send forth his angels, and they shall gather out of his kingdom all things that offend, and them which do iniquity; And shall cast them into a furnace of fire: there shall be wailing and gnashing of teeth. Then shall the righteous shine forth as the sun in the kingdom of their Father. Who hath ears to hear, let him hear.

Then the church went to sleep, and Satan came and sowed tares in the church. In the beginning, the tares were indistinguishable from the Christians; so God said to leave them in the church unless when they are pulled out, some of the Christians might be rooted out with them. In the end, God will remove the tares. Many of our new translations of the Bible call the tares "weeds," but this is not correct. When tame oats are planted in a field, and some wild oats grow up in the field also, one cannot distinguish the plants until they put on the seed. The tame oats seed will have one rounded edge on one end and a pointed edge on the other end, and the wild oats seed will have a sucker mouth on one end and a pointed edge on the other end. Thus you will know them by their fruit.

The key in this parable is that the church went to sleep.

First Thessalonians 5:6–8 says:

> Therefore let us not sleep, as do others; but let us watch and be sober. For they that sleep sleep in the night; and they that be drunken are drunken in the night. But let us, who are of the day, be sober, putting on the breastplate of faith and love; and for an helmet, the hope of salvation.

Romans 13:11 says:

And that, knowing the time, that now it is high time to awake out of sleep: for now is our salvation nearer than when we believed.

I believe that the church has been lulled into sleep and in this sleep has not been fully conscious of the work of the enemy Satan as he has planted his tares in the church. The church is losing its saltiness, and because iniquity abounds, the love of many has waxed cold. The church has become desensitized to the unrighteousness of the world, just as Lot in Sodom and Gomorrah allowed his spirit to be vexed by the immorality around him.

Matthew 13:31-32 says:

Another parable put he forth unto them, saying, The kingdom of heaven is like to a grain of mustard seed, which a man took, and sowed in his field: Which indeed is the least of all seeds: but when it is grown, it is the greatest among herbs, and becomes a tree, so that the birds of the air come and lodge in the branches thereof.

The next parable is of the mustard seed, which is the smallest seed. It is planted, becomes a tree, and the birds come to feed in the tree and off the tree. They nest in the tree, and their droppings are the only thing that they leave at the tree. These are the people that come into the church, take the food and the shelter, but they give nothing to the church. They take from the church and leave their foul droppings in the church.

Matthew 13:33 says:

Another parable spoke he unto them; The kingdom of heaven is like unto leaven, which a woman took, and hid in three measures of meal, till the whole was leavened.

The next parable is the leaven that was placed in the church until it had completely filled the church. In the Bible, leaven is always associated with sin. So we now find that sin has been introduced into the church. When we look at this church, there is a whole lot more wrong with it than there is right with it. Most of us would not have or would not desire this mess, let alone sacrifice for this church. Now before you get the wrong idea that I do not like the church, that is the farthest thing from my heart and my mind. If one finds a baby that is dirty, puts it in a tub, and washes the baby, the water will become dirty. One does not throw the baby out with the bathwater.

When I think of Noah's Ark, it did not have any ventilation, and it had only one window. It was closed and had hundreds of animals that needed to be cared for every day. These animals continued to urinate and defecate, so the ark must have become very unpleasant to live in. But it was the only thing afloat and the only place left with life. So given the choice, I would have wanted to be on the ark. The church may not be perfect, but it is the best thing afloat for the Christian and a lost and dying world.

Matthew 13:44 says:

> Again, the kingdom of heaven is like unto treasure hid in a field; the which when a man has found, he hides, and for joy thereof goes and sells all that he has, and buys that field.

The next parable says the kingdom of heaven is like a treasure hid in a field. When a man finds the treasure, he hides it, goes and sells all that he has, and buys the field. Jesus looked down from heaven and saw the church as a treasure, and He bought it with His life.

Matthew 13:45–46 says:

> Again, the kingdom of heaven is like unto a merchant man, seeking goodly pearls: Who, when he had found one pearl of great price, went and sold all that he had, and bought it.

The next parable is about a merchant man that is looking for pearls. When he finds one of a great price, he goes and sells all that he has and buys this pearl. Again, this is Jesus looking for a pearl which is the church, and He purchased this pearl with His blood. I am completely overwhelmed by God's mercy, long- suffering, grace, and unconditional love which are so abundant. He gave this incredible sacrifice of His only Son for my salvation which is so undeserved.

Matthew 13:47–50 says:

Again, the kingdom of heaven is like unto a net, that was cast into the sea, and gathered of every kind: Which, when it was full, they drew to shore, and sat down, and gathered the good into vessels, but cast the bad away. So shall it be at the end of the world: the angels shall come forth, and sever the wicked from among the just, And shall cast them into the furnace of fire: there shall be wailing and gnashing of teeth.

The next parable is about a net that is cast into a sea. Every kind is gathered in the net, and then there is a sorting of the contents; the good is retained, and the bad is castaway. God says at the end of the world that His angels will come and sever the wicked from the just; the wicked will be cast into the lake of fire for eternal judgment. What God is saying to us is that it is not our place to judge others nor to try to form a perfect church but rather to be sure that we walk the talk. Our concern is about our lives and our relationship with Jesus Christ. If we will yield our lives to Jesus Christ and let Him live in us and through us, then we will walk in the Spirit. God will use us to reach a lost and dying world because they will know we are Christians by our love for one another.

CHAPTER 29

Recent Years

I did not realize that it had been five years since I started to write this book. A lot has happened during that time. My wife was diagnosed with breast cancer eighteen months ago. I really struggled with it. I could not bear the thought of losing her. It drove me to my knees, and I was finally able to give it to the Lord that He was in charge. She was able to have a lumpectomy with a sentinel node biopsy, and there was some metastasis in a lymph node. The breast surgeon felt she was able to remove all the cancer. A year later, Jan had a benign lump near the tumor.

I have had to have a pacemaker put in as my heart stopped. I also had a deep brain stimulator implanted in my brain to control essential tremors.

Several years ago, I found out that one of the surgeries on my back was done by a resident that was not being supervised. He drilled through the spinal cord and cut a lot of the nerves. This has resulted in a lot of damage to the nerves in the spinal cord, lots of very severe pain, as well as weakness in my left leg. In December of last year, the pain level reached ten and stayed there for ten weeks before they could put in a pain pump. The pain pump is controlling the pain but doesn't do anything for the nerve damage which continues to deteriorate.

At 2:00 on Christmas morning, I was lying in bed in complete agony when the Holy Spirit gave me this revelation of the true meaning of Christmas. I was in so much pain that I could not get out of bed to write it down. I told the Lord He would have to bring it back to me when I was able to get up. This revelation is recorded in chapter 32 of this book.

On another occasion, I kept passing out, and after insisting on seeing a vascular surgeon, the surgeon told me that the ultrasound showed blockage of the carotid arteries and that I needed surgery as soon as possible to prevent a stroke. He needed a CAT-scan with dye before the surgery could be done. My wife was praying at 12:15, just as they were injecting the dye. He told me to go directly to his office after the test. The vascular surgeon came in and asked me if I had an iPhone. He put the video of the CAT-scan on my phone and told me watch the video. There was no plaque at all in the arteries. He was in complete shock as God had cleaned out my arteries. *Praise the Lord!*

Beside all the medical issues in recent years, Jan and I have been extremely blessed to be able to enjoy many family vacations with our children and grandchildren. It has been wonderful living in the country with family nearby. We enjoyed horses for a while and have been raising steers for many years. It has been a pleasure to be a part of the Melissa Volunteer Fire Department first as a firefighter and then as the chaplain. Our son Mark along with Jan and I own The Martin Place art gallery and framing shop in McKinney, Texas. I help with framing, and we display some of my photos and Jan's paintings. I have maintained my veterinary license, and occasionally, I practice veterinary medicine. We are thankful for all of God's blessings and the many friends we have made through the years.

CHAPTER 30

Testimony Written by Tatum Martin

On November 19, 2018, I (Tatum) had just finished getting ready for my sorority's formal event. Heading out to my friend's car, I started down the seven stairs at the front of my dorm. At the very first step, my foot slipped forward, and I started falling face first down the steps. I went from the first step to the very bottom, and I took all the weight of the fall on my left knee. My hands didn't even get scraped. My knee had a pretty good scrape which was about the size of a half-dollar. I slapped some Neosporin, a Band-Aid, and some ice on it; and I moved on with the evening. I came home Tuesday afternoon and had an eight-hour workday on Wednesday. My knee was getting progressively worse. Walking over a store and standing behind a register would not help.

I spent Wednesday night at my grandparents', and the knee was getting to be much worse. It had begun to swell a little, so my uncle gave me a machine to circulate cool water on my knee overnight. When I woke up the next morning, my knee hurt so much I could hardly put any weight on it. I got a pair of crutches from the closet and hobbled around the kitchen, trying to help with the Thanksgiving lunch. As we neared the end of the meal, and it was time to go, I was almost in tears. I had no clue how I was going to make it through the Thanksgiving sale eight-hour shift I had coming up. I was frantically searching for things to help my knee.

Eventually, I came across a package of ACE bandage wrap and went to ask my grandpa how to wrap it. When I brought it over, he asked me if I wanted to pray about it. In my head, I thought to myself, *Absolutely not, crazy man. God's not going to fix my knee. Just wrap it so I can get to work!* Out loud, though, I responded, "All right, let me sit next to you on the couch so I can hear what you pray."

He placed his right hand over my knee and prayed aloud that God might heal me. Instantly, the swelling decreased, and I could easily and with no pain bend my knee. I was able to work that evening and the Black Friday sale with no pain thanks to the Lord healing my knee.

* * * * *

The night before Tatum was healed, God showed me as her grandfather that he wanted Tatum to experience the fullness of Christ's death on the cross, that by his stripes we are healed. I knew that when I prayed for Tatum, she would be healed, and it would have a life-changing effect upon her, causing her to have a deep hunger for the Word of God and a newfound trust in God.

CHAPTER 31

Recap of an Ordinary Man Walking with an Extraordinary God

God has blessed my wife and I. Three of our sons and their families live in the area—James and his wife, Lena; Charlie and his wife, Cory, and Mark. Steven and his wife, Jenniffer, live in Oklahoma. We have three great daughters-in-law, Lena, Cory, and Jenniffer. Our six incredible grandchildren, Tatum, Kimberly, Kylah, David, Christy, and Rachel have been such a blessing to us. Tatum married Micah Hays January 1, 2021, in our den with a small family ceremony because of COVID, and I had the privilege of marrying them. Our grandchildren give this old man a lot of pleasure, and they are a great help with the farmwork that I can no longer do. We are currently fattening three steers to eat.

I am eighty years old now. When I was seventy, I asked God what was left because I felt that I had been put out to pasture. God turned me to this scripture in Psalms.

Psalm 71:17–18 says:

> O God, you have taught me from my youth: and hitherto have I declared your wondrous works. Now also when I am old and gray- headed, O God, forsake me not; until I have

shown your strength unto this generation, and your power to everyone *that* is to come.

This may be the most difficult chapter to write because the topic is easily misunderstood. Even in the first-century church apostasy had started to invade the church. Paul, James, Peter, and Jude dealt with it in their writing to the churches. Jesus offended the priests, Pharisees, and the Sadducees because they did not want the truth, and they rejected Jesus as being the Son of God. It is not my point or purpose to offend anyone, and I want to make it very clear I believe in the church and wholeheartedly support the church and pastors who are called of God and are preaching the Word of truth. I am in favor of Bible schools and seminaries that teach the truth. However, many of these entities have gone astray from the truth and are blind to their error because they are so indoctrinated by tradition and man's doctrine. I hope you will read this, prayerfully understanding the love which I have for God and His truth. Because of these errors, I hope to give some insight in how this is taking place.

When I received Jesus as my Savior and Lord, there was not anything that I wanted more than to be like Him and to serve Him. I immediately began to read my Bible and anything and everything that I was told would help me to accomplish this task. The more I read and studied, the more uptight and confused I became. A pastor told me that if he looked at my life, he would not want to be a Christian because I was so uptight. Now there were things taking place in my life that were very positive. God had taught me to pray for the sick, and they were healed. God showed me how to use His Word, and He delivered a woman from demon-possession. He taught me to hear His voice and to discern people's needs. But the things I learned about Bible study, prayer, witnessing, and overcoming sin were not working. It came to a head when Dr. Reeves had a friend come into the animal hospital, took him through the bridge to life, had him pray the sinner's prayer, and told him he was saved. I knew his friend was not saved and was totally confused.

I called Dr. Reeves out of the room and told him that the man was not saved. Six months later, the man came back and told us that he had accepted Jesus the night before at his church. He told us that he left our place totally confused, but he had started to go to church and came to understand salvation and had received Jesus the night before. Up to this point, I was sure I could serve Jesus in my flesh because I didn't know any other way. Jesus spent three years trying to get the disciples to stop walking by sight and in the flesh to no avail. Peter was absolutely convinced he could die for Jesus until he denied Him three times.

Luke 22:31–32 says:

> And the Lord said, Simon, Simon, behold, Satan has desired to have you, that he may sift you as wheat: But I have prayed for you, that your faith fail not: and when you are converted, strengthen your brethren.

Peter had to get out of the fleshly walk and be converted to walk in the power of the Spirit, which came after Jesus was crucified and resurrected. Peter had now entered a whole new way of serving God in the mighty power of the Spirit. Jesus also spoke of a rest in our ability to serve Him.

Matthew 11:28–30 says:

> Come unto me, all *you* that labor and are heavy laden, and I will give you rest. Take my yoke upon you, and learn of me; for I am meek and lowly in heart: and you shall find rest unto your souls. For my yoke is easy, and my burden is light.

Hebrews 3:7–4:16 says:

> Wherefore (as the Holy Ghost says, Today if you will hear his voice, Harden not your hearts, as in the provocation, in the day of temptation in the wilderness: When your fathers tempted me, proved me, and saw my works forty years. Wherefore I was grieved with that generation, and said, They do always err in their heart; and they have not known my ways. So I swore in my wrath, They shall not enter into my rest.) Take heed, brethren, lest there be in any of you an evil heart of unbelief, in departing from the living God. But

exhort one another daily, while it is called today; lest any of you be hardened through the deceitfulness of sin. For we are made partakers of Christ, if we hold the beginning of our confidence steadfast unto the end; While it is said, Today if you will hear his voice, harden not your hearts, as in the provocation. For some, when they had heard, did provoke: howbeit not all that came out of Egypt by Moses. But with whom was he grieved forty years? *was it* not with them that had sinned, whose carcasses fell in the wilderness? And to whom swore he that they should not enter into his rest, but to them that believed not? So we see that they could not enter in because of unbelief. Let us therefore fear, lest, a promise being left *us* of entering into his rest, any of you should seem to come short of it. For unto us was the gospel preached, as well as unto them: but the word preached did not profit them, not being mixed with faith in them that heard *it*. For we which have believed do enter into rest, as he said, As I have sworn in my wrath, if they shall enter into my rest: although the works were finished from the foundation of the world. For he spoke in a certain place of the seventh *day* on this wise, And God did rest the seventh day from all his works. And in this *place* again, If they shall enter into my rest. Seeing therefore it remains that some must enter therein, and they to whom it was first preached entered not in because of unbelief: Again, he limits a certain day, saying in David, Today, after so long a time; as it is said, Today if you will hear his voice, harden not your hearts. For if Jesus had given them rest, then would he not afterward have spoken of another day. There remains therefore a rest to the people of God. For he that is entered into his rest, he also has ceased from his own works, as God *did* from his. Let us labor therefore to enter into that rest, lest any man fall after the same example of unbelief. For the word of God *is* quick, and powerful, and sharper than any two-edged sword, piercing even to the dividing asunder of soul and spirit, and of the joints and marrow, and *is* a discerner of the thoughts and intents of the heart. Neither is there any creature that is not manifest in his sight: but all things *are* naked and opened unto the eyes of him with whom we have to do. Seeing then that we have a great high priest, that is passed into the heavens, Jesus the Son of God, let us hold fast *our* profession. For we have not a high priest which cannot be touched with the feeling of our infirmities; but was in all points tempted like as *we are, yet* without sin. Let us therefore come boldly unto the throne of grace, that we may obtain mercy, and find grace to help in time of need.

When we learn to be led by the Spirit and to walk in the Spirit, we enter a walk that is directed by God that is eternal, and that leads to a heavenly vision and direction. When Dr. Reeves' friend came back and told us that he had just got saved, it was a wake-up call because we were dealing with eternal souls with eternal consequences.

So I went to the Lord that night and told God that everything that I had learned from man didn't seem to be working. God told me that I needed to get to *know Him* in His nature, character, and personality, and to do that, I would have to stop my ministries and spend my time with Him. I also needed to enter into His rest.

Galatians 1:11–12 says:

> For I certify you, brethren, that the gospel which was preached of me is not after man. For I neither received it of man, neither was I taught it, but by the revelation of Jesus Christ.

The problem in the church is they are taught the doctrines of men and church traditions, just as the priests and the Pharisees were so ingrained in their doctrines and traditions that they could not see truth when it stood in front of them. The Pharisees were educated men in church doctrine and tradition but not in the truth of God's Word.

Isaiah 29:13 says:

> Wherefore the Lord said, Forasmuch as this people draw near me with their mouth, and with their lips do honor me, but have removed their heart far from me, and their fear toward me is taught by the precept of men.

John 14:26 says:

> But the Comforter, *which is* the Holy Ghost, whom the Father will send in my name, he shall teach you all things, and bring all things to your remembrance, whatsoever I have said unto you.

First John 2:27 says:

> But the anointing which you have received of him abides in you, and you need not that any man teach you: but as the same anointing teaches you of all things, and is truth, and is no lie, and even as it has taught you, you shall abide in him.

No wonder Jesus called fishermen and uneducated men to be His disciples because they did not have to unlearn a lot of doctrine and tradition. The problem today is that young men and women go to seminary to learn to be ministers, and they are taught man's doctrine because these men were taught by other men. When they don't know what a scripture means, instead of waiting on God's revelation, they get together and read the commentaries to decide what they think is the best interpretation. They are too proud to admit they don't know what the scripture means, thus false doctrines are started and now become what most believe are the truth.

I waited fifty years for God to bring His revelation to a scripture that I refused to accept what the commentaries had to say that it meant. They were wrong, and when God's revelation came, it was absolutely mind-boggling. I will share it later as it fits into a topic I want to cover. I admit that this seems to be a logical way to educate pastors, but God's Word says He will lead us into all truth.

John 8:32 says:

> And you shall know the truth, and the truth shall make you free.

Galatians 1:10 says:

For do I now persuade men, or God? Or do I seek to please men? For if I yet pleased men, I should not be the servant of Christ.

God always has a better way. The truth will not always please men. People are always asking me for my opinion on scriptures. I always tell them that I do not have an opinion because my opinion will not hold any weight with God, so let's see what God's Word says about it.

Ephesians 3:16–21 says:

That he would grant you, according to the riches of his glory, to be strengthened with might by his Spirit in the inner man; That Christ may dwell in your hearts by faith; that you being rooted and grounded in love, May be able to comprehend with all saints what is the breadth, and length, and depth, and height; And to know the love of Christ, which passes knowledge, that you might be filled with all the fulness of God. Now unto him that is able to do exceeding abundantly above all that we ask or think, according to the power that works in us, Unto him be glory in the church by Christ Jesus throughout all ages, world without end. Amen.

What an incredible prayer that the spirit will strengthen our inner man that we might have Christ's love and knowledge and be filled with the fullness of God. I keep going back to this prayer because I can't pray a prayer in my flesh that even comes close to this prayer.

I have a book written by Bryan Stuckey from twenty-seven sermons I preached titled *Born of the Water Born of the Spirit*. It goes into great detail how the spiritual birth is identical to the physical birth. There is great emphasis on the Word of God, and we must understand God's Word says what it says. You do not have to read between the lines to understand God's Word. God's Word does not change. It is always the same, and if we have the Holy Spirit, we have the Author of the Word. The same Holy Spirit that wrote the Word can and will bring revelation of the Word. In 1 Peter 2:2, it tells us that we are to desire the sincere milk of the Word.

First Peter 2:2 says:

As newborn babes, desire the sincere milk of the word, that you may grow thereby.

In Hebrews 5:11–14, it tells us we need to go into the meat of the Word that we might discern good and evil.

Hebrews 5:11-14 says:

Of whom we have many things to say, and hard to be uttered, seeing you are dull of hearing. For when for the time you ought to be teachers, you have need that one teach you again which *be* the first principles of the oracles of God; and are become such as have need of milk, and not of strong meat. For everyone that uses milk *is* unskillful in the word of righteousness: for he is a babe. But strong meat belongs to them that are of full age, *even* those who by reason of use have their senses exercised to discern both good and evil.

First, in studying the Word, I must be willing to admit I could be wrong in my understanding of the Word; otherwise, I am not teachable and I don't want the truth. Second, every time I read the Word, I need to read it as if I have not read it before. That is the only way that I am open to God to bring new revelation of His Word.

Isaiah 28:9–13 says:

Whom shall he teach knowledge? and whom shall he make to understand doctrine? *them that are* weaned from the milk, *and* drawn from the breasts. For precept *must be* upon precept, precept upon precept; line upon line, line upon line; here a little, *and* there a little: For with stammering lips and another tongue will he speak to this people. To whom he said, This *is* the rest *wherewith* you may cause the weary to rest; and this *is* the refreshing: yet they would not hear. But the word of the Lord was unto them precept upon precept, precept upon precept; line upon line, line upon line; here a little, *and* there a little; that they might go, and fall backward, and be broken, and snared, and taken. Wherefore hear the word of the Lord, you scornful men, that rule this people which *is* in Jerusalem.

Several years ago, God spoke to me the concept of line upon line and precept upon precept, and I started reading the Bible from Genesis through Revelation. Each time I read through the Bible, God gave me a different theme that is found in every book. Examples might be grace, long-suffering, God's holiness and mercy. These are just a few examples, but it really opens the continuity of God and made God more real and intimate. I try to read the entire Bible three to four times a year. I am not saying this to brag, but if you love someone, you want to spend time with them. It is not all that amazing. If you read three and one-third chapters a day, which takes about twenty minutes, you can read through the Bible in a year. This is by no means the only way to study the Bible. Each person should find what works for them to develop that personal relationship with God.

Luke 17:20–21 says:

> And when he was demanded of the Pharisees, when the kingdom of God should come, he answered them and said, The kingdom of God comes not with observation: Neither shall they say, Lo here! or, lo there! for, behold, the kingdom of God is within you.

Jesus told the Pharisees that the kingdom of God was in them. I have been troubled by this for fifty years, but Jesus said it, so it had to be true. I could not accept the commentaries that said it had to be in the midst. "It could not be said of a self-righteous, Christ-rejecting Pharisee, that the kingdom of God, as to its spiritual content, was within him." I waited fifty years, and God, this past year, showed me that the kingdom was in the Pharisees. Stay with me on this.

Deuteronomy 30:14 says:

> But the word is very near unto you, in your mouth, and in your heart, that you may do it.

Romans 10:17 says:

So then faith comes by hearing, and hearing by the Word of God.

Romans 1:19-25 says:

Because that which may be known of God is manifest in them; for God has showed *it* unto them. For the invisible things of him from the creation of the world are clearly seen, being understood by the things that are made, even his eternal power and Godhead; so that they are without excuse: Because that, when they knew God, they glorified *him* not as God, neither were thankful; but became vain in their imaginations, and their foolish heart was darkened. Professing themselves to be wise, they became fools, And changed the glory of the uncorruptible God into an image made like to corruptible man, and to birds, four-footed beasts, and creeping things. Wherefore God also gave them up to uncleanness through the lusts of their own hearts, to dishonor their own bodies between themselves: Who changed the truth of God into a lie, and worshipped and served the creature more than the Creator, who is blessed forever. Amen.

The Word of God states that God's Word and faith is in every man. Romans 12:3 says:

For I say, through the grace given unto me, to every man that is among you, not to think of *himself* more highly than he ought to think; but to think soberly, according as God has dealt to every man the measure of faith.

Romans 10:8–13 says:

But what saith it? The word is near you, even in your mouth, and in your heart: that is, the word of faith, which we preach; That if you shall confess with your mouth the Lord Jesus, and shalt believe in thine heart that God has raised him from the dead, you shall be saved. For with the heart man believes unto righteousness; and with the mouth confession is made unto salvation. For the scripture says, Whosoever believes on him shall not be ashamed. For there is no difference between the Jew and the Greek: for the same Lord over all is rich unto all that call upon him. For whosoever shall call upon the name of the Lord shall be saved.

The word of faith is in your mouth and heart, and if you believe that Jesus is the Son of God and confess with your mouth, you will be saved and thus have the kingdom within you. A big part of God's promises is conditional. You must believe that Jesus is the Son of God and confess Him with your mouth as Lord.

Romans 7:9 says:

For I was alive without the law once: but when the commandment came, sin revived, and I died.

Matthew 13:11–17 says:

He answered and said unto them, Because it is given unto you to know the mysteries of the kingdom of heaven, but to them it is not given. For whosoever has, to him shall be given, and he shall have more abundance: but whosoever has not, from him shall be taken away even that he has. Therefore speak I to them in parables: because they seeing see not; and hearing they hear not, neither do they understand. And in them is fulfilled the prophecy of Esaias, which says, By hearing you shall hear, and shall not understand; and seeing you shall see, and shall not perceive: For this people's heart is waxed gross, and *their* ears are dull of hearing, and their eyes they have closed; lest at any time they should see with their eyes, and hear with their ears, and should understand with their heart, and should be converted, and I should heal them. But blessed are your eyes, for they see: and your ears, for they hear. For verily I say unto you, That many prophets and righteous *men* have desired to see *those things* which you see, and have not seen *them*; and to hear *those things* which you hear, and have not heard *them*.

Because the Pharisees did not believe that Jesus was the Son of God and rejected Him, God rejected the Pharisees and took the Word of faith from them. A profound truth was revealed that the kingdom of God is within you. God's word says what it says. This truth was revealed as I prayed and waited on God.

First Peter 3:20 says:

> Which sometime were disobedient, when once the longsuffering of God waited in the days of Noah, while the ark was a preparing, wherein few, that is, eight souls were saved by water.

This verse for the last nine months has really troubled me because Jesus said before He returned, it would be as the days of Noah and Lot. Luke 17:22–30 says:

> And he said unto the disciples, The days will come, when you shall desire to see one of the days of the Son of man, and you shall not see *it*. And they shall say to you, See here; or, see there: go not after *them*, nor follow *them*. For as the lightning, that lightens out of the one *part* under heaven, shines unto the other *part* under heaven; so shall also the Son of man be in his day. But first must he suffer many things, and be rejected of this generation. And as it was in the days of Noe, so shall it be also in the days of the Son of man. They did eat, they drank, they married wives, they were given in marriage, until the day that Noe entered into the ark, and the flood came, and destroyed them all. Likewise also as it was in the days of Lot; they did eat, they drank, they bought, they sold, they planted, they built; But the same day that Lot went out of Sodom it rained fire and brimstone from heaven, and destroyed *them* all. Even thus shall it be in the day when the Son of man is revealed.

Noah took approximately one hundred years to build the ark, and in that time, he did not have one single convert. We all get caught up in the fact that Noah and his family were saved from the flood, but we do not look at the millions of people that died.

Genesis 6:5–8 says:

> And God saw that the wickedness of man *was* great in
> the earth, and that every imagination of the thoughts of his
> heart *was* only evil continually. And it repented the Lord that
> he had made man on the earth, and it grieved him at his
> heart. And the Lord said, I will destroy man whom I have
> created from the face of the earth; both man, and beast, and
> the creeping thing, and the fowls of the air; for it repents me
> that I have made them.

God states that every imagination of man's heart was only evil
continually.

The people of this time had walked in the flesh and its desires for
so long that they had completely lost any concept of God's holiness. I
didn't know how many people there were in Noah's time, but there had
to be several million at least. What bothers me is these people believed
they were right with God. God was grieved that man had turned their
hearts and lives from a loving God. All these people that died in the
flood ended up in hell. If that doesn't break your heart and wake you up
to what's going on in our world today, I don't know what it will take.

Millions died in the flood without God because of their self-
righteousness. We are experiencing the same thing today when men
are willing to settle for man's doctrines and traditions rather than a
committed trust in God's Holy Word.

Revelation 3:14–22 says:

> And unto the angel of the church of the Laodiceans write;
> These things says the Amen, the faithful and true witness, the
> beginning of the creation of God; I know your works, that
> you are neither cold nor hot: I would you were cold or hot.
> So then because you are lukewarm, and neither cold nor hot,
> I will spue you out of my mouth. Because you say, I am rich,
> and increased with goods, and have need of nothing; and
> know not that you are wretched, and miserable, and poor,
> and blind, and naked: I counsel you to buy of me gold tried
> in the fire, that you may be rich; and white raiment, that

you may be clothed, and that the shame of your nakedness do not appear; and anoint your eyes with eye salve, that you may see. As many as I love, I rebuke and chasten: be zealous therefore, and repent. Behold, I stand at the door, and knock: if any man hear my voice, and open the door, I will come in to him, and will sup with him, and he with me. To him that overcomes will I grant to sit with me in my throne, even as I also overcame, and am set down with my Father in his throne. He that has an ear, let him hear what the Spirit says unto the churches.

The church of Laodicea has become the predominant church of today, a church with a watered-down gospel that resembles God's church, where men draw near to God with their mouths, but their hearts are far from Him.

Luke 13:24–30 says:

Strive to enter in at the strait gate: for many, I say unto you, will seek to enter in, and shall not be able. When once the master of the house is risen up, and has shut to the door, and you begin to stand without, and to knock at the door, saying, Lord, Lord, open unto us; and he shall answer and say unto you, I know you not whence you are: Then shall you begin to say, We have eaten and drunk in your presence, and you have taught in our streets. But he shall say, I tell you, I know you not whence you are; depart from me, all *you* workers of iniquity. There shall be weeping and gnashing of teeth, when you shall see Abraham, and Isaac, and Jacob, and all the prophets, in the kingdom of God, and you yourselves thrust out. And they shall come from the east, and *from* the west, and from the north, and *from* the south, and shall sit down in the kingdom of God. And, behold there are last which shall be first, and there are first which shall be last.

Matthew 7:21–29 says:

Not everyone that says unto me, Lord, Lord, shall enter into the kingdom of heaven; but he that does the will of my

Father which is in heaven. Many will say to me in that day, Lord, Lord, have we not prophesied in your name? and in your name have cast out devils? and in your name done many wonderful works? And then will I profess unto them, I never knew you: depart from me, you that work iniquity. Therefore whosoever hears these sayings of mine, and does them, I will liken him unto a wise man, which built his house upon a rock: And the rain descended, and the floods came, and the winds blew, and beat upon that house; and it fell not: for it was founded upon a rock. And everyone that hears these sayings of mine, and does them not, shall be likened unto a foolish man, which built his house upon the sand: And the rain descended, and the floods came, and the winds blew, and beat upon that house; and it fell: and great was the fall of it. And it came to pass, when Jesus had ended these sayings, the people were astonished at his doctrine: For he taught them as *one* having authority, and not as the scribes.

Jesus gave a very strong warning. The gospel being preached in most churches today is a watered-down gospel that does not preach repentance. True repentance is brokenness and the full knowledge that I deserve to go to hell. It is not the episode where a young child hits another child, and the mother tells the child they need to tell the other child they are sorry. The child says, "No," and the mother says, "You go tell that child you're *sorry*."

So the child goes and says, "I'm sorry," but there is no conviction of sorrow. Instead of true repentance, this is the scenario that if you want to go to heaven, ask Jesus to forgive you of your sins and to come into your heart, and you will be saved. Then we tell them they are saved, and they cannot lose their salvation. Once saved, always saved.

Isaiah 28:15–18 says:

Because you have said, We have made a covenant with death, and with hell are we at agreement; when the overflowing scourge shall pass through, it shall not come unto us: for we have made lies our refuge, and under falsehood have we hid ourselves: Therefore thus saith the Lord God, Behold, I lay in

Zion for a foundation a stone, a tried stone, a precious corner *stone*, a sure foundation: he that believes shall not make haste. Judgment also will I lay to the line, and righteousness to the plummet: and the hail shall sweep away the refuge of lies, and the waters shall overflow the hiding place.

Jeremiah 6:14 says:

They have healed also the hurt o*f the daughter* of my people slightly, saying, Peace, peace; when t*here is* no peace.

Jeremiah 8:11 says:

For they have healed the hurt of the daughter of my people slightly, saying, Peace, peace; when *there is* no peace.

I call this a fire insurance policy that will burn with them in hell. There is nothing about making Jesus Lord, keeping His Word, and spending time in His Word. More emphasis is given to joining the church and joining a life group. These are all good things, but you must make a commitment to God, spend time in prayer, and study His Word.

Hebrews 5:9 says:

And being made perfect, he became the author of eternal salvation unto all them that obey him.

James 1:12–16 says:

Blessed *is* the man that endures temptation: for when he is tried, he shall receive the crown of life, which the Lord has promised to them that love him. Let no man say when he is tempted, I am tempted of God: for God cannot be tempted with evil, neither tempts he any man: But every man is tempted, when he is drawn away of his own lust, and enticed. Then when lust has conceived, it brings forth sin: and sin, when it is finished, brings forth death.

Romans 6:11–23 says:

Likewise reckon you also yourselves to be dead indeed unto sin, but alive unto God through Jesus Christ our Lord. Let not sin therefore reign in your mortal body, that you should obey it in the lusts thereof. Neither yield you your members as instruments of unrighteousness unto sin: but yield yourselves unto God, as those that are alive from the dead, and your members *as* instruments of righteousness unto God. For sin shall not have dominion over you: for you are not under the law, but under grace. What then? shall we sin, because we are not under the law, but under grace? God forbid. Know you not, that to whom you yield yourselves servants to obey, his servants you are to whom you obey; whether of sin unto death, or of obedience unto righteousness? But God be thanked, that you were the servants of sin, but you have obeyed from the heart that form of doctrine which was delivered you. Being then made free from sin, you became the servants of righteousness. I speak after the manner of men because of the infirmity of your flesh: for as you have yielded your members servants to uncleanness and to iniquity unto iniquity; even so now yield your members servants to righteousness unto holiness. For when you were the servants of sin, you were free from righteousness. What fruit had you then in those things whereof you are now ashamed? for the end of those things *is* death. But now being made free from sin, and become servants to God, you have your fruit unto holiness, and the end everlasting life. For the wages of sin *is* death; but the gift of God is eternal life through Jesus Christ our Lord.

I feel it is necessary to speak to the doctrine of once saved, always saved. I met my wife, and she belonged to the Baptist church which embraces this doctrine. I became a dyed-in-the-wool Baptist, believing their doctrines because they were taught by Brother Harry, our pastor, who had graduated with advanced degrees from Dallas Theological Seminary. I was not saved at the time, but when I got saved, I still embraced the doctrine.

Then I took four senior high school boys out to the Fed Mart parking lot in Dallas, Texas, to witness one Friday night, and we led two girls and one boy to the Lord, who then attended church Sunday morning. The deacons did not like their children going to the parking lot to witness as they associated it with Pentecostal doctrine and not Baptist doctrine. I was called into the pastor's office and told in no uncertain terms if I took the boys out to the parking lot again that I would be told to leave the church.

The boys came Friday night, gung-ho to go out to the parking lot to witness. I told them what the pastor had told me. They said they would go of their own accord. I could not let them go without adult supervision and knew this was God's will, so I went with them this time. They split up as individuals, and several people accepted Christ; some were in church Sunday morning. I was called into the pastor's office on Monday morning and told we would not be allowed in the church again.

So the next week, we went down the road to an Assembly of God church. They teach that you can lose your salvation. So I set out to prove them wrong.

As I began to search the Scriptures, I could not find one scripture that definitively supported the doctrine "once saved, always saved," so I called Brother Harry, and he could not give me a scripture either. But I found a multitude of scriptures to support that you could lose your salvation. I listed a couple scriptures above. I have been in many Sunday school classes, and a member would say, "I know we believe once saved, always saved, but I read a scripture that indicates that you can lose your salvation."

There were three common responses to this statement. The most common was to ignore the statement and go on; the second was to try explaining the scripture away; And the third was to state that our doctrine was well established by scholars and was not to be questioned. Now we know God's Word changes not, and someday, we will be held accountable for the truth. Three years later, we were in Oklahoma City on Sunday, and we went to hear Brother Harry. That Sunday, he told his Baptist church that he had been teaching them false doctrine, and he asked them for forgiveness. He said he had been teaching "once saved, always saved," and it could not be confirmed in the Scriptures. He went on to quote a lot of scriptures to show that you could lose your salvation and how.

It goes to show that if you want the truth, you must search the scriptures and wait for God's revelation. I want to bring up one other point. If you believe in free will, then you cannot believe "once saved, always saved" because you would no longer have free will after you are saved. Now I'm going to quote the scariest verse in the Bible, Revelation 22:19, which says, "And if any man shall take away from the words of the book of this prophecy, God shall take away his part out of the book of life, and out of the holy city, and from the things which are written in this book."

To teach "once saved, always saved," you would have to take a multitude of scriptures out of the Bible. I have heard a TV celebrity say he uses Wite-Out. If he doesn't like a scripture, he whites it out. May I remind you the Logos (Word) is God. I fear for a lot of preachers because they are the blind leading the blind right into hell because of their error.

I beg that you do not reject what you just read. We will look at several more passages in the Bible.

John 8: 31–32 says

> Then said Jesus to those Jews which believed on him, If you continue in my word, then are you my disciples indeed; And you shall know the truth, and the truth shall make you free.

The Word of God is truth and if we understand the Word, we will know the truth. We are going to look at the lives of the disciples and especially Peter's as there is more written about him.

The parable about the ten virgins that took their lamps to meet the bridegroom was previously quoted in Chapter 28 from Matthew 25:1–13. Five of the virgins took vessels of oil with their lamps, and five virgins just took their lamps. I have always wondered about this parable. I had surgery on May 28th, and I can never sleep the first two nights after the surgery as the drugs they use wire my brain. So, as I laid in bed meditating on God's Word, God brought the parable to my mind, and He said He would reveal the meaning to me.

John 14:5–6 says

> Thomas said unto him, Lord, we know not where you go; and how can we know the way? Jesus said unto him, I am the way, the truth, and the life: no man comes unto the Father, but by me.

Back to the virgins and the lamps. The way is believing in Jesus, the truth is Jesus, and the light is the resurrected Christ. Jesus took our sins on the cross, died in our place, and went to hell to pay for our sin. He thus fulfilled the law when he died for our sins and paid the debt in hell separated from God the Father. Having fulfilled the law and conquering death, He was not resurrected as the son of man, but as the Son of God with a new glorified immortal body.

Romans 5:10 says

> For if, when we were enemies, we were reconciled to God by the death of his Son, much more, being reconciled, we shall be saved by his life.

Jesus spent three years trying to get the disciples to stop walking by sight and in the flesh. They, like all the virgins, recognized that Jesus was the Son of God. Thus, they took the lamps. There probably was not a man more determined to follow Jesus than Peter, but he was trying to do it in the flesh and with his mind. In his mind he knew that Jesus was the Son of God, but he thought Jesus had come to set up his kingdom on earth at his first coming, and he did not realize that Jesus had to be crucified and then resurrected as the Son of God. The five foolish virgins recognized Jesus was God's Son, but it was with their minds and in their self-righteousness. They did not take any oil which is the Holy Spirit that resurrected Jesus as the Son of God.

Luke 22:31–34 says

> And the Lord said, Simon, Simon, behold, Satan has desired to have you, that he may sift you as wheat: But I have prayed for you, that your faith fail not: and when you are converted, strengthen your brethren. And he said unto him, Lord, I am ready to go with you, both into prison, and to

death. And he said, I tell you, Peter, the cock shall not crow this day, before you shall thrice deny that you know me.

Jesus fed the five thousand. But when it came time to feed the four thousand, the disciples told Jesus they could not do it instead of seeing how much bread they had and bringing the bread to Jesus. They were still walking in the flesh. We see Jesus do miracles today and we do not believe He can do it again.

Mark 8:14–18, 21 says

> Now the disciples had forgotten to take bread, neither had they in the ship with them more than one loaf. And he charged them, saying, Take heed, beware of the leaven of the Pharisees, and of the leaven of Herod. And they reasoned among themselves, saying, It is because we have no bread. And when Jesus knew it, he said unto them, Why reason you, because you have no bread? perceive you not yet, neither understand? have you your heart yet hardened? Having eyes, see you not? and having ears, Hear you not? and do you not remember? And he said unto them, How is it that you do not understand?

If we have no oil to put in our lamps, our hearts will become hardened, and we will continue to walk by sight in our self-righteousness and our flesh. We will not walk in the Spirit because we have no oil, the Spirit of God.

Mark 16:9–11, 13–14 says

> Now when Jesus was risen early the first day of the week, he appeared first to Mary Magdalene, out of whom he had cast seven devils. And she went and told them that had been with him, as they mourned and wept. And they, when they had heard that he was alive, and had been seen of her, believed not. And they went and told it unto the residue: neither believed they them. Afterward he appeared unto the eleven as they sat at meat, and upbraided them with their unbelief and hardness of heart, because they believed not them which had seen him after he was risen.

The disciples were like the five foolish virgins before they saw Jesus in His new resurrected body; then they believed. Thus, when Jesus said, "I am the life", we must believe that He is the resurrected Son of God.

Romans 10:17 tells us that faith comes by hearing and hearing by the Word. As the lamps with oil go out, so we must keep our vessels of oil full that we may have eternal life. That can be done by feeding on the Word of God daily. After the resurrection of Jesus, the disciples believed that Jesus was the Christ, the Son of God. He filled the disciples with the Holy Spirit (their vessels with oil) before Pentecost.

John 20:22 says

> And when he had said this, he breathed on them, and said unto them, Receive you the Holy Ghost:

After he had filled their vessels with oil (Holy Spirit), He told the disciples to tarry until they were baptized with the Holy Spirit. They would receive power to be His witnesses and preform the works of God. Jesus is the way, the truth, and the resurrected life. After Peter saw Jesus resurrected as the Son of God and was converted, he went from walking by sight in the flesh to walking in the Spirit and being led by the Spirit. On the day of Pentecost, Peter preached with great power under the anointing of the Holy Spirit.

Hebrews 2:4 says

> God also bearing them witness, both with signs and wonders, and with divers miracles, and gifts of the Holy Ghost, according to his own will?

John 1:12 says

> But as many as received him, to them gave he power to become the sons of God, even to them that believe on his name:

Now this ordinary man spent five years believing that Jesus was God's Son, but trying to serve Him in the flesh, doing good deeds and living in self- righteousness. When I realized I had no power to be a son of God, I realized I was dead without hope.

John 5:25 says

> Verily, verily, I say unto you, The hour is coming, and now is, when the dead shall hear the voice of the Son of God: and they that hear shall live.

I was like the very dry bones in Ezekiel 37. When Ezekiel spoke the words of God to the dry bones, they became living souls. I realized I was a wretched man without hope. My only solution was asking for God's mercy and receiving Jesus Christ as my Savior; that is what I did. I surrendered my life to Jesus and made Him Lord.

I Corinthians 15:54

> So when this corruptible shall have put on incorruption, and this mortal shall have put on immortality, then shall be brought to pass the saying that is written, Death is swallowed up in victory.

Now this ordinary man is no longer an ordinary man but is a joint heir with Christ if I endure to the end. Hallelujah, praise the Lord that He can take an ordinary man and transform me into the image of Christ, to dwell with Him forever where this mortality will put on immortality, this corruptible flesh will put on incorruptible, and I will have the divine nature of God's Son.

CHAPTER 32

The True Meaning of Christmas

On Christmas morning of December 2021, I had been in severe pain of level ten for over four weeks, and at 2:00 in the morning, I was in complete agony when the Holy Spirit brought this incredible revelation. It just flowed. I told God, "I need to write this down now so I won't forget it, but I am in so much pain I can't get out of bed, so I need you to bring it back in the morning."

I was able to get up Christmas morning, got my wife's notepad, and started to write as the Holy Spirit flowed through me to write. It was an incredible experience to write what God was giving me. I have shared it with several people and watched many of them weep as they read it. Several have told me that they needed it that day. All I can say is to God be the *glory*.

As I was writing it, my wife asked me what I was writing. I told her that when I finished, she could read it. She read it and responded, "This had to be the Holy Spirit because you can't write like that." Thus an ordinary man's walk was led by an extraordinary God.

* * * * *

When Jesus consented to become the Son of Man, the Word became flesh when He was born of a virgin named Mary; and He dwelt among man. He was born in a stable with His only visitors being the shepherds. Now for the first time, the light was going to shine in the darkness, and the glorious light of God was going to be revealed to man to make a way out of sin into God's light. He would be the living water that would create a well of water springing up unto eternal life. He would be the bread that came down from heaven, and whosoever would eat of this bread (being His flesh) and drink of His blood would have eternal life. Jesus came to show man how to live in the Spirit and walk in the Spirit. Jesus came to redeem man that while man was yet a sinner, He died for him.

God the Father expressed His incredible magnificent love to man by the sacrifice of His Son on the cross. He opened the doors of heaven by this great sacrifice that we might spend eternity with the Great I Am. God sent His Son to die on the cross, take our sin upon His flesh, and descend into hell to pay the penalty for sin once and for all.

Because Jesus believed that God could and would resurrect Him from hell if He lived a perfect life, by faith, He was resurrected from hell. He now sits on the right hand of God and is waiting for the final day of redemption of His adopted brothers and sisters to spend eternity in glory with Him, the Father, and the Holy Spirit.

ABOUT THE AUTHOR

Ernest S. Martin grew up on a large ranch in North Dakota where his family had a dairy and raised both commercial and registered Herefords. They grew wheat, durum, barley, oats, and alfalfa hay. Growing up on a farm and ranch gave Ernest insight into the scriptures as many illustrations in the Word of God are related to sheep, goats, and growing grain.

While in high school, Ernest studied a curriculum geared to be an engineer but changed to veterinary medicine at North Dakota State University. He received his DVM from Oklahoma State University. While doing post-doctoral research at OSU, he met his wife, Jan, who was doing graduate work in chemistry. They were married eleven weeks later in 1966.

After moving to Dallas, Texas, Ernest eventually had his own animal hospital. He received Jesus as his Savior on August 21, 1970, and soon started an outreach Bible study for hippies. This outreach became a church, which Ernest pastored while still practicing veterinary medicine. After selling his veterinary practice at age sixty-two, he went to firefighter school and became a volunteer firefighter, and he is currently the chaplain of the Melissa Fire Department. Ernest and his wife, Jan, have four sons, five granddaughters, and one grandson.

www.ingramcontent.com/pod-product-compliance
Lightning Source LLC
Chambersburg PA
CBHW021612120626
46545CB00001B/184